AGRICULTURE, GROWTH AND REDISTRIBUTION OF INCOME

CONTRIBUTIONS
TO
ECONOMIC ANALYSIS

190

Honorary Editor:
J. TINBERGEN

Editors:
D.W. JORGENSON
J. WAELBROECK

NORTH-HOLLAND
AMSTERDAM • NEW YORK • OXFORD • TOKYO

AGRICULTURE, GROWTH AND REDISTRIBUTION OF INCOME

Policy Analysis with a General Equilibrium Model
of India

N.S.S. NARAYANA
Indian Statistical Institute, Bangalore

Kirit S. PARIKH
Indira Gandhi Institute of Development Research, Bombay

T.N. SRINIVASAN
Yale University, New Haven

1991

NORTH-HOLLAND
AMSTERDAM • NEW YORK • OXFORD • TOKYO

in association with

ALLIED PUBLISHERS LIMITED
New Delhi Bombay Calcutta Madras Nagpur
Ahmedabad Bangalore Hyderabad Lucknow

Publishers:

ELSEVIER SCIENCE PUBLISHERS B.V.
Sara Burgerhartstraat 25
P.O. Box 211, 1000 AE Amsterdam, The Netherlands

*Co-publishers and Sole Distributors for
India, Sri Lanka, Nepal and Bangladesh:*

ALLIED PUBLISHERS LIMITED
P.O. Box 7203, 13/14, Asaf Ali Road
New Delhi – 110002, India

Distributors for the United States and Canada:

ELSEVIER SCIENCE PUBLISHING COMPANY, INC.
655 Avenue of the Americas
New York, N.Y. 10010, U.S.A.

Library of Congress Cataloging-in-Publication Data

Narayana, N. S. S.
    Agriculture, growth, and redistribution of income : policy
analysis with a general equilibrium model of India / N.S.S.
Narayana, Kirit S. Parikh, T.N. Srinivasan.
      p.   cm. -- (Contributions to economic analysis ; 190)
    Includes index.
    ISBN 0-444-88667-2
    1. Agriculture and state--India. 2. Income distribution--India.
3. Equilibrium (Economics)   I. Parikh, Kirit S. II. Srinivasan, T.
N., 1933-   . III. Title. IV. Series.
    HD2073.N37 1991
    338.1'854--dc20
                                                          91-16806
                                                              CIP

ISBN: 0 444 88667 2

PRINTED IN THE NETHERLANDS
(Indian edition: Printed in India)

INTRODUCTION TO THE SERIES

This series consists of a number of hitherto unpublished studies, which are introduced by the editors in the belief that they represent fresh contributions to economic science.

The term "economic analysis" as used in the title of the series has been adopted because it covers both the activities of the theoretical economist and the research worker.

Although the analytical methods used by the various contributors are not the same, they are nevertheless conditioned by the common origin of their studies, namely theoretical problems encountered in practical research. Since for this reason, business cycle research and national accounting, research work on behalf of economic policy, and problems of planning are the main sources of the subjects dealt with, they necessarily determine the manner of approach adopted by the authors. Their methods tend to be "practical" in the sense of not being too far remote from application to actual economic conditions. In additon they are quantitative.

It is the hope of the editors that the publication of these studies will help to stimulate the exchange of scientific information and to reinforce international cooperation in the field of economics.

The Editors

कृषितो नास्ति दुर्भिक्षम्

Krishito Naasti Durbhiksham

For one who toils there is no hunger

An old Sanskrit aphorism

Acknowledgements

The research work reported in this book was initiated at the International Institute for Applied Systems Analysis (IIASA), Laxenburg, Austria as a part of its Food and Agriculture Program (FAP). Though the bulk of the work was carried out over a number of years at IIASA, a lot of research and writing was also done at the Indian Statistical Institute, New Delhi and Bangalore and at the Indira Gandhi Institute of Development Research, Bombay. We gratefully acknowledge the support of these institutions.

The development of the model has benefited enormously from the comments and criticism of many of our colleagues of the FAP at IIASA. We want to particularly acknowledge our intellectual debt to Michiel Keyzer with whom we have had many fruitful discussions. Other colleagues whose contribution we want to specifically acknowledge are Csaba Csaki, Guenther Fischer, Klaus Frohberg, Ferenc Rabar and Mahendra Shah. We also wish to thank Jan Morovich and Laslo Zeold for computational assistance and R. Radhakrishna and K.N. Murthy for the demand system a modified version of which is used in the model.

Our profound thanks are due to the library staff of IIASA and of the Indian Statistical Institute, Bangalore for their hearty cooperation in meeting with our requirements which were sometimes exacting.

We thank Maulik Parikh for helping us with editorial corrections.

Finally for entering, revising and beautifying many versions of the various chapters on the word processor, we thank Barbara Hauser, T.S. Mahesh Mohan and B.S. Phaniraj. K. Arvind also helped us with computer work. We thank A. Ganesh Kumar for his help in proof-reading.

Bombay, December 1989

N.S.S. Narayana
Kirit S. Parikh
T.N. Srinivasan

Contents

List of Tables

List of Figures

1

A Framework for Policy Analysis

1.1   Guiding Principles of India's Development

The Directive Principles of State Policy of the Indian Constitution, although not enforceable by any court, express the philosophy and the objectives that "are nevertheless fundamental in the governance of the country and it shall be the duty of the State to apply these principles in making laws" (Article 37, The Constitution of India). Interestingly, most of the articles enunciating these principles (as amended from time to time) urge the state to strive to secure "a social order in which justice, social, economic and political shall inform all the institutions of the national life" and "to minimize inequality in income, status, facilities and opportunities, amongst individuals and groups"(Article 38), and to ensure "that the ownership and control of the material resources of the community are so distributed as best to subscribe the common good; that the operation of the economic system does not result in the concentration of wealth and means of production to the common detriment" (Article 39). Article 41 seeks to make effective provisions for securing the right to work, to education and to public assistance in case of unemployment, disability, sickness, etc.

The Principles assign the raising of the level of nutrition and the standard of living of the people and the improvement of public health as some of the primary duties of the state (Article 47). The development of agriculture and animal husbandry along modern scientific lines is also assigned to the state (Article 48). The provision of Free and Compulsory education for all children under the age of fourteen within ten years of the commencement of the Constitution (Article 43) and equal pay for equal work for both men and women (Article 38) are other notable goals that the state should achieve.

The strong egalitarian and redistributive thrust of these principles is evident. It is also clear that a dominant role of the state in the economic sphere is implicit in them. Although the objectives of these principles are yet to be attained, that they continue to be evoked in political and public policy debates is a testament to their appeal. Indeed the government resolution establishing the Planning Commission for articulating a national development strategy explicitly invoked these principles. The very first Five Year Plan set out the task of development as to "translate . . . the goals of social and economic policy prescribed in the Directive Principles of the Constitution . . . into a national programme based upon the assessment of needs and resources" (as quoted in Draft Sixth Five Year Plan 1979-83). Indeed, achieving rapid development with social justice is the problem of Indian development. Yet the policies that can succeed in promoting such growth are not obvious. Policies that at first blush appear to do so can turn out to be ineffective if not inappropriate because of the interaction between private responses and public policies and their ultimate effects in a complex economy.

The possibility that the growth of national income brought about by planned development may not be equitably shared was suggested as early as 1960, long before the same issue was raised elsewhere in the world, in the Indian Parliament by the late Rammanohar Lohia, a socialist member. The response by Prime Minister Nehru is worth quoting:

> . . . it is said that the national income over the First and Second Plans has gone up by 42 per cent and the per capita income by 20 per cent. A legitimate query is made where has this gone? It is a very legitimate query; to some extent of course, you can see where it has gone. I sometimes do address large gatherings in the villages and I can see that they are better-fed and better-clothed, they build brick houses . . . Nevertheless, this does not apply to everybody in India. Some people probably have hardly benefited. Some people may even be facing various difficulties. The fact remains, however, that this advance in our national income, in our per capita income has taken place, and I think it is desirable that we should enquire more deeply as to where this has gone and appoint some expert committee to enquire into how exactly this additional income that has come to the country or per capita has spread.

Nevertheless, concern that the growth process may have been unequalizing led Pandit Nehru's government to appoint a Committee under the Chairmanship of Professor P.C. Mahalanobis to study the distribution of income and standards of living in India. Later other reports such as the Hazari Report, and The Dutt Committee Report, questioned whether the system of controls on private industrial development led to a concentration of economic power. Whether additional layers of controls established on the recommendation of these committees, such as through the Monopolies and Restrictive Trade Practices Commission have in fact led to any appreciable reduction in concentration or have simply added another source of delay and inefficiency is another matter. Nevertheless, exploring alternative policies that promote rapid development with social justice is the main theme of this book.

1.2   Problems in Policy Formulation

Needless to say, the objectives of the policy-maker will play a dominant role in policy formulation. Although it is said that the objective of government policy in a democratic society is to promote the welfare of the people, it is difficult to translate this into operational terms. To begin with there are the deep problems of moral and economic philosophy. First, what is the welfare indicator of an individual? Should it be a function of his consumption of various goods and services over time or of the characteristics of such goods or of the abilities that the goods and services consumed enable him to achieve? (See Sen 1983a, 1983b). Second, even if one were to agree on a welfare measure at the individual level, how does one aggregate the measures relating to different members of society? Indeed, what constitutes society for this purpose — citizens of voting age, all citizens living at a point in time, or all present and future citizens? Third, if present and future generations are to be included, should they be treated in the same way or are there reasons for assigning a lower weight for the welfare of later generations? Fourth, if the size of the future generation is in part determined by voluntary choices made by the present, would not the welfare of the future generation be reflected in that of the present? The celebrated Possibility Theorem of Arrow (1963) suggests that in general it may be impossible to aggregate individual preferences into a social preference ordering that satisfies some desirable properties.

One way out of the philosophical bind is to abandon the search for complete and consistent aggregation of individual preferences (Sen 1979). More simply put, there may be an agreement among individuals in a society about the ordering of a subset of alternatives though they may differ on others. For example, all individuals may agree that faster aggregate of growth is preferable to slower, less poverty to more, more stable and sustainable growth path to less stable and unsustainable, etc., while they may disagree on trade-offs among them and on other social objectives. This suggests that, at a minimum, policies may have to be designed in a context of multiple objectives, with no agreed trade-off among them.

It is again evident that a choice of policies is constrained by the social, political, administrative and economic framework. Conceptually, it is helpful to think of policy formulation as a choice among alternative combination of values to be assigned to a set of policy instruments subject to the constraints imposed by the socio-political-economic framework. Even this conceptualization is not free of difficulties, since the distinction between objectives, instruments and constraints is not clear-cut. For example, the achievement of self-reliance (somehow measured) could be either classified as an objective or as one of the constraints on the choice of policy; that is, any policy that does not achieve a specified minimal degree of self-reliance could be ruled out altogether. To take another example, increasing state ownership of means of production (nationalization) can be deemed an objective in itself or merely as an instrument to achieve other objectives. Indeed, it is not uncommon to find instances in which what were once instruments become objectives e.g. the past expansion of the public sector was an instrument for ushering in socialism. Now it is viewed by some in India regardless of its performance as sine-qua-non of socialism! It is like a Guru who is supposed to show the path to God being worshipped as God himself! Nevertheless, despite all its ambiguities, the conceptualization in terms of objectives, instruments and constraints is a powerful analytical stepping stone.

A change in the existing levels of any policy instrument can have effects (favourable or unfavourable) on one or more objectives. This is illustrated in Figure 1 with respect to a number of instruments and objectives. Here, the effect of each policy instrument on the set of objectives is considered one at a time. Equally, a policy can have an impact on some or all the constraints. In a typical policy problem, the choice may involve many instruments which in turn means that it is important to consider the mutual interaction among them. In other words, the effects on an objective or constraint of a set of policies need not be additive. They can reinforce (super additive) or counter-act (sub-additive) each other. A satisfactory approach to policy analysis should account for these.

1.3   Desiderata for Policy Analysis

It is useful at the outset to lay out a minimal set of formal requirements on the formulation of policies. To avoid repetition, from now on, the word policy will be used generally to denote a policy (e.g.investment policy) and, more loosely, to denote the level at which the associated instrument is set (e.g. investment level). In view of the possible interaction among policies in their effect on objectives, the first requirement is mutual consistency among the set of policies proposed for consideration. A set of policies is said to be mutually

Policy Instrument	Objective			
	Growth	Equity	Stability	Sustain- ability
Investment Level	↑	↑↓	↓	
Income Tax	?	↑?		
Indirect Tax	↑	↓	↓	
Irrigation	↑	↓	↑	↓
High yield varieties	↑	↓	↓?	↓
Fertilizers	↑	↑↓		↓
Mechanization	↑?	↓		
Land ceiling and redistribution	↑↓	↑		↑↓
Tenancy reforms	↑	↑		↑?↓
Public food distribution	↓	↑	↑	↑
Procurement of foodgrains	↓	↑		
Buffer stock operation	↓?		↑	↑
Food aid	↑↓?	↑	↑	↓

↑ Furthers objective.
↓ Adverse effect on objective.
? Questionable effect.

Fig. 1.1 Some conceivable effects of policy instruments

consistent with respect to a set of objectives if their combined effect is in the desired direction with respect to at least one objective. Although this sounds almost banal, its importance and the difficulty of checking for mutual consistency can hardly be exaggerated. Unless one has a reasonably well-articulated and empirically specified 'model' of the complex relationship between the policies and the objectives over the proposed range of changes in the levels at which the instruments of policy are to be set, checking for mutual consistency is nearly impossible. Consider, for example, investment and public distribution policies of Figure 1. Since each affects each of the three objectives in a direction opposite to that of the other, if we assume for simplicity that their joint effect is the sum of individual effects, depending on the strength of these effects, it is conceivable that some proposed levels of investment and public distribution end up in reducing growth, worsening the equity of the outcomes and destabilizing the system, i.e., being mutually inconsistent! To repeat, the interaction among policies can be exceedingly complex, and assuming that a set of policies is mutually consistent merely because a partition of the set revealed that each element of the partition was consistent taken by itself can be misleading.

The second requirement is feasibility. A set of policies is said to be feasible if it satisfies all the relevant constraints. If our model of the system is complete in the sense of encompassing the constraints imposed by the social, political, administrative and economic framework, then there is nothing further to be said. On the other hand, if one is working with a partial model, in which a subset of relevant constraints is excluded, then of course, a set of policies not violating any of the included constraints need not necessarily be feasible. Since no model of the real world can be complete, feasibility of a policy set is often presumed rather than proven, if it does not violate any of the included constraints and informal analysis suggests that it is unlikely to violate any other relevant but excluded constraint.

The third requirement is one of efficiency. A set of consistent and feasible policies is said to be efficient if there is no alternative set of consistent and feasible policies that advances each objective at least as much, and at least one objective to a greater extent in the desired direction. Clearly, in the choice among policies from a social point of view, the search can be restricted to efficient policy sets. It is also clear that consistency and feasibility, while necessary, are not sufficient for a set of policies to be efficient. It is likely that different policy-makers may weigh different objectives differently in their evaluation. But, even if they do, an inefficient set of policies will receive no consideration from any policy-maker. A fortiori, if all policy-makers agree on a social welfare function that incorporates their agreed weights, one can define an optimal set of policies as the set among those that are efficient which maximizes the social welfare function. One may note that since the notion of feasibility itself is not well defined for an incomplete model, questions of efficiency and optimality do not arise. Thus, for the formal model of this book, which is an incomplete one, the relevant notion is that of mutual consistency of policy.

In this book, the analytical model constructed is that of the economic system of an open and mixed economy, i.e., an economy in which private and public sectors co-exist in most spheres of economic activity and the economy trades in commodities with, and receives capital inflows from, the rest of the world. The socio-political-administrative system is not formally modeled, although such consideration may be informally brought in occasionally. Before we turn to the specific issues in modeling an open and mixed economy, we describe briefly the political and administrative framework of economic policy-making in India.

1.4 Planning for National Development

The Government of India, by a resolution promulgated in 1950, established a Planning Commission as an advisory body to the Central Government and charged it with the task of formulating plans for national development. Such plans had been formulated even before independence, notably by a committee of the Indian National Congress headed by Pandit Nehru, by a group of entrepreneurs and businessmen, and even by the colonial government in its final years (Hanson 1966). However, there was opposition to state-initiated planning among some of the influential leaders of post-independence government including the first Indian Governor-General, C.Rajagopalachari, and the Deputy Prime Minister Sardar Patel. It is perhaps the expectation of strong political opposition that led to the establishment of the Planning Commission through the fiat of a government resolution rather than through any of the formal means that would have required approval by Parliament. The political authority, if not legitimacy, that the Planning Commission would have had, had it been created through an Act of Parliament, was sought through the creation of the National Development Council in which the Chief Ministers of all the States were members. The Council discussed and approved development plans formulated by the Commission, although the Council itself has lost some of its prestige over the years.

The constitutional distribution of legislative powers between the Centre and the States assigned almost all matters relating to agriculture exclusively to the States. Although through the Five Year Plans and Central assistance to States on plan account, some measure of balanced development among States was sought to be achieved, there still are wide inter-State disparities in agricultural performance, only a part of which could be attributed to agro-climatic differences or to differences in initial endowments of infrastructure like irrigation.

The legislative powers relating to industries are assigned to the Centre by law by Parliament which declared such control by the Union to be expedient in the public interest. Legislation with respect to trade and commerce in, and the production, supply and distribution of, the products of such industries can be enacted by either the States or the Centre. Foreign trade and commerce is exclusively in the legislative province of the Centre. Apart from these constitutionally-mandated divisions, industrial development is governed by the industrial policy resolutions of the Government of India of 1948 and 1956. These resolutions divided the industries into three groups: those which will be established or expanded exclusively in the public sector, those reserved for exclusive development by the private sector and those which could be developed by either the public or the private sector.

The philosophy underlying the reservation of some industries in the public sector was that public control of certain key sectors of the economy (the so called "commanding heights") will enable the State to direct the development of the entire economy along a desired path. Thus, key infra-structural industries such as Railways, Telecommunications, Electricity-generation etc. were to be in the public sector. Also the industries supplying key industrial raw materials like steel were reserved to the public sector. It was expected that through an appropriate pricing policy for the output of the public sector, not only could the development of other industries be significantly influenced but also resources for investment in the public sector could be generated from profits of the public sector enterprises. The extent to which these expectations were realized is another story altogether. In any case, in the analytical framework of this book, all non-agricultural activities in the economy have been aggregated into a single sector. The differences, if any, in the objectives and operations of public and private sector enterprises do not figure in the analysis. However, public investment as a whole plays a role in it.

An important objective of the Indian development strategy is the promotion of self-reliance. By this it was meant that India's dependence on the rest of the world for capital, equipment and technology needed for her development should be minimized. In practice, it was interpreted more rigidly and a development strategy of import substitution wherever possible regardless of costs was adopted. The inward-oriented import substitution strategy, its costs and benefits, are not discussed here at length. However, the implications of eliminating trade barriers and varying external resource flow from eliminating it altogether (total self-reliance), at one extreme, to quadrupling it at the other extreme are analyzed.

Thus, one sees the Indian economy as a mixed economy in which millions of private decision-makers, consumers and producers react to government policy. Their ingenuity in adapting to the government's regulatory policies have often made many of them ineffective. This has resulted in the use of a large variety of policy instruments, the mutual consistency of which with the objectives, at least with those often repeated in public rhetoric by political leaders, is not obvious. It is in this context that we see the need for model for policy analysis that integrates the behavioral responses of the various economic agents in the economy and which distinguishes the variety of policy instruments often used in the country. The applied general equilibrium model of an open economy presented here is, we believe, such a model and hence useful for policy analysis.

1.5   Modeling an Open and Mixed Economy

By definition, in a mixed economy, a significant part of the economy is controlled by private decision-makers. This means that state control over the economy has to be exercised in part through instruments of state policy (such as taxes) that affect private decisions. The interplay of the reactions of many private decision makers to changes in state policy determine its outcome. Policy-evaluation has to be done in such a context. More generally, it means that the state in choosing its actions has to treat private behavior as constraints. In almost all economies, mixed or otherwise, an overwhelming proportion of aggregate consumption expenditure is allocated by private consumers. In mixed economies, production of some of the commodities and the associated investment relating to capacity creation for such production are decided by private producers. For modeling their decisions, one needs to specify their objectives, i.e., what they seek to achieve through their decisions as well as the constraints they face in making their choices.

In an economy where most consumable commodities are bought and sold, it is natural to assume that private consumers choose their most preferred consumption basket from the set of such baskets that they could have consumed, given the prices they face and their total consumption-expenditure, which in turn is determined by how much they decide to save out of their disposable income. In a market economy disposable income of consumers is the difference between the income they earn from their labor supply to the market as well as from the earnings from any non-labor assets they own and the direct taxes they pay to the government. The proportion of disposable income that households choose to save will in turn be influenced by the households' preferences between present consumption and future consumption and the returns they expect to receive (allowing for risk) on the assets (financial and non-financial) in which they choose to hold their savings. Clearly the menu of available alternative investment opportunities and their risk-return characteristics determine the portfolio of assets held by households. Where savings and investment decisions are so modeled, the model acquires the main characteristic of a dynamic one. Otherwise, it remains a static model, and the savings and investment decisions are essentially exogenously specified.

Private producers in a dynamic model of a market economy can be presumed to maximize the present value of their enterprise through appropriate output, input and investment (including investment in inventories) decisions. In particular this implies that they maximize appropriately defined after-tax profits each period, the profits being a function of their choice of outputs, inputs, investment (and its financing through debt and equity) and the current and expected future prices including interest rates, and subject to any constraints that they face such as input and output quotas, compulsory sales to government, etc.

In general, the decisions of private producers and consumers can be described either in reduced form as functions of the variables that they cannot influence (i.e. variables exogenous to their decisions) such as predetermined capacities, income or wealth, the relevant prices, and government policy instruments or in structural form in which their objectives and constraints are specified in terms of decision variables as well as exogenous variables.

To close the model, one needs to specify the time path of exogenous variables. A subset of exogenous variables such as capacities available for utilization in each period, initial wealth (net value of assets and liabilities) and inventories are the result of past decisions. As such these are predetermined and hence exogenous for current decision. Another subset, namely, the levels at which the government policy instruments are set, while exogenous to private decisions are subject to choice by government. One can either pursue a positive analysis in which the aim is to draw out the implications of exogenously specified values of government policy variables or a normative analysis in which a government objective function and constraints on its choices are specified. The policy instruments are then presumed to be set at levels that maximize the objective function subject to the constraints being satisfied.

The remaining set of variables, exogenous to private decisions but endogenous to the economy as a whole, are commodity and asset prices and returns on financial instruments. A subset of prices are those relating to internationally-traded goods. If the economy is a sufficiently small trader in the world markets for all its traded goods and if the government intervenes in trade only through tariffs, then the domestic prices of these commodities are determined by world prices and tariffs. If the government imposes trade quotas rather than tariffs on some internationally-traded commodities, then the domestic prices of such traded commodities, the prices of non-traded commodities, prices of domestic factors (wage rates, capacity rentals, etc.) and rates of return on assets are endogenous. These are determined through a set of economy-wide or systemic constraints, namely, that supply (from domestic production and imports) equal demand (domestic and export) for each commodity and financial instrument and that the trade deficit not exceed the level that can be financed through exogenous foreign aid and capital inflows. Thus, these system-wide constraints determine the endogenous net trade flows for internationally-traded commodities which are not quota-constrained, and prices for all other commodities and factors as well as returns on financial instruments.

The above approach to modeling a mixed economy emphasizes its three essential features: the behavioral response of the private segment of the economy to public policy choices as well as to market prices and, in turn, the feed-back effects of these responses on public policy choices mostly through their impact on government revenues and expenditures and also through government liabilities (currency and public debt) in so far as these figure in the choice of assets in which the private sector holds its wealth, and, finally, the fact that for each commodity, factor or financial instrument supply from all sources together must equal demand, again from all sources put together.

The last feature describes the general equilibrium aspect of the model, that is, each endogenous variable such as a price could in principle influence the supply or demand of each and every commodity, factor or financial instrument, although the strength of this influence will vary across commodities, factors and instruments. In a dynamic model such influence extends over time as well. That is, today's price of a commodity may influence not only its current, but also its future, demands and supplies and those of other commodities. For example, even if the elasticity of demand for every other commodity with respect to the price of rice is negligible, if the economy produces mostly rice, then the price of rice will influence the income of consumers significantly and, through the income effect, the price of rice will influence the current demand for all other commodities, current savings and investments, and through them the future course of these variables. Clearly, if interdependence within the economy is pervasive and strong as it is likely to be in a moderately complex economy, a general equilibrium approach is essential. Policy analysis based on a partial approach, equilibrium or otherwise, can be misleading since it ignores spill-over or feed-back effects.

APPLIED GENERAL EQUILIBRIUM

An applied general equilibrium model (AGM) is an empirical version of the analytical model of a mixed economy described above. It specifies the functional forms for the various behavioral responses, the numerical values of the parameters occurring in them and the variables exogenous to the model (such as world prices for traded commodities). Usually the specified parameter values are partially drawn from econometric studies and in part determined in a way that the data relating to some base period including the actual prices that prevailed in that period represent an equilibrium set.

1.6   Policy Analysis with an AGM

An AGM is a flexible tool for policy analysis. In principle the impact of any policy that affects the behavioral responses can be analyzed with the help of an AGM model. The following are only illustrative and not exhaustive:

(i) Foreign trade, aid and capital inflow policies. As discussed earlier, tariffs imposed on traded goods determine their domestic prices given their world market prices. Thus any policy that imposes or changes tariffs, by changing domestic prices of such traded commodities, changes the demands and supplies of all other commodities. To restore equilibrium, other endogenous prices and variables have to adjust. The consequences of the move to a new equilibrium including change in the welfare of consumers constitute the impact of the tariff policy. An imposition of a quota or changes in existing quotas, on the other hand, affects the systemic constraint on the quantity of supply and demand for those commodities. To restore equilibrium once again the endogenous variables have to adjust. Changes in aid or capital inflow levels affect the systemic constraint on trade balance.

The process of adjustment to changes in policy variables can be constrained in some way if it is of analytical interest. This illustrates the flexibility of an AGM as an analytical tool. An example will clarify this. Consider the adjustment to a change in the availability of external resources through changes in, say, foreign aid levels. It usually involves changes in the endogenously determined net imports of traded commodities which are not quota-constrained. If, for some reason, it is decided that some endogenous net imports should not be allowed to change from their initial values, then, in effect, these imports no longer are endogenous and their initial levels become quota-constraints in the new equilibrium. Thus the burden of adjustment to restore equilibrium subsequent to a change in aid levels falls on the remaining set of endogenous variables.

(ii) Redistributive policies. In a general equilibrium, the distribution of income among individuals depends on the distribution of ownership of the primary factors and assets and the equilibrium factor prices and returns on assets. Any policy-induced change in the ownership of assets or wealth is, of course, a redistributive policy - it will usually change the equilibrium factor

prices and returns on assets thereby changing income distribution as well. More generally any policy that changes equilibrium factor rewards and asset returns has a redistributive effect, some of which can be unforeseen and surprising. Without a model of the AGM type and computing the new equilibrium subsequent to a policy change the distributional effects cannot be analyzed even qualitatively. Besides studying redistributive effects of policies that are adopted for other reasons, policies which are introduced primarily as redistributive devices are of interest. Such policies will include, without by any means exhausting all redistributive policies, income or consumption subsidies for well defined subgroups of consumers and employment creation for particular subgroups.

(iii) Public investment and consumption policies. Adjustment to any changes in government expenditure on investment or consumption in general involves changes in endogenous variables that change government revenue in an offsetting way. Once again, one can constrain the adjustment only to a particular subset of endogenous variables. For example, if the entire schedule of income tax rates is endogenous and will adjust to changes in government expenditure, one may wish the rates applicable to particular subgroups not to change at all. In such a case, the rates that are not allowed to change become exogenous.

1.7 Scope and Plan of the Book

The objective of this book is the analysis of policy alternatives that promote growth and structural transformation while ensuring social justice. The analysis is mainly, though not exclusively, focussed on agriculture. The time horizon of analysis extends until the end of the twentieth century. The tool of analysis, is an Applied General Equilibrium Model of the Indian economy.

Chapter 2 sets the stage by reviewing the performance of Indian economy, and agriculture in particular since independence in maintaining a fairly steady growth in aggregate output in the context of a perceptible slow-down in the growth of the net sown area.

Chapter 3 provides a technical description of the AGM model of India called AGRIM, (for Agriculture, growth and redistribution of income model) and describes its empirical (data and econometrically estimated relationships) underpinnings.

Chapter 4 sets out the scheme of analysis to be followed in subsequent chapters. It describes the base or reference scenario of the model for the period 1980-2000 and the crucial assumptions about the time path of exogenous variables such as population, its rural-urban composition, trends in the growth of the net sown area, the deficit in external trade, etc. The impact of a change in any policy (or set of policies) from its course in the reference scenario is assessed through the changes induced in a set of performance indicators relative to the reference scenario. The indicators used for this purpose and their relevance are described. Chapters 5 to 11 contain the core of the book, an analysis of the impact of alternative policy scenarios.

Chapter 5 considers public distribution policies relating to foodgrains.

Chapter 6 considers, to an extent, yet another fiercely- debated policy problem of orientation towards the rest of the world, whether trade policy should be outward-oriented and liberal or inward-oriented and restrictive. The consequences of varying the levels of external assistance are also analyzed.

Chapter 7 analyzes another policy oriented towards the alleviation of rural poverty: the creation of productive assets through rural works programmes in which unemployed and underemployed rural workers are provided employment, usually at a real wage below the ruling market real wage. Wages are also paid in foodgrains in the food-for-work version of the rural works programme.

Chapter 8 is devoted to the analysis of a policy issue that has been extensively debated in the literature, namely, the sensitivity of agricultural performance to movements in terms of trade between the agricultural and non-agricultural sectors.

Chapter 9 analyzes the policy of subsidizing chemical fertilizers, one of the important inputs in agriculture.

Chapter 10 is concerned with investment in irrigation.

Chapter 11 concludes the book drawing out the policy lessons from the previous chapters. It also compares the model and conclusions of the book with other studies in the literature addressing some of the same set of policy problems.

2

Indian Economy and Agriculture Since Independence

The development of the Indian economy has been guided by the course charted by the Planning Commission. The First Five Year Plan covered the period 1951-56 and altogether six five year plans and four annual plans (for the period 1966-69 and 1979-80) have been completed. The seventh plan was launched in 1985-86. Table 2.1 describes some of the achievements.

It is evident from Table 2.1 that per capita income grew at a rather modest rate of about 1.6% per annum on the average in nearly 34 years. Although the structure of the economy shifted away from its dependence on agriculture, the economy is by no means industrialized. The average rate of growth of value added in manufacturing has been an unimpressive 5.1% per year and manufacturing accounted for only 16.3% of GDP in 1984-85 representing a minuscule increase of about 1% over its value in 1950-51. A more or less constant rate of growth of aggregate national output was achieved at increasing costs in terms of capital formation as can be inferred from the increase in the rate of gross capital formation from 10.0% of GNP in 1950-51 to 23.4% in 1984-85. Part of the explanation for such a rising incremental capital output ratio is of course the structural change towards more capital intensive activities that occurs in the normal course of development. However, there is substantial evidence that the inward-looking industrialization strategy of development pursued by the planners is the significant cause of the low rate of growth despite increasing investment (Ahluwalia 1985. Bhagwati and Desai 1970 , Bhagwati and Srinivasan 1975, 1984).

Some indicators of agricultural development are seen in Table 2.2. The substantial growth in the output of food and fibres over nearly three and a half decades is evident. There has been rapid technical change (popularly known as the green revolution) in the production of cereals, with nearly 60% of the cultivated area in 1985 being devoted to the so-called high yielding varieties introduced in the late 60s. Even though there was a phenomenal growth in the use of chemical fertilizers starting from a negligible base in 1950, the intensity of usage in 1984-85 at less than 50 kg. per hectare of land is still modest by developed country standards. There was roughly a doubling of the proportion of the cultivated area that is supplied with irrigation during this period. Agriculture accounted for 31% of India's exports in 1981-82 in value terms compared to 26% in 1950-51, and its importance in imports has fallen substantially from 35% to 10% mainly because of self-sufficiency in foodgrains. Indeed, compared to the imports which were nearly 10% of domestic availability in 1950-51, India exported a small volume of foodgrains in 1984-85. However, the imports of edible oils in recent years have been substantial, indicating the relatively poor growth in the output of oilseeds. Another area of even more dismal performance is in the production of pulses. There is no significant trend in output growth; annual fluctuations have been large with a peak output of 13.2 million tons in 1958-59 and a low of 8.6 million tons in 1979-80. Possibilities of imports from the rest of the world are limited.

More grain was bought by the government in 1984-85 than it distributed at subsidized prices through ration shops. This excess procurement was essentially a reflection of the fact that the government in effect ran a price support operation with the attendant accumulation of stocks. The foodgrains distribution subsidies inclusive of carrying costs of stocks and the subsidies on the use of fertilizers have become substantial, accounting for more than a tenth of total non-developmental expenditure of the Central and State Governments put together.

Ever since a poverty line of Rs.20 per capita per month in urban areas and Rs.15 in rural areas (1960-61 prices) on consumption expenditure was defined by a committee appointed by the Planning Commission in 1960, there has been an ever-increasing literature on estimating the trends in poverty and testing a number of explanatory hypotheses (see Bhattacharya et al. (1985) and Tendulkar (1987) for an overview). If we use simple head count measure, namely, the proportion of population with consumption expenditure below the poverty line, no trend is seen in rural or urban poverty in annual data from the sixties until 1973-74. The two subsequent observations for 1977-78 and 1982-83 show a sizeable fall in rural areas from 46.1% in 1973-74 to 40.1% and 33.2% respectively. In urban areas, the figure rises from 38.7% in 1973-74 (which represents a significant fall from an average of over 45% in the previous decade) to 39.56% in 1977-78 only to fall to 34.87% in 1982-83. Whether or not the recent fall is a statistical artifact, two things are clear: India is still a country of the poor most of whom are rural residents and that four decades of development have not made any major dent in the proportion of poor in the population.

India's development strategy has not succeeded in creating rapidly growing employment opportunities outside agriculture. Confining to the male work force to avoid problems of the changing definition of worker between censuses, the share of the male labor force in agriculture has declined marginally from 69.51% in 1961 to 66.69% in 1981. In fact, there has been only marginal decline in a period of more than a century since the first population census in 1861! Another indicator of this failure is that in the twelve years between 1973 and 1984 employment in private industry grew by a grand total of 7% while that in the public sector industry grew by 41%. In industries under the control of the state and quasi government bodies, the rate of growth at 60% was more

TABLE 2.1 Salient features of Indian economic development

	1950-51	1984-85
Per capita GNP (at 1970-71 prices, Rupees)	486.6	831.2
Output of foodgrains(million metric tons)	55.0	145.5
Share of agriculture in nominal GDP (%)	50.1	31.5
Share of manufacturing in nominal GDP (%)	15.3	16.3
Population (millions)	359.0	739.0
Share of rural population (%)	83.0	77.0*
Share of gross domestic savings in GDP(%)	10.2	22.9
Share of exports to GDP (%)	6.5	6.3
Share of gross domestic capital formation (%)	10.0	24.4

Average annual rates of growth (%)**	1950-51 1964-65	1967-68 1984-85
GDP	3.92	3.77
Population	2.01	2.27
Per capita GNP	1.91	1.50
Agricultural value added(at 1970-71 prices)	2.43	2.41
Manufacturing value added(at 1970-71 prices)	6.40	5.27
Wholesale prices	2.62	8.67

* Relates to 1981
** Based on semi-logarithmic time trends except for manufacturing value added which is based on end-point comparisons. The years 1965-66 and 1966-67 have been omitted because of distortions due to serious shocks to the economy such as two successive and severe droughts in 1965-66 and 1966-67, a war with Pakistan in 1965 and the devaluation of the rupee in June 1966.

Sources: Government of India: *Economic Survey*, 1986-87 and earlier years; Central Statistical Organisation: *National Accounts Statistics* January 1986 and earlier years; Reserve Bank of India: *Report of the Committee to Review the Working of the Monetary System*, 1985.

rapid than in the public sector as a whole. There are reasons to believe that the relatively rapid growth in public sector employment is largely due to overstaffing.

TABLE 2.2 Salient features of Indian agriculture and its development

	1950-51	1984-85
Land development		
Arable land (million hectares)	186.70	181.00
Per capita arable land (hectares)	0.52	0.25
Gross sown area (million hectares)	131.90	171.40
Net sown area (million hectares)	118.80	143.00
Cropping intensity	1.10	1.20
Gross irrigated area (as a percentage of gross sown area)	17.10	35.30
Area under high yielding varieites (as percentage of gross sown area under five major cereal crops)	n/a[1]	58.70
Average farm size (hectare)	3.05	n/a
Draft power		
Draft animals (millions)	66.00	81.00[4]
Tractors (stock in thousands)	8.60	276.00[2]
Chemical fertilisers (kilogram per hectare of gross sown area)		
Nitrogenous	0.44	31.97
Phosphatic	0.05	11.03
Potassic	0.00	4.90
Human resources		
Cultivators (millions)	78.00[3]	92.00[4]
Agricultural labourers (millions)	43.00[3]	55.00[4]
Output of major crops		
Index of agricultural production (Base: Triennium ending in 1969-70=100)	58.50	155.80[5]
Rice (million tons)	22.10	58.30
Wheat (million tons)	6.80	44.10
Coarse grains (million tons)	16.90	31.20
Pulses (million tons)	9.20	12.00
Cereals (million tons)	45.80	133.60
Foodgrains (million tons)	55.00	145.50
Sugarcane (million tons)	70.50	170.30
Oilseeds (million tons)	5.00	13.00
Cotton (million bales)	2.90	8.50

Jute and mesta (million bales)	4.20	7.80
Agricultural exports (as a percentage of the value of all exports)	26.00	30.70[4]
Agricultural imports (as a percentage of the value of all imports)	34.80	10.50[4]
Foodgrain imports (as a percentage of total net domestic availability)	9.2	−0.03

Public distribution of foodgrains

Procurement (million tons)	n/a	20.10
Distribution (million tons)	n/a	15.80
Stock (million tons)	n/a	21.42
Central Government subsidies on the distribution of foodgrains and fertilisers as a percentage of total non-developmental expenditure of Central and State Governme	n/a	11.63

(1) Not available.
(2) Refers to 1977
(3) Refers to 1971
(4) Refers to 1981.
(5) Refers to 1983 4.

Sources: Ministry of Agriculture, Government of India: *Area and Production of Principal Crops in India,* 1980-81 and earlier issues; Data on arable land obtained from response to questions in Rajya Sabha by the Minister of State for Agriculture (*Times of India*, April 25, 1987, p.14); Ministry of Finance, Government of India: *Economic Survey,*1986-87 and earlier issues.

The industrial sector, although by no means the dynamic sector it was intended to be, has become considerably diversified. In the twenty years between 1959-60 and 1979-80 while net value added in the industry as a whole grew at 5.6% per year, value added in industries producing consumer durables grew at 10.7%, capital goods at 8.1% and intermediate goods at 4.2%. On an input- based classification, chemical-based industries grew at 8.6% per year, metal-based industries at 7.8% while the traditional agro- based industries grew at only 3.2% per year (see K.L. Krishna 1987). It is likely that these trends have only strengthened since 1979-80.

The trends in India's foreign trade reveal a mixed picture - of some modest successes and large failures. India's share in the world trade has been continuously declining from 2.4% in 1948 to less than 0.5% in 1986. Other smaller countries such as the Republic of Korea with virtually no manufactured exports in 1960, when India exported $630 million worth of such goods, have left India way behind since then. In 1983, Korea exported $22.2 billion worth of manufactured exports as compared to India's $5.1 billion. However, the structure of exports in terms of commodities and destinations has been diversified. From negligible shares in the 1950s, traditional exports such as engineering goods, jewellery based on diamonds or precious stones, garments, etc., accounted for nearly 50% of the total value of exports in 1984-85. Trade with Eastern Europe and developing countries has expanded much faster than the total trade since 1950. The commodity composition of imports has also changed drastically. Share of food in total imports in 1983 was only 7% as compared to 22% in 1965. Share of machinery has declined from 37% to 17% during the same period indicating the extent of import substitution. India's external debt has continued to grow with public and publicly-guaranteed long-term debt amounting to $22.4 billion in 1984 as compared to $7.9 billion in 1970. However, the debt service burden as a percentage of exports of goods and services is a modest 13.8% in 1984 as compared to 35.8% in the case of a heavily indebted country such as Brazil.

Finally, turning to indicators of health status, life expectancy at birth increased from 32.5 years (31.7 years) during 1941-51 for males (females) to 54.1 (54.7) years in 1980. Infant mortality during the same period declined from 175 per 1000 live births to 115 (Visaria, 1987).

3

A Policy Model for Agriculture, Growth and Redistribution of Income (AGRI Model)

TECHNICAL DESCRIPTION

The model we have constructed is described in this chapter. We call the model AGRIM as an acronym for 'agriculture, growth and redistribution of income model'. In our model there are two broad groups of commodities: agriculture and non-agriculture. There are three sets of agents: producers, consumers, and the government which, through its policies, can influence domestic supplies, prices, foreign trade, etc. Producers and consumers exchange goods subject to the influence of the government's policy. Thus, there are essentially four components to the model: supply, demand, policy and exchange. The full model can be viewed as a system of interconnecting sub-models relating to these components. The sub-models in the first three components are econometrically estimated while the fourth component deals with the computation of equilibrium prices. The existence, uniqueness and stability of equilibrium prices and the algorithm for obtaining them through an iterative procedure in the exchange component are described in Keyzer (1981). This chapter discusses the issues and the methodology involved in setting up the supply, demand and policy components of the model.

3.1 Supply Sub-Models

3.1.1 Agriculture

A schematic outline of the sub-models, indicating various steps involved in estimating agricultural production is shown in Figure 3.1. A number of commodities are distinguished in the agricultural sector prior to their necessary aggregation to conform to the sectoral classification of the demand system, domestic exchange and international trade. These include sixteen major crops, nine minor crops, dairy, fishery and livestock products (see Appendix 3.1). In what follows, 't' denotes the time period (year) and Greek, Roman and lower case letters are used to denote parameters of econometric equations.

We start with estimation of crop production. Though one could have specified "reduced form" output supply functions, such a procedure masks farmers' decisions in allocating their limited land resources to various crops and the impact of changes in fertilizer availability, rates of adoption of high yielding variety (h.y.v.) seeds, etc., on crop yields is not transparent. These are very important in the context of agricultural policy analysis. Estimating "reduced form" output supply functions, which incorporate only the net outcome of a number of decisions, is unsatisfactory for simulating the effects of alternative policies.[1] We followed a two-stage procedure, separately estimating the acreage and the yields of each group.

Total area. The total gross cropped acreage in the country under all crops put together is determined first. It is then allocated to various crops. In India, most of the arable land is already under cultivation. A widely accepted estimate of the potential cultivable land limit that can be ultimately reached is about 165 million hectares (m.h.)[2]. In the present model, net sown area (NSA) is specified to reach ultimately the level of 165 m.h. as follows (NSA$_t$ —>165 m.h. as   t —> ∞):

$$NSA_t = 165000/[1 + \exp (a + b(RIAL)_t + c(RIAL)_t^2 + d(TIME)_t]$$

(1)

where

NSA$_t$	=	net sown area in 1000 hectares in year t;
RIAL$_t$	=	rainfall index for all crops in year t (normal = 100);
TIME$_t$	=	1 for the crop year 1950-51; and
exp	=	denotes exponential.

The total gross cropped area (GCA) in the country is the total NSA multiplied by aggregate cropping intensity (ACI). Since ACI depends on the extent of irrigation, let us turn to the irrigated area.

Irrigated area. Strictly speaking, the net irrigated area (NIA) should depend on, among other things, investment in irrigation. But a continuous series of data on irrigation investment is not available.[3] However, a continuous data series is available for agricultural investment as a whole, of which irrigation

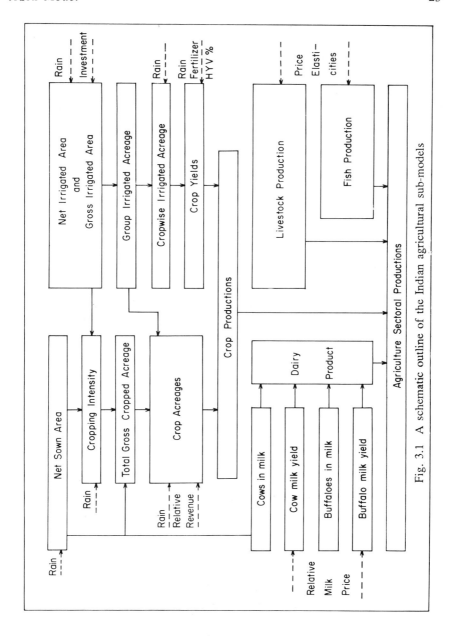

Fig. 3.1 A schematic outline of the Indian agricultural sub-models

investment is a part, the rest belonging to land improvements and purchase of agricultural implements and machinery, etc. Since the latter part was likely to affect the gross irrigated area (GIA) more than the NIA, it was preferred to relate the GIA to agricultural investment. The GIA was specified to be a function of agricultural investment (AGINV), index of all-India rainfall (RIAL), and time (TIME).

$$GIA_t = \alpha + \beta \ RIAL_t + \tau \ AGINV_t + \delta \ TIME_t + u_t \qquad (2)$$

It would have been more natural to use some measure of agricultural capital stock rather than investment in equation (2). Besides such data not being available, many components of agricultural capital are of relatively short duration suggests that investment is likely to be highly correlated with capital stock.

The potential limit of GIA is estimated to be around 113.5 m.h. (see Planning Commission (1981), NCA (1976)). The actual level reached by 1984-85 was 60.5 m.h., i.e., less than 55 percent of the limit. This suggests that there is still a long way to go to reach the limit, and therefore, the ultimate potential was not specified as an asymptote in the functional form for GIA. The ratio of NIA to GIA was assumed to remain constant over time. This was estimated by regressing NIA on GIA with no constant term in the equation.

$$NIA_t = \mu \ GIA_t + u_t \qquad (3)$$

Aggregate crop intensity. Now, the ACI was specified to be a function of the rainfall and the extent of irrigation in the country (that is, the proportion of NIA in NSA), as follows:

$$ACI_t = \alpha + \beta \ (NIA/NSA)_t + \tau \ RIAL_t + \delta \ (RIAL)_t^2 + u_t \qquad (4)$$

One should not take equations (3) and (4) together to imply that since the ratio of GIA to NIA is fixed $(1/\mu)$, ACI varies only because the cropping intensity on unirrigated land varies. Such an inference would be erroneous since the ACI is the result of three types of multiple cropping:[4]

   (i)   Several irrigated crops are grown on the same land;
  (ii)   Several unirrigated crops are grown on the same land;

---

1   For more elaborate arguments see Narayana and Parikh (1981).

2   The net sown area in 1980-81 was 142 m.h., i.e., nearly 85 percent of the potential limit. See Report of the National Commission on Agriculture (NCA) (1976).

3   R.N.Lal (1977) provides these data for some years.

4   See Dharam Narain and Shyamal Roy (1980).

(iii)   Several crops are grown on the same land of which only some are irrigated.

Inclusion of (NIA/NSA) is relevant for explaining (i) and (iii) and rainfall for explaining (ii) and (iii) above, so that both of them together explain the overall aggregate cropping intensity. We now have:

$$GCA_t = ACI_t \ (NSA)_t \tag{5}$$

Groupwise and cropwise irrigated area. Out of all the crops grown in India, sixteen major crops were identified including rice, wheat, maize, jowar and bajra. Of the rest, seven minor crops were identified. The remaining crops fall into two groups: fruits and vegetables and condiments and spices. Treating these two also as minor crops, we have finally sixteen major and nine minor crops. A list of these crops is given in Appendix 3.1.

These twenty-five crops were regrouped into six categories based on their (i) growing season, (ii) type of soil suitable for growth, and (iii) intercrop substitutability. This led to the identification of the following six groups:

   (i)   rice, ragi, jute and mesta;
   (ii)   wheat, gram, barley;
   (iii) maize, jowar, bajra, cotton;
   (iv)   groundnut, sesamum, rapeseed, mustard and other oilseeds;
   (v)   sugarcane;
   (vi)   all other crops.

Only group (v) consists of a single crop (sugarcane), because of its special characteristics. It grows in more than one season, and when it is rationed, that is, when the sugarcane is not planted but is allowed to grow from the stem left in the ground after the first harvest, the same crop can grow in more than one year.

In the first stage the GIA was allocated to the above-mentioned six groups. Gross irrigated area for a group g, $(IA_{gt}, g = 1, 6)$, was specified to be a function of its own value in the previous year $(IA_{gt} - 1)$, and a rainfall index relevant for the leading crop in that group $(RAIN_{gt})$. One may argue that relative profitability between the soil-based groups of crops should also have been an explanatory variable in allocating GIA to various groups. In India, irrigation planning seems to be oriented more towards alleviating risks of uncertain rainfall than maximizing productivity. Traditionally, regions with more assured rainfall received comparatively less priority in irrigation development. The inclusion of the variable IA_{gt-1} reflects this aspect. However, while specifying such a function for each group, an additivity constraint that the sum of IA_g over all groups would add up to the total GIA, was imposed. Thus, a linear model involving a simultaneous estimation of g equations (analogous to the Linear Expenditure System of demand) was specified as follows:

$$IA_{gt} = \tau_g(RAIN)_{gt} + \delta_g IA_{gt-1}$$
$$+ \alpha_g[GIA_t - \Sigma\tau_g(RAIN)_{gt} - \Sigma\delta_g(IA)_{gt-1}] + u_{gt}; \; g=1,..6 \qquad (6)$$

with $\Sigma\alpha_g = 1$.

It may be noted that equation (2) was simultaneously estimated with equation (6).

At the second stage, each IA_g was allocated to individual crops, within group g. For this purpose, a linear model analogous to (6) with an additivity constraint was specified as follows:[5]

$$IC_{gkt} = \beta_{gk} + \tau_{gk}(RAIN)_{gkt} + \delta_{gk}(IC)_{gkt-1}$$
$$+ \alpha_{gk}[IA_{gt} - \Sigma\beta_{gk} - \Sigma\tau_{gk}(RAIN)_{gkt} - \Sigma\delta_{gk}(IC)_{gkt-1}]$$
$$+ u_{gkt} \qquad (7)$$

with $\Sigma\alpha_{gk} = 1$, where

IC_{gkt} = irrigated area of kth crop in g^{th} group.

Acreage under crops. The estimation of farm supply response, i.e., farmers' decisions on acreage allocation to various individual crops, is an important step in developing an agricultural policy model. Agricultural policy affects the supply of agricultural output—both its crop composition and the output of each crop. Agricultural supply, however, is an outcome of the production decisions of a large number of farmers. The time lag between the commitment of major inputs and the harvest of a crop is an important characteristic of agricultural production. Once they sow a crop, farmers can affect the output to be obtained months later only to a limited extent. Besides, the sowing decisions have to be made in an uncertain environment regarding the weather during the growing season and the price the crop will fetch after harvest. Our approach to modeling farmers' decisions reflects these aspects. A detailed report of our modeling approach and estimation of acreage response can be found in Narayana and Parikh (1981). Only a brief description highlighting some of the more important issues is given below.

Our basic postulate is that a farmer's desired allocation of the land among competing crops depends on crop specific rainfall, expected relative revenue

---

5 See Appendix 3.6.

of various crops, and technological features. Past allocation decisions may also constrain the extent to which land can be shifted from crop to crop.

Two important points are to be noted. These are :

(a) In traditional agriculture with unchanging technology, relative crop prices can reasonably be assumed to reflect relative profits earned by farmers in allocating an acre to one crop rather than to another. However, if technology is not stagnant but is continually changing, the year-to-year changes in the farmers' land allocation decisions are due not only to variations in prices, but also to variations in yields per unit of land because of technical progress. As such, the gross revenue per hectare in growing one crop relative to that of competing crops is a more appropriate proxy for relative profits than relative prices.[6]

(b) Farmers observe prices and revenues over time and are also aware of any random shocks which may be of only short-run nature. All these factors influence the process by which the farmers estimate expected revenues in the future. A model of this process should also reflect them.[7] We postulate the process of the formation of revenue expectation for each crop to be an Auto-Regressive Integrated Moving Average (ARIMA) process. Such a model implies that farmers, in expecting their revenue, take into account not only the past realized revenues, but also the extent by which their expectations differed from the actual realizations in the past. These crop revenue expectation equations are as follows:

$$\pi_{kt}^{*} = \pi_{kt} - W_{kt} = \phi_{1k}\pi_{kt-1} + \phi_{2k}\pi_{kt-2} + \phi_{3k}\pi_{kt-3} + \ldots + \mu_{k}$$
$$+ \theta_{1k}W_{kt-1} + \theta_{2k}W_{kt-2} + \theta_{3k}W_{kt-3} + \ldots \qquad (8)$$

where

π_{kt} = $(WPI)_{kt} \cdot YLD_{kt}$;
WPI_{kt} = wholesale price index of crop k;
YLD_{kt} = yield of crop k;
W_{kt} = a random disturbance assumed to be white noise.
        (* refers to expected value.)

The rainfall variables are crop specific indices with the index value for normal rainfall being set at 100. An irrigation variable was used to reflect technological factors. Depending on the crop, the corresponding group spe-

---

6 Often, the possible negative correlation between price and yield prohibits using them as two separate explanatory variables.

7 The traditional Nerlovian adaptive expectation model does not adequately satisfy this requirement. For a discussion of this point see Narayana and Parikh (1981).

cific irrigated area (IA_g or IA_g as a proportion of GIA) was used as one of the variables in explaining the cropped acreage because the rate of inter-crop substitution as well as multiple cropping intensity could depend upon the availability of irrigation.

Formally, the acreage response model is specified as follows:

$$A^*_{gkt} = a_{gk}\left(Z^*_{gkt}\right)^{b_{gk}} \left(R_{gkt}\right)^{c_{gk}} \left[\frac{IA_g}{GIA}\right]_t^{d_{gk}} \left[\frac{IA_{sc}}{GIA}\right]_t^{e_{gk}} . (GIA)_t^{f_{gk}} . V_{gkt} \; \ldots \quad (9)$$

$$A_{gkt} = \left(A^*_{gkt}\right)^{\tau_{gk}} . \left(A_{gkt-1}\right)^{\left(1-\tau_{gk}\right)} \quad\quad\quad (10)$$

where

(i) A_{gkt}^* and A_{gkt} denote long-term desired (equilibrium) acreage and actual acreage respectively of crop k in group g;

(ii) IA_{sc} is the irrigated area of sugarcane;

(iii) Log V_{gkt} is a random error term assumed to be (independently and identically) normally distributed with mean zero and a constant variance;

(iv) R_{gkt} is the crop-specific rainfall index; and

(v) Z_{gkt}^* is the expected revenue of crop k in group g relative to that of its competing crops k_1 and k_2, i.e.,

$$Z^*_{gkt} = \pi^*_{gkt} / (\pi^*_{gk1t}.\pi^*_{gk2t})^{\frac{1}{2}}; \; \text{or alternatively}$$

$$= \pi^*_{gkt} / \frac{1}{2} (\pi^*_{gk1t} + \pi^*_{gk2t}) \quad\quad\quad (11)$$

where π_{gkt}^* are as shown in equation (8).

From (9) and (10), a reduced form can be obtained as follows:

$$\begin{aligned}
\text{Log } A_{gkt} =\; & a_{gk}.\tau_{gk} + (1-\tau_{gk})\log A_{gkt-1} + b_{gk}.\tau_{gk}\log Z_{gkt}^* \\
& + c_{gk}.\tau_{gk}\log R_{gkt} + d_{gk}.\tau_{gk}\log [IA_g/GIA]_t \\
& + e_{gk}.\tau_{gk}\log [IA_{sc}/GIA]_t + f_{gk}.\tau_{gk}[\log (GIA)_t] \\
& + \tau_{gk}\log V_{gkt}
\end{aligned} \quad (12)$$

As a first step, equation (8) was estimated for all the major sixteen crops using Box-Jenkins methodology[8] and the estimates of expected revenues and relative revenues from (11) were computed. In the next step, these estimates were

---

8   See Box and Jenkins (1970).

used in estimating (12). For these results, and their detailed discussion, the reader is referred to Narayana and Parikh (1981).

In the case of minor crops ($k = 18,25$), the following model was estimated. Let

$$RESD_t \equiv \Sigma \ A_{kt} \tag{13}$$

where A_{kt}, the gross cropped area of kth crop, was specified as:

$$A_{kt} = b_k \cdot RESD_t + V_{kt}; \ k = 18,25 \tag{14}$$

However, in the model simulation, RESD was fixed at

$$RESD_t = 0.2(GCA)_t \tag{15}$$

and the estimated gross cropped acreages of the sixteen major crops obtained from (12) were scaled up (or down) such that

$$\Sigma \ \Sigma \ A_{gkt} = 0.8(GCA)_t \tag{16}$$

Crop yields. Let us now turn to modelling of yields. Given crop acreages, output levels depend mainly on the type of soil, the type of seeds (local or high yielding varieties (h.y.v.)) and the pattern of input application (fertilizers, pesticides, etc.). Compared to developed countries, the extent and quality of irrigation as well as the levels of fertilizer inputs are low in India.[9]

However, both irrigation and fertilizer application have been very important factors in determining crop yields. Particularly since the introduction of high yielding varieties during the mid-sixties, the rate of their adoption also became important in determining yield. Thus crop yields depend mainly on the three control variables: irrigation, h.y.v. adoption rate, and fertilizer application, apart from natural factors such as rainfall.

The bio-technology of h.y.v. cultivation in the country is mainly confined to only five cereal crops: rice, wheat, jowar, bajra and maize. The rate of adoption of h.y.v. is far higher in the case of rice and wheat compared to that of jowar, bajra and maize. In the late sixties, the percentage of area under h.y.v. varied between three to seven for all the five crops. But by the late seventies, nearly seventy-five percent and forty percent of the areas of wheat and rice, respectively were sown with h.y.v., whereas only about twenty-five percent of the areas under jowar, bajra and maize were sown with h.y.v. Though fertilizer is known to be applied to a number of crops, again rice and wheat are major fertilizer consuming crops, together accounting for more than

---

9 Aggregate fertilizer intensity in India by 1980 was only 21 kg. of nitrogen, 7 kg. of phosphatic and 4 kg. of potassic fertilizer nutrients/hectare of gross cropped area.

sixty percent of the total fertilizer used in the country[10]. Jowar, bajra and maize together account for another ten percent and sugarcane accounts for another six percent. All the other crops share the remaining twenty to twenty five percent.

Such a diverse pattern of input applications among crops led us to three different approaches in estimating yield functions: one for rice and wheat, another for jowar, bajra and maize, and a third for other crops. We estimate yield functions of rice and wheat simultaneously because of these two crops compete for a large share in the total limited quantity of fertilizers.

We have time series data on the area under irrigation, rainfall and prices (all crop-specific) and for the five cereals mentioned above, the percentages of area under h.y.v. Data on yield, however, are available only as average yield and separate time series of data on yield for h.y.v. or yield for irrigated land are not available. Time series are also available on the total fertilizer used on all crops in the country. We have no time series on crop specific fertilizer levels applied, though there are one or two cross section surveys giving the information for a year or two.[11]

Rice and wheat. We distinguished three types ($i = 1, 3$) of yield functions corresponding to three cultivation regimes of seed variety and water use for the two crops ($k = 1, 2$) as follows (the time subscript t is omitted for ease of presentation).[12]

Let

   i = 1 denote local seeds sown on unirrigated land;

       = 2 denote local seeds sown on irrigated land;

       = 3 denote h.y.v. seeds sown on irrigated land.

Let

   S_{ik} = proportion of the area under i^{th} type in the total area of crop k;

   A_k = total area of crop k (hectares);

   $A_{ik} = S_{ik}.A_k$;

   f_{ik} = fertilizer intensity (tons/hectare) on A_{ik};

   R_{ik} = crop specific, land specific rainfall;

---

10   For a cross section survey data on crop specific fertilizer application for the year 1972, see Sarvekshana (1978).

11   See Sarvekshana (1978).

12   Generally, h.y.v. are sown only on irrigated land implying h.y.v. area is less than or equal to irrigated area. However, of late, wheat farmers are growing h.y.v. on unirrigated land also. We assumed, however, that all h.y.v. are grown only on irrigated land so that unirrigated h.y.v. area is set to zero.

R_k = crop specific aggregate rainfall;

P_k = output price of crop k;

F_{rw} = fertilizer (nitrogen nutrient) allocated to rice and wheat together;

F = total fertilizer (nitrogen) used on crops in the country;

YLD_{ik} = yield on i^{th} type seed water regime under crop k and;

YLD_k = aggregate yield of crop k,

so that

$$YLD_k \equiv \Sigma \ S_{ik} \ YLD_{ik} \tag{17}$$

Let us postulate the yield in period 't' to be a function of fertilizer intensity, separately for each type of land, as follows:

$$YLD_{ikt} = a_{ik} + b_{ik}f_{ikt} + c_{ik}f_{ikt}^2 + d_{ik}R_{ikt} + U_{ikt}$$

$$= YLD_{ikt}^* + U_{ikt} \tag{18}$$

so that YLD_{ikt}^* represents the expected yield.

Now posing the following constrained maximization problem that value of output is maximized for each period t subject to a constraint on fertilizer availability for that period

$$\text{Max } L_t = \Sigma \ P_{kt}[\Sigma \ A_{ikt}(YLD_{ikt}^*)] - LMDA_t \ [\Sigma \ \Sigma A_{ikt}f_{ikt} - F_{rwt}] \tag{19}$$

and using the first order conditions for a maximum and after some relevant substitutions we can solve for fertilizer intensity on each type of land as

$$f_{ikt} = [LMDA_t/P_{kt} - b_{ik}] \ / \ (2.c_{ik}) \tag{20}$$

where $LMDA_t$, the shadow price of the fertilizer, is given by

$$LMDA_t = \frac{2F_{rwt} + \Sigma \left[A_{kt}\left\{ \Sigma' \frac{S_{ikt}b_{ik}}{c_{ik}} \right\} \right]}{\Sigma \left[A_{kt}\left\{ \Sigma \frac{S_{ikt}}{P_{kt} \ c_{ik}} \right\} \right]} \tag{21}$$

Thus, in principle one can estimate, using a non-linear simultaneous equations approach, all the parameters in equation (18) and hence the fertilizer shadow price $LMDA_t$ and the intensities f_{ikt} by minimizing the sum of the squares of error terms as given by

$$\Sigma \ \Sigma \ (YLD_{kt} - YLD_{kt}^*)^2 \tag{22}$$

where YLD_{kt}^* is the expected value of YLD_{kt}. However, since we have information only on R_{kt} (crop specific aggregate rainfall) but not on R_{ikt} (which is specific to type of land) the above procedure cannot be adopted. To get around this problem, we eliminated R_{ikt} from YLD_{kt}^{*} in the following manner:

Let $YLD_{kt}^{*} \equiv \Sigma\ S_{ikt}\ YLD_{ikt}^{*}$

$$\equiv \Sigma\ S_{ikt}(a_{ik}+b_{ik}f_{ikt}+c_{ik}f_{ikt}^{2}+d_{ik}R_{ikt})$$

$$\equiv \Sigma\ S_{ikt}(a_{ik}+b_{ik}f_{ikt}+c_{ik}f_{ikt}^{2})+\Sigma\ d_{ik}S_{ikt}R_{ikt} \tag{21A}$$

Since data on R_{ikt} are not available, we postulated that

$$\Sigma\ d_{ik}S_{ikt}R_{ikt} = d_{k}R_{kt} + V_{kt}$$

where V_{kt} is assumed to have an expected value of zero and a constant variance. Then substituting in (21A) and taking expectation of V_{kt} we get

$$YLD_{kt}^{*} = \Sigma\ S_{ikt}(a_{ik}+b_{ik}f_{ikt}+c_{ik}f_{ikt}^{2}) + d_{k}R_{kt}$$

We then substituted the above in (22) and minimized. Unfortunately, the resulting parameter estimates did not appear sensible, perhaps due to a high multicollinearity between fertilizer use, irrigation and rate of h.y.v. adoption.

We have, however, a large body of data, based on Simple Field-Trials (SFT) on farmers' fields, on the yield responses to fertilizer levels applied. These data are available separately for the three types of regime in the case of rice, wheat, jowar, bajra and maize. Parikh and Srinivasan et al (1974) and Parikh (1978) analyzed these data and estimated fertilizer response functions (18) for several crops under each type of regime. Using these estimated fertilizer response parameters, we reduced the estimation problem to scaling these SFT-determined yield estimates to conform to the observed actual yield levels in the aggregate for each crop. That is, equation (19) was modified by bringing in these scale factors s_{k}. Now the problem is

$$\text{Max } L_{t} = \Sigma\ P_{kt}A_{kt}(YLD_{kt}^{**}) - LMDA_{t}(\Sigma\ \Sigma A_{ikt}f_{ikt}\text{-}F_{rwt}) \tag{19A}$$

where

$$YLD_{kt}^{**} = s_{k}[\Sigma S_{ikt}(a_{ik}+b_{ik}f_{ikt}+c_{ik}f_{ikt}^{2})] + d_{k}R_{kt} \tag{18A}$$

The estimation was carried out minimizing the error sum of squares

$$\Sigma\ \Sigma\ (YLD_{kt} - YLD_{kt}^{**})^{2}$$

with respect to s_{k} and d_{k}. 's_{k}' can be viewed as a crop-specific aggregate scale factor reflecting farm yields under actual field condition in the country as a whole compared to yields obtained under experimental conditions on *that part of the country* which is covered by the SFT. Note that s_{k} and d_{k} are the only parameters to be estimated now, since all other parameters are exogenously specified. It may be noted that in this part of the exercise, time-series of F_{rw} was obtained by setting

$$F_{rwt} = m.F_t \tag{23}$$

for all time periods, where m was set at 0.6202 based on Sarvekshana (1978). The details of obtaining the parameters, a_{ik}, b_{ik} and c_{ik} from the SFT data and of estimation of yield functions of major cereals are given in Narayana and Parikh (1987).

Bajra, jowar and maize. For these crops the response parameters based on technical data from SFT were relied on, and only the scale factors and the coefficients corresponding to rainfall were estimated. The yield functions for these crops were separately estimated using Ordinary Least Squares. The postulated functions were as follows:

$$
\begin{aligned}
YLD_{kt} = s_k \, [(a_{1k}+a_{2k}I_{kt}+a_{3k}H_{kt}) &+ (b_{1k}+b_{2k}I_{kt}+b_{3k}H_{kt})f_{kt} \\
&+ (c_{1k}+c_{2k}I_{kt}+c_{3k}H_{kt})f_{kt}^2] + d_k R_{kt} + u_{kt}
\end{aligned} \tag{24}
$$

where I_k and H_k are the proportions of irrigated and h.y.v. areas respectively in the total area of crop k, and f_k and R_k are the aggregate fertilizer intensity (tons/hectare) and rainfall of crop k. Note that the parameters a_{jk}, b_{jk} and c_{jk} were all specified based on SFT data and are exogenous for equation (24). For estimating equation (24) the time series of f_{kt} were obtained as fixed proportions of the total available fertilizer F_t divided by the crop areas. These proportions were 0.0205, 0.0303 and 0.0414 for bajra, jowar and maize, respectively.

Other major and minor crops. For all other crops excluding rice, wheat, bajra, jowar and maize, h.y.v. adoption has been insignificant. However, irrigation and fertilizer could be important to several crops. Thus, for most of these crops, yield functions were postulated and estimated simply with fertilizer intensity and/or irrigation intensity as main explanatory variables. Crop-specific rainfall was also used as an explanatory variable in some cases.

However, there are some crops (especially minor crops) whose yields have remained stagnant, fluctuating around a stationary mean. In all such cases, a simple auto-regressive process of the first or second order was fitted to their yield data.

Thus, in general, the yield functions of all the other major and minor crops were postulated as follows:

$$YLD_{kt} = F_k \, [YLD_{kt-1}, \, I_{kt}, \, f_{kt}, \, R_{kt}, \, Time] \tag{25}$$

where k and t are crop index and time index, YLD_k, R_k, I_k and f_k are yield, rainfall, irrigation intensity and fertilizer intensity of crop k, respectively.

However, not all the explanatory variables were necessarily present in the finally chosen estimated equations. Generation of time series of f_k was based on a fixed proportion of total fertilizer use in the country (see Appendix 3.6).

It is important to note that in all the yield functions discussed above, the fertilizer intensity is measured in nitrogen nutrients. We assume that phosphorus and potash nutrients are used in fixed proportions with nitrogen nutrients. In simulations of the model, total availability of nitrogenous fertilizer is projected exogenously as a function of time. However, fertilizer is used only to the extent that it is profitable.

Also, during simulations, crop specific technical progress factors were introduced exogenously for some crop yields. These details are given in Appendix 3.6.

Let us now turn to outputs of the livestock sector. These include milk, beef, mutton and pork, etc. A complete list of these products is also given in Appendix 3.1.

Dairy. Unfortunately, the data base of the Indian livestock sector is weak. We have a few livestock censuses conducted once in five years. Though FAO's Supply Utilization Accounts give a time series information, the reliability of their data is not fully established. CSO's National Accounts Statistics give time series data on outputs of the livestock sector, but only in value terms and not in physical units. Lack of reliable data precluded any attempt at rigorous econometric estimation. However, from the limited data available it is known that, in India, working animals per net sown hectare have been almost constant at 0.6. Also, the relative composition between cows in milk, total breeding cows and total cattle has been almost constant over time, as with buffaloes in the total animal stock (cattle and buffaloes working and breeding). Of the total milk production in India, roughly 55 percent is buffalo milk, 40 to 42 percent is cow milk and the rest is from goats, etc. Milk yield rates of buffaloes are generally higher than those of cows.

Milk output is modeled here as a function of milk-yielding animal stock, their yield rates and the relative price of milk. Equations (26) and (27) are the postulated milk-yield functions for cows and buffaloes respectively:

$$MYC_t = MYC_0 \ (1 + g_c)^{time} \left[\frac{WPMLK}{WPGRN} \right]^{\eta_c} \qquad (26)$$

$$MYB_t = MYB_0 \ (1 + g_b)^{time} \left[\frac{WPMLK}{WPGRN} \right]^{\eta_b} \qquad (27)$$

where

1. MYC_t and MYB_t are milk yields (tons/year) per cow and per buffalo;

2. MYC_o and MYB_o are base period milk yield rates;
3. g_c and g_b are the trend growth rates in yield rates of cows and buffaloes respectively;
4. WPMLK/WPGRN is the wholesale price index of milk over that of foodgrains; and
5. η_c and η_b are the price elasticities.

Equations (28) and (29) below are the postulated stock-equations for cows and buffaloes giving milk:

Cows in milk:

$$CM_t = P_{cm} \cdot P_{cw} \cdot (TCWA)\,(WBWA)\,(WAPH)_t(NSA)_t \qquad (28)$$

where

CM_t	= cows in milk;
P_{cm}	= proportion of cows in milk in total number of cows;
P_{cw}	= proportion of total number of cows in total number of cattles;
TCWA	= total number of cattle per working bullock;
WBWA	= proportion of working bullocks in total number of working animals; and
WAPH	= working animals per hectare of net sown area (NSA).

NSA was estimated earlier. WAPH was assumed to fall from a rate of 0.6 in 1977 to 0.55 by the year 2000 and a suitable time function was specified accordingly. Values of other parameters, such as P_{cm}, P_{cw}, etc., were all culled out from various data sources and exogenously specified.

Buffaloes in milk:

$$BM_t = P_{bm}(1+n_{bt})(LVBFL)_{t-1} \qquad (29)$$

where

$LVBFL_t$	= stock of buffaloes in year t;
BM_t	= stock of buffaloes in milk in year t;
n_{bt}	= natural growth rate of buffaloes; and
P_{bm}	= proportion of buffaloes in milk in total number of buffaloes.

The stock of buffaloes in milk was estimated through historical natural growth rate of buffaloes, because (a) the number of working or non-working buffaloes is much less compared to the number of cattle; (b) draft power (relating to work on farms) provided by buffaloes is relatively small compared to bullocks, and (c) buffaloes, their milk yields being higher, are maintained as profitable commercial assets not only by farmers, but by numerous milk-selling entrepreneurs.

Finally, the total milk output function was specified as

$$(MILK)_t = 1.0522 \ [CM_t \cdot MYC_t + BM_t \cdot MYB_t] \tag{30}$$

where the factor 1.0522 accounts for milk obtained from goats and other animals, and is approximately 5 percent of the total quantity of milk from cows and buffaloes.

Livestock Products. The following livestock products were distinguished at the time of estimation: beef, mutton and pork, other meat, hides and skins, eggs and poultry, wool and hair, and other livestock products.

Time series data on the outputs of these products measured at constant prices (1960-61 prices) are available from the National Accounts Statistics (CSO). Semilog time trend functions were fitted to these data as follows:

$$(LSTP)_{jt} = \exp[\alpha_j + \beta_j (TIME)_t + u_{jt}] \tag{31}$$

where j = beef, mutton, etc.

Of these products, hides and skins, wool and hair and other livestock products belong to sector 9 of our ten sector aggregate model (to be discussed later). Sector 9 output is measured in constant monetary units (US $). However, the rest of the products, such as beef, have to be measured in physical units. From various other data documents (mainly from FAO's Supply Utilization Accounts), information on the prices of these products of the year 1960-61 was obtained. These prices were used in converting the estimates of $(LSTP)_j$ to physical units.

It is obvious that the output projections being based on simple time trends are not functions of the stock of animals. They are not responsive to the product prices either. However, in simulations of the model, these estimated equations (31) were later slightly modified to make outputs responsive to prices by stipulating exogenously specified elasticities of supply with respect to prices. For these details see Appendix 3.6.

Fish production. We have data on fish production in physical units. Of the total fish production in the country, the proportion of marine fish is about two-thirds, the rest being inland fish.[13] However, in our model, these two categories were not distinguished. We regressed the number of fishing boats (on which data are also available) on total fish production as follows:

$$FISHQ_t = \alpha + \beta \ (BOAT)_t + u_t \tag{32}$$

and BOAT (the number of boats) was separately specified as a time trend in

---

13   See various volumes of Bulletin on Food Statistics and Indian Agriculture in Brief.

simulations of the model. However, this specification also was revised later to introduce price sensitivity. See Appendix 3.6.

This completes the discussion of all commodities in the agricultural sector. Let us turn to non-agriculture.

Non-agriculture. In our model, all non-agricultural commodities were aggregated into one sector. For such an aggregated non-agriculture sector in a developing country like India where many subsectors often produce output below capacity level for want of spare parts, inputs or demand, the conventional production function approach is inadequate. It is necessary to characterize the sector in a way that leads to investment and capacity expansion even in the face of persistent idle capacity. The basic idea in our approach is that the non-agriculture sector expands capacity so as to minimize expected cost of production to meet future demand which is uncertain.

The sub-model to estimate non-agricultural production is as follows:

The *cost per unit* of non-agricultural production was assumed to depend on the deviation between the desired capacity output, QC_{dt}, and actual output, Q_t. Thus the *total cost*, C, was specified as:

$$C(Q_t, QC_{dt}) = Q_t[\alpha_o + \alpha_1(QC_{dt}-Q_t) + \alpha_2(QC_{dt}-Q_t)^2] \tag{33}$$

where the term in parentheses in r.h.s. is the cost per unit. Minimization of the expected costs (i.e., by writing equation (33) in terms of expected values and minimizing) over QC_{dt} gives us the cost minimizing desired capacity, QC_{dt}, as follows:

$$QC_{dt} = V(Q_t)/E(Q_t) + E(Q_t) - \alpha_1/2\alpha_2 \tag{34}$$

where $V(Q_t)$ is the variance of Q_t and $E(Q_t)$ is the expected output level.

Now, α_1 was assumed to be zero, so that

$$QC_{dt} = E(Q_t) + V(Q_t)/E(Q_t) \tag{35}$$

We could assume:

(i) $V(Q_t)$ is constant over time, and
(ii) expected actual output generally equals expected demand for the good, so that

$$E(Q_t) = E(Y10DD_t) \tag{36}$$

where Y10DD is the demand for non-agriculture in the country as a whole. Then, the desired increment in the capacity output follows as:

$$\begin{aligned} DK_{dt} &= \text{desired capacity output increment} \\ &= QC_{dt} - QC_{a,\,t-1} \end{aligned} \tag{37}$$

where $QC_{a,t-1}$ is the actual capacity output created until the previous year.

However, there could be a problem of the availability of investible resources in achieving the desired capacity levels. These resources are limited by savings[14] available for investing into non-agriculture and the efficiency of capital use. Thus, the potential increment in the capacity output is:

$$DK_{pt} = \text{potential capacity output increment}$$
$$= SNAG_t / ICOR_t \tag{38}$$

where

$SNAG_t$ = resources available to invest in non-agriculture; and
$ICOR_t$ = incremental capital output ratio (a parameter reflecting efficiency of capital use).

Now, obviously the actual capacity output increment is:

$$DK_{a,t} = \text{actual capacity output increment}$$
$$= \text{Min}[DK_{dt}, DK_{pt}] \tag{39}$$

and output capacity actually created is

$$QC_{at} = QC_{a,t-1} + DK_{at} \tag{40}$$

Given this capacity QC_{at}, and the demand, $Y10DD_t$, the actual output, Q_t, is determined as

$$Q_t = \text{Min}[QC_{a,t}, Y10DD_t] \tag{41}$$

Finally, the capacity utilization UC_t is determined as

$$UC_t = Q_t / QC_{a,t}$$

The demand for non-agriculture (see equation (36)) was estimated in two ways as follows:

(a) The demand for non-agricultural output was specified as a function of expected price of non-agriculture relative to that of agriculture, per capita agricultural GDP in the current year (to account for the non-agricultural inputs needed by agriculture) and per capita total GDP in the previous year (to account for the income effects). The following regression equation was estimated:

$$\frac{Y10DA_t}{POPN_t} = \left[\alpha_{nd} + \beta_{nd}\left(\frac{GDPAG}{POPN}\right)_t + \tau_{nd}\left(\frac{PNA*}{PA*}\right)_t + \delta_{nd}\left(\frac{TGDP}{POPN}\right)_{t-1} \right] + u_t \tag{42}$$

---

14   Including any foreign resources.

where

$Y10DA_t$	= non-agricultural GDP;
GDPAG	= agricultural GDP;
TGDP	= total GDP;
POPN	= Population
PNA* & PA*	= expected price indices of non-agriculture and agriculture respectively[15].

Strictly speaking the dependent variable should have been per capita non-agricultural GDP *plus* per capita net imports of non-agricultural goods rather than per capita non-agricultural GDP. It was decided to use only GDP since for a large economy such as India's net imports meet only a small proportion of the total demand.

(b) Another way to estimate the total demand is to estimate each of its individual components. These are:

    (i) human consumption of non-agriculture;

    (ii) intermediate consumption of the non-agricultural commodity by agriculture;

    (iii) investment demand;

    (iv) public final consumption by the government; and

    (v) export demand.

Thus,

$$Y10DB_t = (HHCNAG_{t-1})(PGR_t)(GRT_t^{\eta}) + (CINTEN_{t-1})(GRA_t)$$

$$+ (INVEST_{t-1}+EXP10_{t-1}+PUBFCE_{t-1})GRT_t \qquad (43)$$

where

$Y10DB_t$	= expected total non-agricultural demand;
$HHCNAG_{t-1}$	= households' consumption of non-agriculture in period t–1;
PGR_t	= population growth rate from period (t–1) to period (t);
GRT_t	= growth rate in total GDP from period (t–2) to period (t–1);
η	= expenditure elasticity for non-agriculture demand;
$CINTEN_{t-1}$	= intermediate consumption of non-agricultural commodity by agricultural sector in year (t–1);
GRA_t	= growth rate in agricultural GDP from period (t–1) to period t;

---

15   These were estimated as ARIMA schemes using Box-Jenkins methodology.

INVEST$_{t-1}$ = investments from the previous year;

EXP10$_{t-1}$ = net exports of non-agricultural commodity in period (t–1); and

PUBFCE$_{t-1}$ = public final consumption of non-agricultural commodities in period (t–1).

In equation (43), GRT$_t$ is a proxy for the expected growth rate in total GDP between periods (t-1) and t or, put another way, we are assuming static expectation with respect to the growth rate of total GDP.

The entire right-hand side of equation (43) is the expected total demand for non-agriculture.

In simulations of the model, E(Y10DD$_t$) was specified as:

$$E(Y10DD_t) = Max[Y10DA_t, Y10DB_t] \qquad (44)$$

where Y10DA$_t$ is the estimated value of the dependent variable in equation (42).

Next, the incremental capital output ratio (ICOR) in equation (38) was specified as:

$$ICOR_t = 6/b^t \qquad (45)$$

where b, exogenously fixed as 1.01, is a technical progress parameter. Thus ICOR is assumed to *decline* from a base value of 6 in 1970 to 4.45 in 2000. However, the Indian data over 1950-80 reveal that the actual ICOR has increased over time and was in the range of 6-8 in the late seventies. On the other hand, the Planning Commission in their Sixth Five-Year Plan (1979-84) assumed the ICOR to be 4.7. Our assumption is a compromise between the recent past and the Planning Commission's optimism.

Finally, one must recognize that part of the non-agricultural output is generated in the rural areas and the income from that accrues to rural population. For this, the rural share in non-agricultural production is exogenously fixed as follows:

YNAR$_t$ = Rural Non-agricultural Production

$$= YNAR_{t-1} + b_{rn}(Q_t - Q_{t-1}) \qquad (46)$$

We have no direct data to estimate b$_{rn}$. Based on indirect data from National Accounts Statistics (CSO), NCAER(1980), etc., b$_{rn}$ was exogenously specified as 0.4.

Having described the essential features of the supply sub-models we turn to the sectoral aggregation of our model. There are ten sectors in the model: nine agricultural sectors and one non-agricultural sector. This sectoral aggregation was based on the following two main considerations:

(a) This model for India is one of the many models of the Food and Agriculture Program (FAP) of the International Institute for Applied Systems Analysis (IIASA). FAP's task is to put together a linked system of several national models (covering eighty percent of the world) and use the system of models to perform a global general equilibrium analysis of policies towards alleviation of poverty, growth and development, international trade and interdependence. For linking national models into a global system, all the national modelers had to agree on a sectoral aggregation.

(b) Consumer demand equations of the model were based on consumer expenditure surveys. These surveys distinguish far fewer commodities than the number for which production data are available. But the market clearance condition of the general equilibrium approach requires that the supply and demand for each commodity be equated. This necessarily forces the use of an aggregation procedure that ensures that at the sectoral level, demand and supply refer to the same aggregate.

Both these considerations led to the following commodity aggregation (units of measurement are given in brackets):

Sector 1:   Wheat (thousand tons);
Sector 2:   Rice (thousand tons);
Sector 3:   Coarse grains (thousand tons) consisting of bajra, barley, jowar, maize, ragi and small-millets;
Sector 4:   Bovine and ovine meats (thousand tons of carcass weight) consisting of beef and mutton;
Sector 5:   Dairy products (thousand tons of fresh milk equivalent);
Sector 6:   Other animal products (thousand tons of protein equivalent) consisting of eggs, poultry, pork and fish;
Sector 7:   Protein feeds (thousand tons of protein equivalent) consisting of cakes of all oilseeds;
Sector 8:   Other food (million 1970 US dollars) consisting of sugar, oils of groundnut, cotton, rape and mustard, sesamum, coconut and other oilseeds, gram and other pulses, tea, coffee, fruits and vegetables and condiments and spices;
Sector 9:   Non-food agriculture (million 1970 US dollars) consisting of cotton lint, raw jute, raw mesta, tobacco, sannhemp, rubber, hides and skins, wool and hair and other livestock products; and
Sector 10: Non-agriculture (million 1970 US dollars).

Most of our output estimates were in physical units. Some commodity outputs were valued in Indian rupees at some base year prices. Appropriate wholesale price indices were used in bringing them to a common base year (1970) prices. Depending on the commodity and the sector to which it belonged either a base year wholesale price was used in converting the value output to physical units or a base year exchange rate (assumed to be Indian Rs. 7.5 per US dollar in 1970) was used in converting the value output in 1970 Indian rupees to 1970 US dollars.

3.2 Demography

One of the important uses to which the model was to be put, was to analyze policies towards reduction of poverty and income redistribution. For this purpose, the population of the nation was distributed into ten consumer expenditure classes: five in rural and five in urban areas. For both rural and urban areas, the values of per capita annual consumer expenditure limits defining these classes at the base year (1970) prices were as follows:

| Class number | | Expenditure range |
Rural	Urban	
1	1	$\leq$ Rs. 216
2	2	> Rs. 216 $\leq$ Rs. 336
3	3	> Rs. 336 $\leq$ Rs. 516
4	4	> Rs. 516 $\leq$ Rs. 900
5	5	> Rs. 900

These boundaries are updated every year to correspond to the equivalent income at target prices. The details of this updating are given in Appendix 3.2.

The total population of the country was projected at an exogenous growth rate as:

$$POPN_t = POPN_{t-1}(1+n_t) \qquad (47)$$

where n_t is the exogenously fixed natural growth rate. Similarly, the proportions of urban population (UPOP) in the total population and of rural non-agricultural population (RNPOP) in the rural population (RPOP) were exogenously specified as time trends as follows:

$$UPPRN_t = \text{Proportion of urban population in } POPN_t$$
$$= UPPRN_o(1+g_u)^{time} \qquad (48)$$

and

RNPRN$_t$ = Proportion of rural non-agricultural population in RPOP$_t$

$$= \text{RNPRN}_o(1+g_m)^{\text{time}} \tag{49}$$

where g_u and g_m are growth rates.

3.3 Distribution of Endowments and Population among Consumer Expenditure Classes

Each individual derives his income from productive activity as well as from transfers from the government. He spends it on the purchase of commodities, on taxes paid to the government and saves the rest. We now turn to the process of income generation and of its distribution among our ten consumer expenditure classes. More precisely, we describe the process by which the size of the population in each class, its average income and its consumption expenditure are determined.

Income from productive activity comes from the production of agricultural and non-agricultural outputs and accrues to the primary factors (land, labour and capital) employed in production. The claim of an individual for a part of this income stream, his "income entitlement" so to speak, depends on the extent of his ownership of the factors of production and on factor prices. If data were available on the amount of land, labour and capital owned by an average member of each expenditure class in the base year and if one can specify the evolution of the population in each class, its ownership patterns and factor prices over time in each run of the model, it would be trivial to determine the class-wise income distribution. Unfortunately, with our data base such a direct approach is not feasible. Another problem implicit in the direct approach to the determination of income distribution in any general equilibrium model is one of simultaneity: income distribution influences demand and hence the determination of market clearing equilibrium factor and commodity prices and these prices in turn influence income distribution. In what follows, this simultaneity has been evaded by using exogenously specified "target prices" (to be discussed later) in determining income distribution while demand is specified as a function of income at "target" prices and market prices of commodities. At equilibrium market prices, supply equals demand though these prices may differ from the "target" prices that determined incomes. In practice, these differences turned out to be insignificant and were ignored. As will be seen below, factor ownership pattern only indirectly influences the income distribution.

Specifically at a given set of target sectoral relative prices the total agricultural income and non-agricultural income are determined. The non-agricultural income is then split into rural and urban components as per an exogenously specified proportion.[16] Given these agricultural, rural non-agricultural and urban non-agricultural incomes, aggregate consumption expenditures were computed, using aggregate consumption functions estimated separately for rural and urban regions. These functions, estimated using NCAER(1980) data, relate aggregate mean consumption expenditure to aggregate income under the assumption that consumption and income are jointly and lognormally distributed.

Let C,Y be an individual's consumption and income (at target prices) and CBAR, YBAR be mean or expected values of C and Y over all individuals; and $c = \log C$ and $y = \log Y$; and let c and y be jointly normally distributed, so that

$$c = a_1 + a_2 y + v \tag{50}$$

where

$$y \sim N(\mu_y, \sigma_y^2) \tag{51}$$

$$v \sim N(0, \sigma_v^2) \tag{52}$$

so that

$$c \sim N[\mu_c = a_1 + a_2\mu_y, \ \sigma_c^2 = \sigma_v^2 + a_2^2\sigma_y^2] \tag{53}$$

In estimating a_1, a_2, σ_y^2 and σ_v^2, separately for rural and urban areas grouped data from NCAER (1980) on income, savings and population proportions and the data from National Accounts Statistics (CSO) on total national private disposable income, private final consumption expenditure and private household savings were used. These data are for the year July 1975 to June 1976. For a detailed discussion of the reliability of these data, the mathematics and statistics of the procedure used in estimating the parameters, etc., the reader is referred to Narayana, Parikh and Srinivasan (1984) some details of which are also given in Appendix 3.4 here. It suffices to note here that rural parameter estimates were used for agricultural and rural non-agricultural households and urban estimates for urban non-agricultural households in our model.

In simulations with the model, CBAR for each period was obtained from the relation

$$\log CBAR = a_1 + a_2 \log YBAR + \frac{1}{2}\left[\sigma_v^2 \alpha_2 (1 - \alpha_2)\sigma_r^2\right] \tag{54}$$

---

16   See equation (46).

given the estimates of YBAR for that period from supply modules, σ_y^2 and σ_v^2.[17]

The assumption that the distribution of (C,Y) is bivariate log-normal can be used to derive the proportion of total population, consumption expenditure and income accounted for by households within any specified expenditure class. Thus

PP_j = proportion of population in j^{th} expenditure class

$$= \phi \left[\frac{\log (XPL_{j+1}) - \mu_c}{\sigma_c} \right] - \phi \left[\frac{\log (XPL_j) - \mu_c}{\sigma_c} \right] \tag{55}$$

PC_j = proportion of aggregate consumption expenditure accounted for by the jth expenditure class

$$= \phi \left[\frac{\log (XPL_{j+1}) - \mu_c}{\sigma_c} - \sigma_c \right] - \phi \left[\frac{\log (XPL_j) - \mu_c}{\sigma_c} - \sigma_c \right] \tag{56}$$

and

PY_j = proportion of aggregate income accruing to the jth exenditure class

$$= \phi \left[\frac{\log (XPL_{j+1}) - \mu_c}{\sigma_c} - RHO_{cy}.\sigma_y \right]$$

$$- \phi \left[\frac{\log (XPL_j) - \mu_c}{\sigma_c} - RHO_{cy}.\sigma_y \right] \tag{57}$$

where XPL_j are the expenditure limits[18] and RHO_{cy} is the correlation coefficient between c and y and $\phi(X)$ is the cumulative distribution function of the standard normal distribution.

These proportions were obtained separately for agricultural, rural non-agricultural and urban non-agricultural households for each of the rural and urban expenditure classes. Using the respective population proportions, the exogenously given totals of agricultural, rural non-agricultural and urban populations were split into corresponding classwise components. The physical output of each of the nine agricultural sectors was split into classwise rural income

---

17   We will return to this point later.

18   In the simulation runs these limits get updated from year to year on account of price changes. See Appendix 3.2.

"endowments" as per the agricultural income proportions. Rural and urban non-agricultural outputs were split into corresponding classwise non-agricultural endowments using the respective income proportions.

It is worth mentioning that

(a) This approach provides indirect estimates of classwise savings by subtracting classwise mean consumption from mean income:

$$ZCBAR_j = \text{mean per capita consumption of } j^{th} \text{ class}$$
$$= CBAR(PC_j/PP_j) \tag{58}$$

and

$$ZYBAR_j = \text{mean per capita income of } j^{th} \text{ class}$$
$$= YBAR(PY_j/PP_j) \tag{59}$$

(b) On the face of it, it may look odd that the agricultural expenditure classes get the same proportion of the total of each agricultural output. But this is purely an arithmetical device to ensure that the sum of the value of the endowments assigned to each class equals its share of total income.

(c) As mentioned earlier the class-wise endowments and populations were derived using the target sectoral relative prices. In this sense these are expected levels. However, the equilibrium relative prices are determined in the model using the framework of an exchange economy in which domestic production is predetermined and fixed during the exchange. Hence, the equilibrium incomes and expenditures are endogenous, and an inconsistency between the expected and equilibrium proportions (population, income and expenditure) can arise if the equilibrium relative prices deviate significantly from their targets. Of course, even then, for each class its income-expenditure balance is met.

(d) Any redistributive policy implies income subsidies for some groups which need to be accounted for in determining the population distributions. We do account for these effects.

The parameters a_1, a_2, σ_y^2 and σ_v^2 were estimated separately for rural and urban areas from NCAER (1980) data and used in equation (54) in computing CBAR, given the YBAR that emerged from the supply sub-models.[19] Thus, YBAR, and hence CBAR, changes from year to year while σ_y^2 (and σ_v^2) remain fixed. This implies that CBAR, and consequently the various proportions [equations

---

19　It must be remembered that equation (54) was used separately for agricultural, rural non-agricultural and urban non-agricultural households.

(55), (56) and (57)], change only with a change in the aggregate mean income, and class-wise distribution remains fixed. However, the government may wish to pursue policies oriented towards income redistribution such as a change in structural features of the economy like asset-holding, land reforms, etc., across various income groups. A provision was, therefore, made in the model to allow for variations in σ_y^2 under redistributive policies.

A survey by the National Sample Survey Organization (NSS 1972) and the Reserve Bank of India (RBI 1971-72) give data on a number of wealth variables relating to rural households consisting of cultivator households, non-cultivator households of which a part consists of agricultural labour households, and non-agricultural rural households. Data on cultivator households and non-cultivator households are available according to 15 size-classes of land owned. Data are also available on the values of agricultural plant and equipment owned by the households in each size-class. Besides, information on the land owned by each ownership size-class, land leased out and land leased-in as a percentage of the owned land in the size-class is also available. Non-cultivator households supply agricultural labour and they do not themselves cultivate any land. However, cultivator households, particularly those from the lower size-classes, also supply agricultural labour.

Taking these structural features into account, an "income entitlement coefficient" for each size-class could be derived, which is the share of a particular farm-size-class in the total income. Formally, the computation of these coefficients involved the following two steps:

Step 1: Agricultural output ($VOLAG_t$) and agricultural GDP ($GDPAG_t$) were decomposed as follows:

$$VOLAG_t = \Sigma PRAW_{it}^* . Q_{it}$$
$$= GDPAG_t + INNON_t + FEEDLS_t \tag{60}$$

and

$$GDPAG_t = WAGES_t + INTRST_t + RENT_t + PROFIT_t + SELFEM_t + DEPR_t \tag{61}$$

where with subscript t referring to the year,

$PRAW_{it}^*$ = target relative price of ith sector output for the year t;
Q_{it} = i^{th} sectoral output;
$INNON$ = intermediate consumption of non-agricultural goods in agricultural production;
$FEEDLS$ = feed of livestock;

WAGES   = wage payments;
INTRST = interest payments;
RENT   = rent payments;
PROFIT = profit payments;
SELFEM = mixed income of self-employed; and
DEPR   = depreciation.

INNON and FEEDLS were based on fertilizer usages and costs, other non-agricultural inputs and exogenously assumed feed proportions. WAGES and others were exogenously fixed as proportions of GDPAG at their respective averages over a period of eight years, 1970-71 to 1977-78, from the data from the National Accounts Statistics (CSO).

Step 2: For the sth farm-size class (s=1, . . . 15), let

$TAO_{s,t}$ = proportion of land owned in total agricultural land;

$TRENT_{s,t}$ = proportion of land rented-out in total leased out land;

$TAOP_{s,t}$ = proportion of effective land operated in total land;

$TPEOP_{s,t}$ = proportion of plant and equipment owned in the total plants and equipment used in agriculture;

$AGLAB_{s,t}$= proportion of agricultural labourers in the total agricultural labour force.

Thus,

$$\Sigma \, TAO_{s,t} = \Sigma \, TRENT_{s,t} = \Sigma \, TAOP_{s,t} = \Sigma \, TPEOP_{s,t} = \Sigma \, AGLAB_{s,t} = 1 \tag{62}$$

Now, the income entitlement coefficient for s^{th} farm-size class $INC_{s,t}$ could be written as:

$$
\begin{aligned}
INC_{s,t} \quad &= \; [TAOP_{s,t}(SELFEM_t)+TPEOP_{s,t}(DEPR_t) \\
&\quad + AGLAB_{s,t}(WAGES_t) \\
&\quad + TRENT_{s,t}(RENT_t+INTRST_t+PROFIT_t)] \; \frac{1}{GDPAG_t}
\end{aligned}
\tag{63}
$$

Note that

$$\Sigma \, INC_{s,t} \; = \; 1$$

Since the total agricultural income and agricultural population are known, it is possible to revise $\sigma_y{}^2$ for the agricultural households every year using these income entitlement coefficients,[20] once we specify the way any policy might affect the proportions TAOP, etc. Unfortunately, the data base for implementing this for rural and urban non-agricultural sectors is not available. As such, $\sigma_y{}^2$ was exogenously fixed at its estimated value for these two groups.

3.4 Demand Sub-Model: Private Final Consumption

Private final consumption demand was estimated as a Piecewise Linear Expenditure System, i.e., a separate linear expenditure system (LES) for each expenditure class of the rural and urban populations was estimated. Time series of cross-section data from NSS Reports on consumer expenditure surveys were utilized in estimating these demand systems.

The data base used in estimating our supply sub-models came mainly from official publications such as *National Accounts Statistics* by the Central Statistical Organization and the *Estimates of Area and Production of Principal Crops* by the Ministry of Agriculture. The National Sample Survey Organization (NSS) is a separate autonomous organization and their surveys are independently conducted.[21] It has been noted by several researchers that the estimates of final consumption by households as estimated from NSS surveys and official data differed. While several explanations have been offered in the literature explaining this discrepancy, we merely note here that

(a) estimates of food consumption based on NSS data are generally higher; and

(b) estimates of total private final consumption expenditures are roughly the same between NSS surveys data and official data.

In the light of (a) and (b), the standard LES equation was slightly modified and estimated by us as follows:

$$P_i \, X_{ij} = c_{ij} \, P_i^I + b_{ij}\left[E_j - \Sigma P_i^I \, c_{ij}\right] + a_{ij} + u_{ij} \tag{64}$$

$$i = 1,10$$

$$j = 1,10$$

---

20 σ_y^2 is given by $\sigma_y^2 = \log\left[1 + \dfrac{\text{Var}(Y)}{\text{YBAR}^2}\right]$. See eqns. (50) to (53).

21 NSS is the only source in India for a detailed data base on consumer expenditure by households.

with

(i) $\Sigma b_{ij} = 1$;
(ii) $\Sigma a_{ij} = 0$;

and where P_i, P_i^1 and E_j are price and price index of the ith sector and total expenditure of the jth expenditure class.[22] c_{ij} and b_{ij} have the usual interpretation of "committed" quantities and marginal expenditure shares. X_{ij} is the private final consumption of the ith commodity by the jth class as per NSS. 'a_{ij}' is the discrepancy between the observed expenditure (dependent variable) and the expected expenditure based on official data (first two terms on the r.h.s.) on the ith commodity by the jth class. The latter is an estimate of the unavailable official data on expenditure of the jth class on the ith commodity. The estimates of a_{ij} thus address point (a) above while restriction (ii) ensures that point (b) holds. However, we assumed that point (b) holds for every expenditure class; and the modified LES system (64) was estimated separately, for all ten expenditure classes. We could have estimated, in principle, all the ten demand systems simultaneously with the restriction that a_{ij} summed over i and j (instead of over i for each j) equals zero. We did not do so because of its cumbersome computational implication.

3.5   Policy Sub-Models

Producers and consumers take production and consumption decisions given the prevailing government policies. The economy is an open economy with the government deciding the level of exports and imports of both agricultural and non-agricultural goods. Within the country, several redistributive programmes are pursued involving the government's intervention in an otherwise free market. Simultaneously, the objective of growth, development and price stability, etc., are sought to be maintained. The role played by the government was modeled as follows:

A. *Procurement.* The government procures annually a part of the foodgrains production directly or indirectly from the farmers at prices set by the government. These procurement prices are announced before harvest and are usually lower than the free market prices at harvest so that farmers are in effect taxed on the amount they sell to the government. However, in exceptionally good

---

22   The required conversion of these estimates from price index terms to price terms was made
     later. Also note that additivity and homogeneity properties are not affected by the intro-
     duction of α_{ij}

years of domestic production, free market prices may fall below announced procurement prices.[23] In that case, farmers are subsidized in their sales of produce to the government up to the ceiling set by the government's procurement quantity targets.

Rice and wheat are the major foodgrains procured. The main considerations in setting the procurement targets are requirement of the public distribution system, storage capacity, etc. However, the actual levels procured may depend on the level of production and procurement prices relative to market price. We tried to incorporate these considerations in our estimation of the procurement functions and chose the best fitting equations. Procurement of rice was estimated (eqn. 65) as a function of the difference between the target amount of distribution and existing buffer stocks (the larger the difference the greater the effort at procurement) and production level of rice.

$$PRORCE_t = \alpha_r + \beta_r.Q_{rt} + \tau_r.(DIST_t - STOK_{t-1}) + u_{rt} \tag{65}$$

where

PRORCE = quantity of rice procured;
Q_r = quantity of rice produced;
DIST = public distribution target for foodgrains (see eqn. 70 below); and
$STOK_{t-1}$ = public buffer stock of foodgrains at the end of year (t–1).

Wheat procurement was estimated (eqn.66) as a function of its production level and the procurement price of wheat relative to its open market price (the higher the procurement price the more successful efforts to procure).

$$PROWHT_t = \alpha_w + \beta_w.Q_{wt} + \tau_w.(PRPR_{wt}/PRICE_{wt}*) + u_{wt} \tag{66}$$

where

PROWHT = quantity of wheat procured;
Q_w = quantity of wheat produced;
$PRPR_w$ = wheat procurement price announced by the government; and
$PRICE_w*$ = wheat open market price as expected by the farmers.

The government also procures a small quantity of coarse foodgrains. This quantity was simply specified as

$$PROCGR_t = 0.04(PRORCE_t + PROWHT_t) \tag{67}$$

where

---

23   In this case, these prices take on the role of support prices.

PROCGR = quantity of coarse grains procured.

It was not possible to model procurement-price-setting econometrically. A government body, the Agricultural Prices Commission (later renamed the Commission for Agricultural Costs and Prices), sets procurement quantity and price targets. The members of the Commission have been known to disagree on the costs of production and on which class of farmers (rich or poor) actually contributes to procurement. We took the view that production costs, production levels and other relevant factors would be reflected in the movement of wholesale prices and procurement prices respond to changes in wholesale prices. Thus, we set:

$$PRPR_{ft} = PRPR_{f,t-1}\left[1 + 0.65\left[\frac{WPI_{f,t-1} - WPI_{f,t-3}}{WPI_{f,t-1} + WPI_{f,t-2}}\right]\right] \qquad (68)$$

where

$PRPR_f$ = procurement price of foodgrains f (f = rice, wheat and coarse grains); and

WPI_f = wholesale price index of foodgrains f.

The difference between the open market price and the procurement price can be viewed as an implicit tax per unit amount of grains procured. Thus, farmers are viewed as selling their entire output at open market prices and paying a tax at this rate on the part of the output sold to government. This tax effect of procurement was allowed for in the model while allocating the agricultural outputs to various rural expenditure classes. First, the total procurement tax (PROTAX) could be estimated using the expected market clearing prices, i.e., target prices, as follows:

$$\begin{aligned}
PROTAX_t &= PROWHT_t[P_{wheat,t}{}^* - PRPR_{wheat,t}] \\
&+ PRORCE_t[P_{rice,t}{}^* - PRPR_{rice,t}] \\
&+ PROCGR_t[P_{c.grains,t}{}^* - PRPR_{c.grains,t}] \qquad (69)
\end{aligned}$$

where P^* is the target price. Thus, the disposable income of farmers is $GDPAG_t - PROTAX_t$.

By reducing the agricultural outputs allocated to the jth class by a factor of

$$(1 - PROTAX_t/GDPAG_t)$$

it is ensured that the value of the endowments of agricultural outputs of each class equals its disposable income.

B. *Public distribution.* The government distributes several essential commodities (foodgrains in our model) to the public through fair price shops at subsidized prices. These shops are situated all over the country, though mainly in urban areas. Thus, urban population is the main beneficiary (i.e., recipient of the subsidy) of the public distribution system (p.d.s.). Since the need for p.d.s. is deemed more essential in years of scarcity than in years of plenty, the quantity of foodgrains to be distributed was set as follows:

$$\frac{DIST_t}{NPFG_t} = \alpha_d + \beta_d \left[NFGPC_t + NFGPC_{t-1} \right]$$

$$+ \tau_d \left[NFGPC_t - NFGPC_{t-1} \right] \left[\left| NFGPC_t - NFGPC_{t-1} \right| \right]$$

$$+ \delta_d \left(Q_{na} / POPN \right)_t + U_{dt} \qquad (70)$$

where

DIST = quantity of foodgrains to be distributed;
NPFG = net production of foodgrains;
POPN = total population;
NFGPC = per capita NPFG; and
Q_{na} = non-agricultural output.

Average of two years' per capita production is taken to account for the stocks in the distribution channels. The quadratic term which retains the change of sign is used to differentiate the effects of a bad year following a good year and one following a poor year. The p.d.s operates mainly in urban areas. The last bracketed term in (70) captures the effect of the growth in urban incomes.[24] No distinction was made between target and actual distribution levels.

In simulations of the model the quantity of public distribution of foodgrains was constrained from above as follows:

$$DST_t = Min[DIST_t, (0.135.UPOP_t)] \qquad (71)$$

where

DST_t = quantity of public distribution of foodgrains (10^6mt) specified in the model;
$DIST_t$ = quantity (10^6 mt) from eqn. (70); and
$UPOP_t$ = urban population (10^6).

0.135 tons per person per year is the ceiling on the quantity of distribution, imposed exogenously. In the years between 1951 and 1980, the largest ever per capita quantity distributed to the urban population in India through p.d.s. was 145 kg. per year.[25] Since in the simulations weather fluctuations are

---

24   Note that urban share of non-agricultural output was fixed at 0.6 (see eqn. 46) and the share of urban population in the total population (POPN) is varying but only slightly (see eqn. 48).

25   This was during the drought years, 1966 and 1967.

ignored, a lower ceiling of 135 kg. seems reasonable.

The subsidized (ration) prices were specified as:

$$PRR_{f,t} = 0.8P_{f,t}^{*} \tag{72}$$

where

  (i)   f refers to foodgrains sectors 1, 2 and 3 (i.e., wheat, rice and coarse grains);
 (ii) PRR_{ft} = ration price of foodgrains f; and
(iii) $P_{f,t}^{*}$ = targeted relative price of sector f.

The public distribution system could be viewed as providing a subsidy to urban consumers, i.e., consumers can be viewed as buying their entire consumption at open market prices while receiving an income subsidy equal to the difference between the value of their rations at open market price and the subsidized price. This subsidy can be estimated (analogous to $PROTAX_t$ earlier) using target prices and ration prices as:

$$\begin{aligned}
DSTSDY_t &= DSTWHT_t \; [P_{wheat,t}^{*} - PRR_{wheat,t}] \\
&+ DSTRCE_t \; [P_{rice,t}^{*} - PRR_{rice,t}] \\
&+ DSTCGR_t [P_{c.grains,t}^{*} - PRR_{c.grains,t}]
\end{aligned} \tag{73}$$

where $DSTWHT_t$, $DSTRCE_t$ and $DSTCGR_t$ are the quantities of wheat, rice and coarse grains in the total DST_t. These quantities were fixed in the proportions worked out from the procurement and the previous year-end stocks. $DSTSDY_t$ was allocated to various urban expenditure classes as per the urban population proportions. The allocated subsidy to each class was deflated appropriately to express it in the same units as the non-agricultural output and added to its non-agricultural endowments.

  C. *Stocks.* In our model stocks of all commodities are held only by the government either for trade purposes or for selling in the domestic open market or in the fair price shops at ration prices.[26] Stock accumulation and release are policy instruments that can be used by the government in achieving price targets. These stocks are accumulated either by imports or domestic open market purchases or procurement. Target stocks were specified as follows for various sectors (i = 1 to 10):

For i   = 1, 2, 3, 8, and 9

$$STK_{i,t}^{*} = Max \left[STK_{i,t-1} + DLTA \; (Q_{i,t} - FEED_{i,t}) \frac{1}{20}, \; 0.2STK_{i,t-1} \right] \tag{74}$$

---

26   Unfortunately no data exist on private stocks in India.

For i   = 4, 5, 6
$$STK_{i,t}^* = Max[Q_{i,t}/60 , 0.2STK_{i,t-1}] \tag{75}$$

For i   = 7
$$STK_{i,t}^* = Max[0.001.Q_{it} , 0.2STK_{i,t-1}] \tag{76}$$

For i   = 10
$$STK_{i,t}^* = [STK_{i,t-1}+DLTA(Q_{i,t})/20 , 0.2 STK_{i,t-1}] \tag{77}$$

where

$STK_{i,t}^*$ and $STK_{i,t}$	= target and actual stocks of the ith sectoral commodity at the end of year t;
$Q_{i,t}$	= production of sector i;
$FEED_{it}$	= quantity kept aside towards animal feed; and
$DLTA(Z_t)$	= Z_t-Z_{t-1}.

For perishable goods (i = 4, 5 and 6), the target stocks were set at 5 days' supply. For nonperishable goods (i = 1, 2, 3, 8, 9 and 10), the target increase in stocks equalled one twentieth of the year-to-year increases in net production. For sector 7, though its output is nonperishable, stocks are assumed to be zero. However, in setting the target, no stock was allowed to fall below 20 percent of its previous year-end level.

There is one important difference between targets for procurement and public distribution and targets for stocks, trade, etc. The former were assumed to be realized always, since endogenous prices do not influence them except in the case of wheat. For the latter, however, the influence of prices is too important to be ignored so that actual stocks and trade levels are simultaneously determined with prices so that the targets may or may not be realized. However, it is possible to specify exogenously certain minimum and maximum bounds, so that targets become flexible and these bounds define a region within which they are realized. Appendix 3.3 gives the bounds on stocks.

D. *Investment and public consumption.* The fixed capital formation (f.c.f.) for each year in the economy (public and private sectors together) was specified as a fraction of the total gross domestic product (GDP). This fraction was stipulated exogenously (i.e., as a time trend) in the model with an asymptotic value of 45 percent. From this total investment target at current prices, total household savings were subtracted so that the difference represents the extent of financing of investment through public savings and foreign capital inflow. Formally,

$$DESRSV_t = \alpha_{ds}(a_{ds})^{time}[GDP70_t \cdot PRIDX_t] \tag{78}$$

where

$DESRSV_t$ = desired investment (total);
GDP70   = total gross domestic product at base year prices;
PRIDX   = GDP deflator.

α_{ds} and a_{ds} were exogenously fixed at 0.172 and 1.025 respectively. Now the target for the sum of public savings and foreign capital inflow is

$$GCSV_t^* = [DESRSV_t - TSAVE_t]/P_{na,t}^* \qquad (79)$$

where $P_{na,t}^*$ is the target price of the non-agriculture (sector 10), and TSAVE is the savings by households (eqns. (58) and (59)) summed over all expenditure classes.

In simulations, we treated classwise household savings as part of its committed expenditure on the non-agricultural good,[27] so that they are always realized.

To arrive at the total government expenditure, the government expenditure on public consumption has to be added to this GCSV*. Data over recent years show that public final consumption expenditure (PBFCE) is approximately 12-13 percent of the GDP. PBFCE was set as follows:

$$PBFCE_t^* = [PRIDX_t \cdot GDP70_t \cdot (\alpha_{pf} + a_{pf} \cdot TIME)]/P_{na,t}^* \qquad (80)$$

where α_{pf} and a_{pf} were exogenously specified as 0.12 and 0.002 respectively such that by the year 2000, PBFCE would be about 17 percent of the GDP.

In the government's budget, both $GCSV_t^*$ and $PBFCE_t^*$ would enter as a part of the government's total demand.[28]

$$GONI_t^* = GCSV_t^* + PBFCE_t^* \qquad (81)$$

Unless $GONI_t^*$ is also treated as a commitment on the part of the government, its value might not be realized in equilibrium. Again by specifying maximum and minimum bounds, this target variable could be endogenized. By splitting the realized value after exchange into investment and final consumption components, one could exogenously assume either $GCSV_t^*$ or $PBFCE_t^*$ or a proportion of each would be realized depending on the policy being analyzed. In most of our policy scenarios, including the reference scenario, the bounds on $GONI_t^*$ were specified such that this was always realized.

---

27 That is, these expected savings were added to the estimated committed volumes.
28 Since the entire demand system (private and government) obeys Walras' Law, those parts of the government budget not explicitly specified are automatically allowed for once the private sector satisfies its budget constraint.

$GCSV_t$, the realized value of $GCSV_t^*$ after the exchange, is allocated along with household savings (TSAVE) as investment in agricultural and non-agricultural sectors. Data show that the agricultural sector claimed around 22 percent of the total investment (at 1970-71 prices) in 1950-51. In later years, however, this percentage went down. For example, in 1975-76 and 1980-81, the corresponding figures were 14 and 18 percent respectively. In our model the share of the agricultural sector in the total gross investment was specified as follows:

$$SAGR_t = \left[\alpha_{ag} - \beta_{ag} \frac{1}{TIME_t} \right] \left[\frac{PAA_t}{PNA_t} \right]^{n_{ag}} \tag{82}$$

so that the share is determined not just as a time trend but also depends on the barter terms of trade between the agricultural and the non-agricultural sectors.

Here

$SAGR_t$ = share of agricultural investment;
PAA_t = price deflator of agricultural GDP; and
PNA_t = price deflator of non-agricultural GDP.

α_{ag} and β_{ag} were specified to be 0.1909 and 0.1588 such that the time trend part would amount to 0.186 in the year 2000. n_{ag}, the terms of trade elasticity, was exogenously specified to be 0.25. It follows that at base year prices, the agricultural investment is

$$AGINV_t = (SAGR_t) \left[GCSV_t + \frac{TSAVE_t}{P_{na,t}} \right] P_{na,t} \left(\frac{1}{PNA_t} \right) \tag{83}$$

and the non-agricultural investment is

$$NAINV_t = (1 - SAGR_t) \left[GCSV_t + \frac{TSAVE_t}{P_{na,t}} \right] (P_{na,t}) \left(\frac{1}{PNA_t} \right) \tag{84}$$

where $P_{na,t}$ is the price of the non-agricultural commodity. It may be noted that $AGINV_t$ enters into eqn. (2) to determine gross irrigated area and $NAINV_t$, converted into per capita terms, $(SNAG_t)$, enters into eqn. (38) to determine the potential increment in the capacity output of non-agriculture.[29]

E. *Quotas, tariffs and deficit on trade*. In this model, the distinction between balance of trade and balance of payments on current account, as usually understood, is not explicitly maintained. The transfer payments, invisibles

---

29 Both $AGINV_t$ and $NAINV_t$ are also converted into appropriate units, i.e., millions or crores (10^7) of rupees, as required by eqns. (2) and (38).

and capital account transfers, etc., were all accounted in terms of net trade or "transfer across the border" in the form of the non-agricultural commodity. The net balance over all commodities due to trade and/or transfers at the border is referred to, in what follows, as balance of trade or simply as trade deficit.

It is obvious that levels of trade and aid, domestic stocks, domestic consumption and investment are all interdependent. These levels depend on various factors including domestic and international prices, the difference between the two being tariff rates. Targets were set in respect of domestic prices, consumption levels, trade volumes, and stocks.

In the case of trade, commodity-wise import and export bounds, i.e., quotas were set, not explicitly but indirectly, by specifying upper and lower bounds on domestic demands. Total trade deficit was specified to be a fixed percentage of the total GDP. This percentage was exogenously specified as 1.5, a level consistent with past data.

Target prices are always realized as long as the bounds on both trade and stocks are not reached. By setting target domestic prices implicitly targets for tariff rates are set since the world prices are assumed to be known. The principle adopted in the reference and policy scenarios (unless otherwise mentioned) in specifying the target prices is that the domestic price of a commodity should gradually move towards its international price, the pace of this movement varying from commodity to commodity and as permitted by the imposed trade bounds. The procedure used for this is as follows. Recall that the model is solved for each year sequentially and that there are ten commodity sectors in it.

Before setting the target prices in year t, we checked which of the following three possibilities occurred for each commodity.

Case (a). Trade constraint was not binding for the year (t–1) [regardless of what happened in the year (t–2)].

Case (b). Trade constraint was binding for both the years (t–1) and (t-2) and also the trade pattern was the same for these two years, i.e., the commodity was exported (imported) in both the years.

Case (c). Trade constraint was binding for both the years (t–1) and (t–2), but the trade pattern was not the same between these two years, i.e., the commodity was exported (imported) in the year (t–2) but was imported (exported) in the year (t–1).

Target prices ($P_{i,t}^{*}$ i = 1, . . . 10) for the commodities that came under case (a) were specified as a function of its realized domestic price in the previous year ($P_{i,t-1}$) and the international price ($P_{i,t}^{w}$) as follows:

$$P_{it}^{*} = P_{it-1} \left[P_{it}^{w} / P_{it-1} \right]^{1/n_i} \tag{85}$$

$$= \left[P_{it-1}\right]^{(n_i-1)/n_i} \cdot \left[P_{it}^w\right]^{1/n_i} \tag{86}$$

The procedure implies that the target price of a commodity i is steered towards its world price over a period of n_i years from the previous year's realized domestic price.[30] However, since n_i was fixed, while the realized domestic price could vary from year to year, obviously the actual number of years taken for the domestic realized price to reach the international level could differ from n_i.

In the case of (b), target price was set as:

$$P_{i,t}^* = P_{i,t-1} \tag{87}$$

and in the case of (c), as:

$$P_{i,t}^* = \left[P_{i,t-1} + P_{i,t-1}^*\right]^{\frac{1}{2}} \tag{88}$$

The rationale behind this scheme of specification is as follows. The fact that the trade bound is not binding implies that the trade levels (whether imports or exports) can be adjusted to permit changes in the domestic price of the commodity. Thus there is a scope for steering its domestic price closer to the world price.

However, cases (b) and (c) indicate that domestic production and domestic demand at target prices have been inconsistent in the sense that even with imports or exports at their limits, target prices could not be realized. In case (b), changes in target price in the direction of world price are unlikely to be realized and it is set at last year's realized price. In case (c), oscillation may be taking place and target price is set at the average of the past two years' realized prices.

Strictly speaking, cases (a), (b) and (c) do not exhaust all the possibilities. For example, the following can occur:

Case (d). Trade constraint was binding in the year (t-1), but not binding in the year (t-2).

However, this is unlikely to occur unless some external shocks are specially introduced into the system. Also, while case (a) does not rule out the possibility of trade reversals (i.e., though the trade was not binding in the year (t-1) still a reversal of the pattern can occur compared to the year (t-2)), this is unlikely to occur in a well-tuned (calibrated) model.

Appendix 3.3 gives the various minimum and maximum bounds specified exogenously with respect to government policy regarding target prices and trade volumes.

---

30   These exogenously specified values of n_i are given in Appendix 3.3.

F. *Government revenue.* All the operations of the government should be carried out within its income consisting of tariffs, taxes, trade deficit (foreign aid), value of its previous year-end stocks and value of endowments procured, if any, in the current year.

$$\text{GREVN}_t = \text{TARIFFS}_t + \text{BALTAR}_t + \text{TAXES}_t + \text{STKVAL}_t$$
$$+ \text{GENVAL}_t \tag{89}$$

where

  (i) TARIFFS_t = Tariff Revenue = $\Sigma\,[P_{i,t}{}^w - P_{i,t}]E_{i,t};$ (90)
     $E_{i,t}$ = Net exports of commodity i;
     $P_{i,t}{}^w$ and $P_{i,t}$ = World price and domestic price of i;
 (ii) BALTAR_t = Trade deficit = $-\Sigma\,P_{i,t}{}^w E_{i,t};$ and   (91)
(iii) TAXES_t = Tax income = $\Sigma\,\text{CHI}_{jt}\,(\text{YM}_{na,t}{}^j)(P_{na,t}).$ (92)

$\text{YM}_{na,t}{}^j$ is the non-agricultural endowment of jth expenditure class ($j = 1,10$ rural and urban together). Government was assumed to levy a tax only on non-agricultural incomes. CHI_{jt} is the tax rate for j^{th} expenditure class. Richer expenditure classes pay more taxes and the progression in the tax structure was specified exogenously. That is, θ_j in

$$\text{CHI}_{jt} = (1-\phi_t)\theta_j \tag{93}$$

were exogenously specified. ϕ_t and hence the classwise taxation levels are endogenous in the model. The iterative procedure involved in solving for the exchange equilibrium determines the actual value of ϕ_t for which again, a target, minimum and maximum values were exogenously specified before the exchange.

Specifications of θ_j are given in Appendix 3.3.

 (iv) STKVAL_t = Value of the previous year-end stocks with the government
                  = $\Sigma P_{i,t}(\text{STK}_{i,t-1})$ (94)
  (v) GENVAL_t = Value of endowments that accrue to government in the current year including procurement and rationing operations
                  = $\Sigma P_{i,t}(\text{GYM}_{i,t})$ (95)

where

   $\text{GYM}_{i,t}$ = Government's endowment of ith commodity

          = $Q_{i,t} - \Sigma \text{YM}_{i,t}{}^j$ (96)

   $\text{YM}_{i,t}{}^j$ = Endowment of ith commodity with j^{th} expenditure class.

Now, the implicit budget constraint for the government is:

$$GONI_t.P_{na,t} + \Sigma\,(STK_{i,t}).P_{i,t} = GREVN_t \tag{97}$$

$GONI_t$ is the realized total demand by government (see eqn. 81).

3.6 Exchange

In the exchange component, budget constraints of all the expenditure classes explicitly enter together with a budget constraint for the nation as a whole. The household budget constraint for j^{th} expenditure class is:

$$\Sigma\,P_{i,t}X_{i,t}^j + P_{na,t}\left[\frac{S_t^j}{P_{na,t}}\right]$$

$$= (1 - CHI_{jt})\,(YM_{na,t}^j)\,P_{na,t} + \Sigma P_{i,t}.YM_{i,t}^j \tag{98}$$

where

$\quad X_{i,t}^j \quad$ = Consumption of ith commodity by j^{th} expenditure class;
$\quad S_t^j \quad$ = Savings by j^{th} expenditure class; and
$\quad CHI_{jt} \quad$ = $(1-\phi_t)\,\theta_j$ as defined in eqn. (93).

Eqn. (97) and (98) together give us a national budget constraint. It must be noted that also the commodity flows remain balanced during the exchange. That is, for each commodity i,

$$\Sigma YM_{i,t}^j + GYM_{i,t} + STK_{i,t-1} = \Sigma X_{i,t}^j + STK_{i,t} + E_{i,t} \tag{99}$$

The model is solved sequentially for each year from 1971 to 2000. The exchange equilibrium of each year determines that year's actual values of class-wise incomes and their commoditywise consumptions, tax levels, commodity-wise net trade, public buffer stocks, tariffs and domestic prices. If government demand is held fixed, then balance of trade or domestic income tax rate can be the adjusting variable. In most of our scenarios, trade deficit was kept fixed and the tax rate adjusted. In some scenarios, both tax rate and trade deficits were fixed and government demand adjusted. Though one could have let the balance of trade adjust, this was not done in any of the scenarios.

3.7 Scope, Limitations and Concluding Remarks

The model described above is a policy-oriented, price endogenous, comput-able general equilibrium model. It can simulate the consequences of various government policies. It is an open model incorporating foreign trade. Since agriculture is a large sector in the Indian economy, any policy that affects agricultural outputs and incomes has spill-over effects in the rest of the economy and our general equilibrium model captures these effects. Similarly, agriculture plays a significant role in India's exports as well as imports; our model being open, allows us to analyze foreign trade aspects.

The model is Walrasian with no money in the system and only relative prices matter. The government policies are set or revised every year. Some policies can, however, be determined appropriately only in a long-run context. These would be assumed to have been so determined exogenously to our model. In fact, simulation runs of the model should help in determining some of these policies. The model is flexible in that a policy variable can be made exogenous in some and endogenous in other policy runs. For example, one can stipulate exogenously certain taxation levels and endogenize government savings and hence investment levels.

Any model that tries to describe reality in a quantitative empirical way is bound to have some limitations and ours is no exception. The major limitations of the model described above that may have some bearing on the results of policy analysis reported in the following chapters are given below:

1. The savings behaviour in the model assumes that the government is a residual saver which ensures that aggregate investment follows a predetermined path of aggregate savings rate. This is a bit optimistic though not too unrealistic, a characterization of India's economy.

2. The allocation of aggregate investment between agriculture and non-agriculture is not explicitly dynamic in our model. Though it depends on relative prices it is not affected by considerations of relative expected profitability of the two sectors. The allocation is thus not optimal. However, if farmers invest more in agriculture from their own savings and if they do not consider investment in non-agricultural sector as an option and if capital markets are not perfect optimality cannot be expected to prevail.

3. There is no explicit modelling of rural labour market. The assumption we have made is that the share of wages remains constant in real terms in agriculture. This implies a Cobb-Douglas production function with full and instantaneous adjustment of wages when prices change.

4. Income distribution in non-agriculture resulting from production is stable, and changes only through government transfers. Available empirical evidence does suggest a fairly stable income distribution.

5. There is one aggregated non-agricultural sector all of which is tradeable. Thus the model does not have any non-tradeables.

6. Consumer behavior is characterized by separate expenditure systems estimated separately for each of the five rural and five urban groups. The broad pattern of parameters across the expenditure groups seems sensible. Even then it would have been preferable if the demand systems for all the five classes were estimated simultaneously and the parameters were made functions of total expenditure level. The estimated systems could in principle lead to surprising response to policy changes since income distribution is treated in terms of five discrete groups in rural and urban areas.

Before we close this chapter, a few econometric problems involved in estimating the various sub-models may be mentioned. Most of these estimates were based on time-series data. Wherever auto-correlation in the relevant disturbance term was present, a first order auto-correlation scheme was assumed during estimation. Each sub-model relating to group irrigated areas, crop irrigated areas in a group, yield functions of rice and wheat, the linear expenditure system of the various expenditure classes was estimated simultaneously. More details are provided in Appendix 3.4. Other econometric aspects relating to estimation of cropwise acreage, yields of major cereal crops, proportions of expenditure, classwise population and incomes, are discussed in detail in Narayana and Parikh (1981 and 1987) and Narayana, Parikh, Srinivasan (1984).

Among the econometric limitations one should mention that in modelling the parameters of the acreage response equations and the price expectation equations (ARIMA processes) were estimated separately. They should have been estimated simultaneously.

One might argue that in general equilibrium theory everything depends on everything else and hence all of the equations (not just a few sub-models) presented above should have been estimated simultaneously. Though this argument is in principle correct, estimation of hundreds of equations simultaneously is infeasible. Besides, certain niceties involving case-to-case tailor-made specifications would be lost in such a gross simultaneous estimation.

In fact, in order not to underestimate the importance of any simultaneity, the sub-models were carefully developed so that they operate in sequence as a recursive system.

We shall discuss the policy conclusions of this study in the context of these limitations of the model in the last chapter.

Some of the econometric issues in estimating the parameters of the model are discussed in Appendix 3.4. The data sources are listed in Appendix 3.5. The estimated parameters of all the equations are presented in Appendix 3.6.

Appendix 3.1

SECTORS AND COMMODITIES IN THE MODEL

I. Sectors and Units of Measurement for Demand, Exchange and International trade

Number of sectors in the economy: 10

S01 : Wheat (10**3 tons)
S02 : Rice (10**3 tons)
S03 : Coarse grains (10**3 tons)
S04 : Bovine and Ovine Meats (10**3 tons of carcass weight)
S05 : Dairy products (10**3 tons of fresh milk equivalent)
S06 : Other animal products (10**3 tons of protein equivalent)
S07 : Protein feeds (10**3 tons of protein equivalent)
S08 : Other food (10**6 US $ of 1970)
S09 : Non-food agriculture (10**6 US$ of 1970)
S10 : Non-agriculture (10**6 US $ of 1970)

II. Commodities at the Supply Level

(a) *Crops (16 major crops and 9 minor crops)*

Major crops: Bajra, Barley, Sugarcane, Cotton, Groundnut, Gram, Jute, Jowar, Mesta, Maize, Rice, Ragi, Rape and Mustard, Sesamum, Tobacco and Wheat.

Minor crops: Other pulses, Other oilseeds, Small millets, Sannhemp, Rubber, Tea, Coffee, Fruits and Vegetables, and Condiments and Spices.

(b) *Livestock products*

Beef, Mutton and Pork, Other Meat Products, Hides and Skins, Eggs and Poultry, Wool and Hair and Other Livestock Products.

UPDATING OF EXPENDITURE CLASS BOUNDARIES

As already described, the population is grouped each year into ten expenditure classes in the model; 5 in rural and 5 in urban areas.

For both rural and urban, these expenditure class boundaries correspond to a per capita annual consumer expenditure of Rs. 216, Rs. 336, Rs. 516, Rs. 900 and greater than Rs. 900 at the base year (1970) prices. For each year the boundaries are revised to give the same equivalent income.

Updating the expenditure limits of the various expenditure classes, year-by-year, in the model is based on the following methodology:

Let us drop the subscript j corresponding to the expenditure class, and let i and t represent commodity and time-period respectively.

For a given time period let us

$$\text{minimize } \Sigma \, P_i X_i = \text{expenditure} = E(P_i, U)$$

subject to

$$\Sigma \, b_i \log (X_i - C_i) = \log U$$

where

X_i = Quantity bought of commodity i
C_i = Committed quantity of commodity i
b_i = Marginal budget share of commodity i with $\Sigma \, b_i = 1$
P_i = Price of commodity i
U = A chosen level of utility

Setting up Lagrangean:

$$\phi = \Sigma \, P_i X_i - \text{LMDA}[\Sigma b_i \log(X_i - C_i) - \log U]$$

From the first order conditions, we get

$$P_i(X_i - C_i) = b_i \, \text{LMDA} \tag{A.4.1}$$

and

$$\log U - \Sigma b_i \log(X_i - C_i) = 0 \qquad (A.4.2)$$

from which it can be shown that

$$LMDA = U \ \pi(b_i/P_i)^{-b_i} \qquad (A.4.3)$$

Summing (A.4.1) over i and substituting for LMDA, we have for any time period t

$$\Sigma P_{it} X_{it} = U\pi(P_{it} / b_i)^{b_i} + \Sigma P_{it} C_i = E(P_{it}, U) \qquad (A.4.4)$$

A similar expression can be written at base year prices (P_{io}), for the same utility level U. From the base year expression and (A.4.4) we get

$$E(P_{it}, U) = \Sigma P_{it} C_i + [E(P_{io}, U) - \Sigma P_{io} C_i] \ \pi(P_{it}/P_{io})^{b_i} \qquad (A.4.5)$$

If $E(P_{io}, U)$ is the base year expenditure limit (i.e., Rs. 336 and so on) then the corresponding $E(P_{it}, U)$ is the revised expenditure limit at revised prices P_{it} with unchanged utility level.

However, during simulation of the model, two problems arise:

(a) Depending upon the demand function parameters of which expenditure class are used, there can be two different estimates of some $E(P_{it}, U)$. For example, the limit of Rs. 216 could be updated using the parameters of the first and second expenditure classes. In such cases, the average of the two estimates is taken.

(b) Since the actually realized prices would not be known until after the exchange, these expenditure limits are updated using once the targeted prices, and again using the previous-year realized prices and finally the specified expenditure limit is the average of the two.

It may be noted that the same methodology is used later in some policy scenarios in working out what is called "equivalent incomes" of various expenditure classes. Equivalent income at a time period t is defined to be the expenditure (not income) required at base year (1970) prices to achieve the same utility level U_t obtained at prices in year t. This provides a true cost of living index specific to each expenditure class.

Appendix 3.3

GOVERNMENT POLICY SPECIFICATIONS, BOUNDS AND PRICES

(a) Stocks

The minimum and maximum stocks are set as

$$\text{STKMN}_{i,t} = a_{i,mn} \text{ STK*}_{it} \tag{A.3.1}$$

$$\text{STKMX}_{it} = \text{Max } [0.04(Q_{it} + \text{STK}_{it-1}); a_{i,mx}\text{STK*}_{it}] \tag{A.3.2}$$

where STKMN_{it} and STKMX_{it} are the targeted minimum and maximum stocks of ith commodity-sector whose output level is Q_{it}. $a_{i,mn}$ and $a_{i,mx}$ are exogenously specified as follows:

$a_{i,mx} = 1.001$ and $a_{i,mn} = 0.999$ for i = 1,9 sectors; and

$a_{10,mx} = 300$ and $a_{10,mn} = 0.01$.

(b) Consumptions

Let

$$AV_{it} = Q_{it} + \text{STK}_{i,t-1} \tag{A.3.3}$$

The maximum and minimum consumptions of i-th sectoral commodity (XMAX_{it} and XMIN_{it} respectively) are set as follows:

$$\text{XMAX}_{it} = b_{i,mx}.AV_{it}; \qquad b_{i,mx} \geq 1 \tag{A.3.4}$$
$$\text{or } b_{i,mx} \approx 1$$

$$\text{XMIN}_{it} = b_{i,mn}.AV_{it}; \qquad b_{i,mn} \leq 1 \tag{A.3.5}$$

Earlier, it was already stated that XMAX_{it} and XMIN_{it} indirectly indicate trade quotas, i.e.,

Exports $\leq AV_{it} - XMIN_{it} - STK_{it}$; and

Imports $\leq XMAX_{it} + STK_{it} - AV_{it}$.

Two different sets of numbers are considered for exogenously specifying $b_{i,mx}$ and $b_{i,mn}$ as follows:

Sector	Set 1		Set 2	
(i)	$b_{i,mx}$	$b_{i,mn}$	b_{imx}	b_{imn}
1	1.15	0.85	1.15	0.85
2	1.05	0.90	1.05	0.90
3	1.15	0.85	1.15	0.85
4	0.99	0.90	1.25	0.90
5	1.1	0.90	1.25	0.90
6	1.0	0.99	1.25	0.99
7	1.1	0.01	1.1	0.01
8	1.1	0.90	1.3	0.90
9	0.99	0.80	1.3	0.80
10	3.00	0.01	3.00	0.01

Set 2 implies less restricted trade compared to Set 1. The reference run was made using both the sets.

While this is the general procedure followed, however, we check for each i every year whether $XMAX_{it}$ is at least as high as the expected total committed volume (computed at P^*_{it} using the demand equations) over all expenditure groups of the population. If it is not so, then $XMAX_{it}$ is arbitrarily revised upwards.

(c) Prices

Recall that P^*_{it} and P_{it} are the targeted and actually realized prices of i-th sectoral commodity for year t; and n_i is the number of years for i-th commodity's previous year realized prices [P_{it-1}] to reach the world price level.

The exogenous specifications of n_i are:

$n_1 = 5$ for $i = 1, 3$ and 5

$$= 12 \text{ for } i = 2, 4 \text{ and } 10$$
$$= 20 \text{ for } i = 6$$
$$= 4 \text{ for } i = 7$$
$$= 2 \text{ for } i = 8$$
$$= 7 \text{ for } i = 9$$

Next, the bounds on targeted prices P^*_{it} to set maximum and minimum prices ($PMAX_{it}$ and $PMIN_{it}$) are specified as follows:

i =	1	2	3	4	5	6	7	8	9	10
g_{imx} =	1.005	1.005	1.005	1.007	1.07	1.07	1.07	1.007	1.007	1.25
g_{imn} =	0.97	0.97	0.9	0.93	0.93	0.98	0.93	0.93	0.93	0.8

where

$$PMAX_{it} = g_{imx} \; P^*_{it} \tag{A.3.6}$$

and

$$PMIN_{it} = g_{imn} \; P^*_{it} \tag{A.3.7}$$

(d) Retail Prices, Raw Prices and Processing Margins

Almost all agricultural commodities, by the time they reach retail shops from farm gates, get complemented with certain types of non-agricultural goods and services. Rice, wheat, etc., are milled; coffee, tobacco, etc., are packed and tinned; cotton becomes cloth, and so on, apart from the usual transport costs involved. Consumers invariably pay for these services also. Since incomes generated by these processing effects do not accrue to farmers but only to producers of non-agricultural commodity, it is essential that a distinction be made between farm-gate prices ($PRAW_{it}$) that farmers receive and retail prices (P_{it}) that consumers pay. The difference between $PRAW_{it}$ and P_{it} represents the non-agricultural processing costs per unit, which is referred to henceforth as processing margin. Given either of these two, i.e., $PRAW_{it}$ or P_{it} the other can be worked out if the processing margin is known.

The processing margin can be expressed either in terms of (i) value coefficients $PRMV_{it}$, as

$$PRMGN_{it} = P_{it} - PRAW_{it} = PRAW_{it} . PRMV_{it} \tag{A.3.8}$$

where $PRMV_{it}$ could be interpreted as a commodity specific percentage of its raw (farm-gate) price; or in terms of (ii) quantity coefficients $PRMQ_{it}$, as

$$PRMGN_{it} = P_{it} - PRAW_{it} = P_{10,t} . PRMQ_{it} \tag{A.3.9}$$

where $PRMQ_{it}$ could be interpreted as the quantity of non-agricultural goods required to process a unit amount of i-th commodity.

Lack of adequate data caused serious problems in estimating $PRMV_i$ and $PRMQ_i$.[1] In some cases, the data are so scanty that the estimates turned out to be even negative.[2] Based on several data sources and inter-industry tables and somewhat even arbitrarily, the following numbers are specified exogenously as $PRMV_i$:

Sector	$PRMV_i$
1	0.06
2	$0.10 + 0.01443.PNA_t/PRAW_{rice,t}$; ($PNA_t$ = Non-agricultural price index)
3	0.08
4	0
5	0.07
6	0
7	0
8	0.0033
9	$0.4998+0.3(1.035)^{tm76}$; (tm76 = Max [0,year-1976)]
10	0

It may be noted that by definition the processing margin is nil for the non-agricultural (10th) sector. Also, only for sectors 2 & 9 (rice and non-food agriculture), these coefficients are time-variant; for others, they are fixed coefficients.

(e) Tax-rate

The minimum and maximum values of targeted ϕ corresponding to tax rate were specified as:

ϕ min = 0.25
and
ϕ max = 2.00

---

1 One simple way to estimate these coefficients is by working out the difference between output and value added per unit of value added.
2 This is understandable. For example, unprocessed milk is costlier than processed milk since the byproducts like butter, etc., have a value added.

Note:

Tax rate $= (1-\phi)\,\theta_j$

$\theta_j = 0.1, 0.2, 0.4, 0.6, 0.9$ for $j = 1, 5$ rural respectively,

$\theta_j = 0.1, 0.2, 0.5, 0.7, 1.0$ for $j = 1, 5$ urban respectively

(f) Commodity Prices

While projecting the cropwise acreages, etc., cropwise prices are necessary (see eqn. 8). The exchange results in only aggregate realized prices at sectoral level. The cropwise prices from the sectoral prices were derived as:

$$\text{PRICE}_{kei,t} = \text{PRICE}_{kei,t-1}\,[P_{i,t}/P_{i,t-1}] \qquad (\text{A.3.10})$$

where k denotes crop k and i denotes sector 1 to which crop k belongs.

SOME ECONOMETRIC ISSUES IN ESTIMATION

The econometric issues involved in estimating the various sub-models presented in the technical description earlier are discussed in this appendix. The discussion is confined to the relatively complex issues relating to the following:[1]

(a) estimation of crop revenue expectation equation (eqn. 8);
(b) estimation of cropwise acreage response equations (eqn. 12);
(c) estimation of yield functions (eqn. 18) for rice and wheat;
(d) estimation of groupwise and cropwise irrigated area (eqns. 6, 7),
(e) estimation of income distribution and proportions of population in each expenditure class.

(a) Crop Revenue Expectations

The crop revenue equation, written as an Auto-Regressive Integrated Moving Average (ARIMA) process, is as follows (eqn. 8 with crop subscript dropped):

$$\pi_t = \pi_t^* + W_t$$

where

$$\pi_t^* = \phi_1 \pi_{t-1} + \phi_2 \pi_{t-2} + \phi_3 \pi_{t-3} + \ldots + \mu + \theta_1 W_{t-1}$$
$$+ \theta_2 W_{t-2} + \theta_3 W_{t-3} + \ldots \tag{a1}$$

with the asterisk denoting expected value, W_t the white-noise or random disturbance with mean zero; and π_t denoting revenue. Generally, such ARIMA processes are described by the number of auto-regressives (p) and the number

---

1 Equation numbers in brackets are as in the Technical Description (Chapter 3).

of moving averages (q) present in the equation and the degree of differencing (d) applied to make the original "homogeneously nonstationary" series stationary.

For each crop we applied the following ARIMA schemes to estimate equation (a1):

(p, q, d): (1, 1, 0), (1, 2, 0), (2, 1, 0), (1, 1, 1), (1, 2, 1) and (2, 1, 1)

We selected the best of these six schemes, first, by checking certain stationarity restrictions on the estimated parameter values, and second, by applying a chi-square test on the residual auto-correlations.

Appendix 3.6 shows the selected schemes, the results of the estimation and the chi-square test statistic on the residual auto-correlations. See Narayana and Parikh (1981) for more details.

(b) Acreage Responses

The reduced form of the acreage response model is as follows (subscripts for crop and group dropped from eqn.12):

$$\log A_t = a.r + (1-r)\log A_{t-1} + b.r.\log Z_t^* + c.r.\log R_t$$
$$+ d.r.\log(IA/GIA)_t + e.r.\log(IA_{sc}/GIA)_t$$
$$+ f.r.\log(GIA)_t + r.\log V_t \tag{b1}$$

where the definition of the various variables are provided in the main text of the technical description. V_t is a random error term assumed to be independently and identically lognormally distributed with mean zero and a constant variance. Some potential problems in estimating eqn. (b1) are as follows:

First, since the time series data are used auto-correlation in the disturbance term is possible. In such a case, though Ordinary Least Squares (OLS) yields unbiased parameter estimates, sampling variances of these estimates would be underestimated.

Second, in the presence of the lagged dependent variable on the right hand side, with no auto-correlation, OLS leads to estimates that are consistent, but biased in small samples. However, OLS applied in the presence of auto-correlation does not even yield consistent estimates.

Third, since by definition the disturbance term and the dependent variable are correlated, especially under auto-correlation, then V_t would be correlated with the explanatory variable A_{t-1} if V_t is correlated with V_{t-1}. This again leads to inconsistent estimates of parameters.

Fourth, under such circumstances, the conventional Durbin-Watson test for auto-correlation cannot be relied on.

These econometric problems were tackled as follows:

(i)   With 21 observations on each variable for the period 1953 to 1974 one may argue that the sample is large enough to bring the bias, caused due to the presence of a lagged dependent variable, to tolerable levels. But this is a subjective matter since what is tolerable depends on the relevant decision problem and the assessment of the analyst.

(ii) The presence, on the right-hand side, of three or four exogenous variables (such as rainfall, relative revenue, irrigation, and so on) other than the lagged dependent variable helps to reduce the asymptotic biases of the estimates in such cases (see Malinvaud 1970).

(iii) We decided to allow for auto-correlation regardless of the value of the Durbin-Watson test statistic. We assumed the following first-order auto- correlation scheme

$$\log V_t = \text{RHO} \, \log V_{t-1} + U_t$$

with U_t distributed as $N(0, \sigma^2)$.

In searching for RHO that minimizes the sum of squares, we did not use the Cochrane-Orcutt technique since it may lead to a local optimum. We used Hildreth-Lu's scanning technique since this not only assures globally optimal estimates but also, depending on the sample size, estimates close to the maximum likelihood estimates (see Maddala). We estimated eqn. (b1) for 40 values of RHO for each crop, over a range of $-1.00 < \text{RHO} < 1.0$ with a step-size of 0.05 and chose the RHO value that yielded the highest $(R\text{-Bar})^2$. Interestingly, for several crops, the estimates of RHO turned out to be zero implying no auto correlation.

The results presented in Appendix 3.6 were accepted on the basis of

(i)   conformity with the expected signs of the various estimates;
(ii) levels of significance for the computed t-coefficients;
(iii) a high $(R\text{-Bar})^2$.

It may be noted that

(i)   For rice, wheat, groundnut, sugarcane and tobacco, we got acceptable results with $\log A_t$ as the dependent variable.
(ii) For ragi, jute, mesta, gram, barley and sesamum the results became acceptable only when we used the areas of these crops relative to the areas of some other crops in the respective groups instead of A_t. Thus

we estimated relative areas of ragi/rice, jute/ragi, mesta/ragi, gram/ wheat, barley/wheat, sesamum/groundnut and rapeseed and mustard/ sesamum instead of the absolute areas under ragi, jute, mesta, gram, barley, sesamum and rapeseed and mustard. In these cases, A_t in eqn. (b1) represents such relative areas.

(iii) In the case of bajra and maize, the coefficient of the revenue variable turned out to be of wrong sign. However, the regression with a price term instead of the revenue term gave acceptable results.

(iv) In the case of jowar inclusion of neither revenue, nor price, nor yield gave acceptable results. Ultimately, the area under jowar relative to that of maize was used in the regression.

(c) Yield Functions

The yield functions for rice and wheat are:

$$YLD_k = s_k \left[\Sigma S_{ikt}(a_{ik} + b_{ik}f_{ikt} + c_{ik}f_{ikt}{}^2) \right]$$
$$+ d_k R_{kt} + U_{kt} \tag{c1}$$

It was mentioned earlier that the parameters a_{ik}, b_{ik} and c_{ik} (i represents type of land and k, the crop) were taken from Parikh and Srinivasan(1974) and Parikh (1978). Only the parameters s_k and d_k are to be estimated using the available data on aggregate yields (YLD_k), prices (P_k), cropwise and typewise acreages (A_{ik}), fertilizer (F_{rw}), etc. The non-linear least squares procedure adopted here is an iterative one. We start with an initial set of parameters s_k and d_k. Using them along with a_{ik}'s etc., we compute the shadow price associated with the availability F_{rw} of fertilizer from the maximization of the expected value of output as:

$$LMDA = \frac{2F_{rw} + \sum\limits_{k} A_k \left[\sum\limits_{i} \left[\frac{S_{ik} b_{ik}}{c_{ik}} \right] \right]}{\sum\limits_{k} \left[\frac{A_k}{P_k} \sum\limits_{i} \left[\frac{S_{ik}}{c_{ik}} \right] \right]} \tag{c2}$$

and the fertilizer intensities as

$$f_{ik} = \frac{\left[\dfrac{LMDA}{P_k} - b_{ik} \right]}{(2c_{ik})} \tag{c3}$$

for various i and k. This enables us to compute the expected values of the aggregate crop yields (denoted as YLD_{kt}**) as per equation (c1) above. Note that the expected value of U_{kt} is zero. Thus, we have the error sum of squares

$$\Sigma \ (YLD_{kt} - YLD_{kt}**)^2$$

which is to be minimized.

Based on Marquadt's procedure and numerical methods, now the initial parameters are revised and with the revised set of parameters the whole process is repeated. The iteration procedure is stopped when there is no appreciable change in the error sum of squares over a given number of consecutive iterations. This exercise was done only in the case of rice and wheat yield functions. See Narayana and Parikh (1987) for more details. The case of other yield functions is straightforward and not discussed here.

(d)   Groupwise and Cropwise Irrigated Area

The groupwise irrigated area is specified in our model as follows:

$$IA_{gt} = \tau_g(RAIN)_{gt} + \delta_g(IA)_{gt-1}$$
$$+\alpha_g[GIA_t - \Sigma\tau_g(RAIN)_{gt} - \Sigma\delta_g(IA)_{gt-1}] + U_{gt} \qquad (d1)$$

where $\Sigma\alpha_g = 1$, and g and t are group and time subscripts. The total gross irrigated area in the country, GIA, is given by:

$$GIA_t = \beta + a(RIAL)_t + b(AGINV)_t + c(TIME) + U_t \qquad (d2)$$

where the variables were already explained earlier. In total, six (g = 1, 6) groups of crops were distinguished.

The systems of irrigation equations (d1) is analogous to the well-known Linear Expenditure system of demand equation. Equations (d1) and (d2) were simultaneously estimated by assuming that U_{gt} and U_t have the same variance. The procedure of estimation is similar to that for the rice and wheat yield functions; starting with an initial set of parameters, we iterated until convergence to a set of values that correspond to the minimum of the error sum of squares.

The same procedure was adopted in estimating simultaneously the system of equations (eqn. 7) for allocating group irrigated area to crops comprising that group. The linear expenditure system (eqn. 64) of demand allocating total private final consumption expenditures among various commodities was similarly estimated.

(e) Distribution of Population and Income across Classes

Equations (50) to (59) in the main text described the way the expenditure classwise populations and their income entitlements were modeled. Let C and Y stand for individual's consumption and income. Recall that c(=logC) and y (= log Y) are postulated to be jointly normally distributed so that

$$c = a_1 + a_2y + v \qquad (e1)$$

where

$$y \sim N(\mu_y, \sigma_y^2) \text{ and } v \sim N(0, \sigma_v^2) \qquad (e2)$$

then

$$c \sim N(\mu_c = a_1 + a_2\mu_y, \sigma_c^2 = \sigma_v^2 + a_2^2\sigma_y^2) \qquad (e3)$$

Also, let RHO_{cy} be the correlation coefficient between c and y.

It was earlier shown that the knowledge of the parameters a_1, a_2, σ_y^2, σ_c^2 and σ_v^2 is necessary to obtain the proportion of population, consumption and income across prespecified expenditure classes. Thus, we need to estimate a_1, a_2, σ_v^2 along with σ_y^2 and σ_c^2.

We used the income-classwise data reported in NCAER (1980) and applied the method of moments to estimate the parameters.

More precisely, let

$$YBAR_i = \text{mean income of } i_{th} \text{ class} = Y_i/P_i$$

where

Y_i = total income in i_{th} class and
P_i = total population in i_{th} class.

YBAR and CBAR are the overall aggregate income and consumption respectively; then it follows that

$$\text{Variance of Y} = \quad \hat{V}(Y) = \Sigma(YBAR_i - YBAR)^2 . P_i / \Sigma P_i \qquad (e4)$$

$$\text{Variance of y} = \quad \hat{\sigma}_y^2 = \log_e\left[1 + V(Y)/(YBAR)^2\right] \qquad (e5)$$

$$\text{Mean y} \quad = \quad \hat{\mu}_y = \log_e YBAR - \tfrac{1}{2}\sigma_y^2 \qquad (e6)$$

$$\text{Variance of C} = \quad \hat{V}(C) = \Sigma(CBAR_i - CBAR)^2 . P_i / \Sigma P_i \qquad (e7)$$

$$\text{Variance of c} = \quad \hat{\sigma}_c^2 = \log_e\left[1 + V(C)/(CBAR)^2\right] \qquad (e8)$$

Mean c $\qquad = \hat{\mu}_c = \log_e CBAR - \frac{1}{2}\sigma_c^2$ $\qquad$ (e9)

Covariance (C,Y) $\quad = \Sigma\,(YBAR_i - YBAR)(CBAR_i$
$\qquad\qquad\qquad - CBAR).P_i/\Sigma\,P_i$ $\qquad$ (e10)

Correlation
coefficient $\quad R\hat{H}O_{cy} = \dfrac{\log_e\left[1 + Cov(C,Y)/(YBAR.CBAR)\right]}{\sigma_y.\sigma_c}$ $\qquad$ (e11)

Finally,

$$\hat{a}_2 = \log_e\left[1 + Cov(C,Y)/(YBAR.CBAR)\right]/\sigma_y^2 \qquad (e12)$$

$$\hat{a}_1 = \mu_c - a_2\mu_y \qquad (e13)$$

$$\sigma_v^2 = \sigma_c^2 - a_2^2\sigma_y^2 \qquad (e14)$$

NCAER (1980) gives data on precentage distribution of population, income and savings across various income classes separately for rural and urban areas for the year 1975-76. *National Accounts Statistics* (1980) by Central Statistical Organization gives data on the aggregate national personal disposable income and domestic savings by private households. Using this information, computation using (e4) to (e14) gave us the various parameter estimates separately for rural and urban areas. See Narayana, Parikh, Srinivasan(1984) for more details on data problems and estimation.

Appendix 3.5

SOURCES OF DATA

All the data required in estimating the various sub-models described earlier were collected mainly from various issues of the following documents:

(1) Estimates of Area & Production of Principal Crops in India by DES*
(2) Bulletin on Food Statistics by DES
(3) National Accounts Statistics by CSO
(4) Supply Utilization Accounts of the FAO
(5) Wholesale Price Statistics by H L Chandok (1978)
(6) Statistical Abstracts by CSO
(7) Simple Fertilizer Trials data supplied by Indian Agricultural Research Institute, New Delhi.
(8) Economic Surveys by DEA
(9) Household Consumer Expenditure Surveys by NSSO
(10) Household Income and its Disposition by NCAER (1980)
(11) All India Debt & Investment Survey by RBI (1971-72)
(12) Tables on Land Holdings No. 215. All India (26th Round, 1971-72) by NSSO (1976)
(13) Fertilizer Use in Agricultural Holdings (NSS 26th Round), Sarveksh-ana (Oct. 1978) by NSSO
(14) Indian Crop Calendar by DES (1967)
(15) Various Five-Year Plan Documents by Planning Commission of Government of India.
(16) Basic Statistics relating to the Indian Economy by CSO
(17) Indian Agriculture in Brief by DES
(18) Fertilizer Statistics by FAI
(19) World Development Reports by the WB
(20) Rainfall data supplied by the IMD
(21) Rainfall data in "Variations in Crop Output" by S K Ray (1977)

(22)   Statistical Pocket Book — India by CSO

---

*DES	Directorate of Economics & Statistics, Ministry of Agriculture, Government of India
CSO	Central Statistical Organization, Ministry of Planning, Government of India
FAO	Food & Agriculture Organization, Rome (Italy)
DEA	Department of Economic Affairs, Ministry of Finance, Government of India
NSSO	National Sample Survey Organization, Ministry of Planning, Government of India
NCAER	National Council of Applied Economic Research, New Delhi.
RBI	Reserve Bank of India, Bombay
FAI	Fertilizer Association of India, New Delhi
WB	World Bank, Washington, DC
IMD	India Meteorological Department, New Delhi

Appendix 3.6

THE ESTIMATED EQUATIONS AND PARAMETERS OF THE MODEL

Total Area: t: time subscript

1. Net Sown Area (000 hect):

    $$NSA_t = 165000 / [1. + exp (- 0.1144 - 0.0172 \, RIAL_t + 0.00007 \, RIAL_t^2 - 0.0276 \, TIME)] \qquad (*1)$$

2. Gross Irrigated Area (000 hect):

    $$GIA_t = 19135.2 + 5.2369 \, RIAL_t + 4.1667 \, AGINV_t + 626.412 \, TIME \qquad (*2)$$

3. Net Irrigated Area (000 hect):

    $$NIA_t = 0.7731 \, GIA_t$$

4. Aggregate Cropping Intensity:

    $$ACIN_t = 0.8993 + 0.7207 \, (NIA / NSA)_t + 0.0019 \, RIAL_t - 0.000007 \, RIAL_t^2$$

Note:

    RIAL   = Aggregate Rainfall Index over all crops.
    TIME   = Time Variable
    AGINV = Agricultural Investment (Rs. crores at 1970-71 prices)

*1: Estimated in the form of $\log \left[\dfrac{165000}{NSA} - 1 \right] = \alpha + \beta_1 X_1 + \beta_2 X_2 + u$

*2: Estimated simultaneously along with the group irrigated area equations in a nonlinear framework.

5.   Gross Cropped Area (000 hect):

   $GCA_t = (ACIN_t)(NSA_t)$

Group Irrigated Area Allocation

$IA_{gt} = \tau_g \ (RAIN)_{gt} + \delta_g \ (IA)_{gt-1} + \alpha_g \ [GIA_t - \Sigma \ \tau_g \ (RAIN)_{gt}$

   $- \Sigma \ \delta_g \ (IA)_{gt-1}]; \ g = 1,6$

Parameters:

	g	τ_g	δ_g	α_g
1.	Wheat group	− 5.7929	0.8820	0.1783
2.	Rice group	12.9497	0.5475	0.4277
3.	Jowar group	− 5.0285	0.7336	0.1186
4.	Oilseed group	− 2.4442	0.8469	0.0340
5.	Sugarcane	− 3.4414	0.4338	0.1167
6.	Residual	0.	0.6592	0.1247

Note:

   IA_{gt} = Irrigated area of crops belonging to group g

   GIA   = Total gross irrigated area over all crops

   $RAIN_{gt}$ = Rainfall for g^{th} group crops

We considered

   $RAIN_{1t}$ = Rainfall of wheat

   $RAIN_{2t}$ = Rainfall of rice

   $RAIN_{3t}$ = Rainfall of jowar

   $RAIN_{4t}$ = Rainfall of groundnut

   $RAIN_{5t}$ = Rainfall of sugarcane

   $\Sigma \ \alpha_g$ = 1.0

Sugarcane group consists of only sugarcane.

Crop Irrigated Area Allocations

$$IC_{gkt} = \beta_{gk} + \tau_{gk} (RAIN)_{gkt} + \delta_{gk}(IC)_{gkt-1}$$

$$+\alpha_{gk}\left[IA_{gt} - \sum_{k\varepsilon g} \beta_{gk} - \sum_{k\varepsilon g} \tau_{gk} (RAIN)_{gkt} - \sum_{k\varepsilon g} \delta_{gk} (IC)_{gkt-1}\right]$$

Parameters:

No.	Group(g) Crop(k)		β_{gk}	τ_{gk}	δ_{gk}	α_{gk}
	Wheat					
1.		Wheat	0	4.7940	1.2448	0.7823
2.		Barley	0	− 0.2196	1.1098	0.0776
3.		Gram	0	1.6730	1.0679	0.1401
	Rice					
4.		Rice	78.3887	207.969	3.5071	0.9974
5.		Ragi	396.894	− 0.9688	0.5605	0.0026
	Jowar					
6.		Jowar	0	0.4112	0.5242	0.2223
7.		Bajra	0	− 1.3737	0.9531	0.1326
8.		Maize	0	− 5.7523	0.8737	0.5258
9.		Cotton	0	0.2786	0.8716	0.1193
	Oilseeds					
10.		Groundnut	− 19.4319	− 0.2936	−0.3279	0.7511
11.		Rape Mustard	50.9403	0.0733	0.1608	0.2219
12.		Sesamum	29.5937	− 0.0663	0.4734	0.0008
13.		Other oilseeds	− 13.5392	0.1442	0.7782	0.0262

However, due to unsatisfactory prediction performance of the wheat group crop parameters, we revised the irrigated area equations for barley, gram and wheat as follows:

$$IC_{1,barley,t} = 1424.12 - 0.5335 \, RAIN_{barley,t}$$
$$IC_{1,gram,t} = 1156.78 + 0.7921 \, RAIN_{gram,t}$$
$$IC_{1,wheat,t} = IA_{1t} - IC_{1,barley,t} - IC_{1, gram,t}$$

Note:

IC_{gkt} = Irrigated area under crop k in group g in time t

$$\sum_{k\varepsilon g} \alpha_{gk} = 1.0$$

Crop revenue, price and yield expectation functions

Variable (π_r)	ARIMA	ϕ_1	ϕ_2	ϕ_3	m	θ_1	θ_2	w_{1972}	w_{1973}	w_{1974}	x^2
Bajra price	110	0.9364			8.0810	0.7367		31.65	49.58	13.00	6.99
Barja yield	120	0.8473			0.0547	-0.1092	-0.5128	0.452	0.332	0.540	8.21
Barley revenue	121	1.2735	-0.2735			-0.9288	1.4495	16.604	74.763	0.000	4.31
Sugarcane revenue	111	0.4641	0.5359			0.8154		284.605	-14.462	0.000	7.45
Cotton revenue	121	0.5718	0.4282			-0.4374	0.7503	-4.444	18.277	0.000	6.29
Groundnut revenue	211	0.0613	-0.0497	0.9884		0.2528	0.6019	-14.014	153.892	0.000	3.77
Gram revenue	121	0.7787	0.2213			-0.2960	-0.3014	71.154	-5.263	0.000	6.39
Jute revenue	121	0.6927	0.3074			0.1676	0.7676	13.143	-68.96	0.000	5.98
Jowar revenue	121	1.6994	-0.6994			-0.3521	-0.0349	36.258	44.130	0.000	5.76
Mesta revenue	120	0.8447			65.7772	-0.2742		89.186	10.514	105.782	9.30
Maize revenue	111	0.6019	0.3981			0.2145	0.6225	61.995	123.436	0.000	5.77
Maize price	121	1.7914	-0.7914			-0.3660		49.023	65.896	0.000	5.71
Maize yield	120	0.9719			0.0264	-0.9729	1.2282	-0.018	-0.048	-0.041	8.97
Rice revenue	111	0.8705	0.1296			0.9236		65.422	9.374	0.000	7.87
Ragi revenue	111	0.4856	0.5144			1.4122		55.297	36.927	0.000	5.02
Rapeseed and mustard revenue	211	0.0069	0.2066	0.7866		0.4297		27.818	39.435	0.000	9.12

Crop revenue, price and yield expectation functions

Variable (π_τ)	ARIMA	ϕ_1	ϕ_2	ϕ_3	m	θ_1	θ_2	w_{1972}	w_{1973}	w_{1974}	x^2
Sesamum revenue	211	0.5887	-0.4238	0.8351		0.4254		6.685	17.001	0.000	6.67
Tobacco revenue	121	0.2405	0.7595			1.2292	0.9618	8.465	32.876	0.000	5.72
Wheat revenue	211	0.2497	0.4024	0.3480		0.7508		8.749	234.803	0.000	3.06

Notes: $\pi_\tau = \phi_1 \pi_{\tau-1} + \phi_2 \pi_{\tau-2} + \phi_3 \pi_{\tau-3} + m + \theta_1 w_{\tau-1} + \theta_2 w_{\tau-2} + w_\tau$

m = a constant equal to the mean of the series if $d = 0$ in (p:q:d): See appendix 3.4.

w_t = white noise in time t.

Degrees of freedom = number of observations (21) - number of parameters.

x^2: (Chi-sqaure) is based on the residual auto correlations.

Gross Area under Crops

(Note that all variables in equations (1) to (16) below are in logarithmic form.)

(1) AREA (Rice)$_t$ = 3.1854 + 0.2541 [AREA (Rice)$_{t-1}$]
+ 0.0180 (RAIN$_t$)
+ 0.4925 (GIA$_t$)
+ 0.5034 (IASO/GIA)$_t$
+ 0.0305 (RRVN$_t$)

(2) AREA (Wheat)$_t^{++}$ = -1.6769 + 0.2599 [AREA (wheat)$_{t-1}$]
+ 0.0984 (RAIN)$_t$
+ 0.0678 (RRVN$_t$)
+ 0.8081 (GIA$_t$)

(3) AREA (Bajra)$_t$ = 7.6335 + 0.2678 [AREA(Bajra)$_{t-1}$]
+ 0.1213 (RAIN$_t$)
+ 0.0789 [EYLD(Bajra)$_t$]
+ 0.5626 (IASO/GIA)$_t$

(4) AREA (Maize)$_t^{**}$ = 1.1541 + 0.4893 [AREA (Maize)$_{t-1}$]
+ 0.0882 (RAIN$_t$)
+ 0.1230 [EPRC(Maize)$_t$]
+ 0.2104 (GIA$_t$)

(5) [AREA(Jowar)/   = 8.4956 + 0.0341 (RAIN$_t$)
AREA(Maize)]$_t$ − 0.7492 (GIA$_t$)
+ 0.3065 [AREA(Jowar)/
                 AREA(Maize)]$_{t-1}$

(6) [AREA(Gram)/   = 14.5845 + 0.0678 (RRVN$_t$)
AREA(Wheat)]$_t$ − 0.0911 (RAIN$_t$)
− 1.4081 (GIA)$_t$
+ 0.1627 [AREA(Gram)/
                 AREA(Wheat)]$_{t-1}$

(7) [AREA(Barley)/ = 8.7462 + 0.0898 (RRVN)$_t$
AREA(Wheat)]$_t$ − 0.0399 (RAIN$_t$) − 0.9111(GIA)$_t$
+ 0.4320 [AREA(Barley)/
                 AREA(Wheat)]$_{t-1}$

(8) $[AREA(Ragi)/$ $=$ $-0.000003 + 0.1348 \; (RAIN)_t$
 $AREA \; (Rice)]_t$ $\qquad + 0.1167 \; (RRVN)_t$
 $\qquad + 0.2421 \; (IASO/GIA)_t$
 $\qquad - 0.2464 \; (GIA_t)$
 $\qquad + 0.1078 \; [AREA(Ragi)/$
 $\qquad\qquad\quad AREA(Rice)]_{t-1}$

(9) $[AREA(Jute)/$ $=$ $-11.8880 + 0.1717 \; (RAIN)_t$
 $AREA(Ragi)]_t$ $\qquad + 0.5694 \; (RRVN)_t$
 $\qquad + 1.5201 \; (IASO/GIA)_t$
 $\qquad - 0.3301 \; (IACN/GIA)_t$
 $\qquad + 0.9331 \; (GIA_t)$
 $\qquad + 0.3634 \; (AREA(Jute)/$
 $\qquad\qquad\quad AREA(Ragi)]_{t-1}$

(10) $[AREA(Mesta)/$ $=$ $-17.7745 + 0.0397 \; (RAIN)_t$
 $AREA(Ragi)]_t$ $\qquad + 0.3874 \; (RRVN)_t$
 $\qquad + 2.1800 \; (IASO/GIA]_t$
 $\qquad + 1.6926 \; (GIA_t)$
 $\qquad + 0.3091 \; [AREA(Mesta)/$
 $\qquad\qquad\quad AREA(Ragi)_{t-1}$

(11) $[AREA(Cotton)/$ $=$ $-0.000051 + 0.0182 \; (RAIN)_t$
 $AREA(Maize)]_t{}^*$ $\qquad + 0.0654 \; (RRVN)_t$
 $\qquad + 0.9008 \; [AREA(Cotton)/$
 $\qquad\qquad\quad AREA(Maize)]_{t-1}$

Note:

RAIN: Crop specific Rainfall;
RRVN: Crop specific Expected Relative Revenue (ARIMA Process);
GIA: Total Gross Irrigated Area over all Crops;
IASO: Gross Irrigated Area under the soil group of crops to which the crop belongs;
IACN: Gross Irrigated Area under Sugarcane;
IAOSD: Gross Irrigated Area under total oilseed crops;
EYLD(j): Expected Yield of jth crop (ARIMA Process);
EPRC(j): Expected Price of jth crop (ARIMA Process); and
AREA(j): Gross Area under crop j.

(12) $AREA(Groundnut)_t$ = 0.000019 + 0.9530 $[AREA(Groundnut)_{t-1}$
+ 0.0895 $(RAIN)_t$
+ 0.0465 $(RRVN)]_t$

(13) $[AREA(Sesamum)/$ = −0.7785 + 0.0858 $(RAIN)_t$
$AREA(Groundnut)]_t$ + 0.0737 $(RRVN)_t$
+ 0.5489 $[AREA(Sesamum)/$
$AREA(Gr.nut)]_{t-1}$

(14) $[AREA(Rapeseed \& Mustard/$
$AREA(Sesamum)]_t$ = 0.000011 + 0.0787 $(RAIN)_t$
+ 0.1336 $(RRVN)_t$
− 0.1917 $(IASO/GIA)_t$
+ 0.1974 $(IAOSD/GIA)_t$
+ 0.3617 $[AREA(Rapesed \&$
$Mustard)/AREA(Sesamum)]_{t-1}$

(15) $AREA(Sugarcane)_t^+$ = 0.000014 + 0.0949 $[AREA(Sugarcane)]_{t-1}$
− 0.2296 $(RAIN)_t$
+ 0.1989 $(RRVN)_t$
+ 0.7230 $(GIA)_t$

(16) $AREA(Tobacco)_t$ = 3.7282 + 0.1762 $[AREA(Tobacco)_{t-1}]$
+ 0.1559 $(RAIN)_t$
+ 0.1140 $(RRVN)_t$

(Note: Henceforth variables are in logarithmic form only if specified to be so.)

(17) $AREA(S.millets)_t$ = $Exp[0.0262$ + 0.6050 log $[Area(Jowar)_t$
+ Area $(Maize)_t$
+ Area $(Bajra)_t]$
+ 0.0178 log $[Area(Ragi)_t]$
+ 0.2476 log $[Area(Barley)_t]]$

(18) Residual Area[#]: $RESD_t$ = 0.2.GCA_t

(19) $AREA(Other Pulses)_t$ = 0.6294 . $RESD_t$

(20) $AREA(Other Oilseeds)_t$ = 0.1340 . $RESD_t$

(21) AREA(Sannhemp)$_t$ = 0.0072 . RESD$_t$

(22) AREA(Rubber)$_t$ = 0.0079 . RESD$_t$

(23) AREA(Tea)$_t$ = 0.0149 . RESD$_t$

(24) AREA(Coffee)$_t$ = 0.0059 . RESD$_t$

(25) AREA(Fruits & Vegetables)$_t$ = 0.1210 . RESD$_t$

(26) AREA(Condiments & Spices)$_t$ = 0.0492 . RESD$_t$

(27) AREA(Coconut)$_t$ = 0.0305 . RESD$_t$

Crop Yields. j: crop index; t: time subscript (mostly dropped but occasionally used)

Rice and wheat[1]:

1. YLD(j = Rice) $= 0.4238 [(1.8232$
    $+ 16.5570 F_{12} - 79.99 F_{12}{}^2) S_{12}$
    $+ (2.4177 + 32.70 F_{22} - 150.47 F_{22}{}^2) S_{22}$
    $+ (2.4461 + 24.33 F_{32} - 68.30 F_{32}{}^2) S_{32}]$
    $+ 0.0002 RAIN(j)$

2. YLD(j = Wheat) $= 0.7407 [(0.8351$
    $+ 18.3490 F_{11} - 81.84 F_{11}{}^2) S_{11}$
    $+ (1.4001 + 23.4612 F_{21}$
    $- 132.92 F_{21}{}^2) S_{21}$
    $+ (1.73 + 30.9359 F_{31} - 122.17 F_{31}{}^2) S_{31}]$

---

[*] Cropped area under cotton was restricted to be below 1.7 times that of cropped area under maize.

[**] Cropped area under maize was restricted to be below 10% of the total gross cropped area GCA.

[+] Cropped area under sugarcane was restricted to be atleast as much as the gross irrigated area under sugarcane.

[++] Cropped area under wheat was restricted to be below 18% of the total gross cropped area GCA.

[#] Sum of the gross areas of individual crops, rice to small millet (eqns.1 to 17), is scaled up or down to be equal to 80% of the total gross cropped area GCA.

Other crops:

3. YLD(j = Bajra)   = 0.1839[{0.9832
                          + 0.2482 PI(j) + 0.2986 PH(j)}
                          + {10.156 + 0.2 PI(j)
                          + 3.8817 PH(j)} PF(j)
                          − {49.092 − 34.921 PI(j)
                          + 13.039 PH(j)} PF(j)^2]
                          + 0.0018 RAIN(j)

4. YLD(j = Maize)   = 0.6598 [{1.178
                          + 0.3115 PI(j) + 0.4705 PH(j)}
                          + {15.29 + 0.625 PI(j)
                          + 5.665 PH(j) } PF(j)
                          − { 48.75 + 4.87 PI(j)
                          + 16.37 PH(j)} PF(j)^2]
                          + 0.0005 RAIN(j)

5. YLD(j = Jowar)   = 0.5928 [{0.7639
                          + 0.5011 PI(j) + 0.3120 PH(j)}
                          + {15.03 − 7.8743 PI(j)
                          + 4.9243 PH(j)} PF(j)
                          − {62.23 − 31.3041 PI(j)
                          + 0.0741 PH(j)} PF(j)^2]
                          + 0.0003 RAIN(j)

6. YLD(j = Barley)   = 0.8053 + 59.99 PF(j)
                          − 3417.94 PF(j)^2

7. YLD(j = Gram)$_t$ = [0.5775
                          + 0.0242 YLD (j)$_{t-1}$].T(j): up to 1976
                          = [1.015.YLD (j)$_{t-1}$].T(j): beyond 1976

8. YLD(j = Ragi)   = {Exp[−3.6595 +0.9341 log RAIN(j)
                          + 0.5294 log PI(j)
                          + 0.0072 TIME]}.(1.01)

9. YLD(j = Jute)$_t$ = [5.2337+0.2042 YLD(j)$_{t-1}$].T(j)

10. YLD(j = Mesta)$_t$ = [YLD(j)$_{t-1}$] {SPI(9)/SPI(10)}$^{0.25}$

11. YLD(j = Cotton) $= [0.3777 + 1.6607 \text{ PI}(j) + 0.0035.\text{TIME}].T(j)$

12. YLD(j = Groundnut) $= 0.7249 + 2.5126 \text{ PI}(j) - 0.006 \text{ TIME} + 0.0002 \text{ RRIN}(j)^2$

13. YLD(j = Sesamum)$_t$ $= 0.1390 + 0.2703 \text{ YLD}(j)_{t-1}$

14. YLD(j = Rapseed & Mustard) $= 0.3760 + 81.4817 \text{ PF}(j) - 8896.48 \text{ PF}(j)^2$

15. YLD(j = Sugarcane) $= [34.2116 + 644.803 \text{ PF}(j) - 6134.04 \text{ PF}(j)^2].T(j)$

16. YLD(j = Tobacco) $= [\ 0.7202 + 6.7204 \text{ PF}(j) - 52.57 \text{ PF}(j)^2 - 0.00003 \text{ RRIN}(j)^2\ ].T(j)$

17. YLD(j = S.Millets)$_t$ $= 0.4411 + 0.0168 \text{ YLD}(j)_{t-1} - 0.1374 \text{ YLD}(j)_{t-2}$

18. YLD(j = Other Pulses)$_t$ $= \{T(j)\ [0.3626 + 0.1194 \text{ YLD}(j)_{t-1}]\ 0.42\} \left[\dfrac{\text{SPI}(8)}{\text{SPI}(10)}\right]^{0.25}$

19. YLD(j = Other Oilseeds)$_t$ $= [0.0870 + 0.6408 \text{ YLD}(j)_{t-1}]\ T(j).\left[\dfrac{\text{SPI}(8)}{\text{SPI}(10)}\right]^{0.25}$

20. YLD(j = Sannhemp)$_t$ $= 0.2748 + 0.2848 \text{ YLD}(j)_{t-1}$

21. YLD(j = Rubber) $= -0.0069 + 0.0218 \text{ TIME}$

22. YLD(j = Tea) $= 0.8116 + 0.0185 \text{ TIME}$

23. YLD(j = Coffee) $= \text{Exp}\ [-1.3816 + 0.0375 \text{ TIME}]$

24. YLD(j = Fruits & Vegetables)$_t$ $= [5.62.(1.025)^{tm76}].\left[\dfrac{\text{SPI}(8)}{\text{SPI}(10)}\right]^{0.33}$

25. YLD(j = Condiments & Spices)$_t$ $= [0.3435 + 0.4227 \text{ YLD}(j)_{t-1}].(1.01)$

Note:

YLD(j)	= Yield of crop j (tons/hectare)
S_{ij}	= Proportion of ith type land in the total area of jth crop
F_{ij}	= Nitrogen intensity on ith type land of crop j (kg/hect)
j	= 1 for wheat
	= 2 for rice
i	= 1 Unirrigated land with local variety seed
	= 2 Irrigated land with local variety seed
	= 3 Irrigated land with h.y.v. seed
	Unirrigated land with h.y.v. seeds = 0 (assumed)
ΣS_{ij}	= 1
RAIN(j)	= Crop-specific Rainfall Index

*1: Estimated simultaneously in a nonlinear framework and as Zellner's seemingly unrelated equations system

PI(j)	= Proportion of irrigated area of crop j within its total cropped area
PH(j)	= Proportion of h.y.v. area of crop j within its total cropped area
PF(j)	= Nitrogenous fertilizer intensity of crop j (kg/hect)
EXP(K)	= Exponential of $K = e^k$
TIME	= Time variable
T(j)	= Technical progress factor for jth crop
T(j = Barley)	= 1.0 up to 1975
	$= (1.01)^{(year-1976)}$ for later periods
T(j = Gram)	$= \{SPI(8)/SPI(10)\}^{0.25}$

where

SPI(K)	= Price Index of Sector K
T(j = Jute)	= 1.0 up to 1976
	$= \{SPI(9)/SPI(10)\}^{0.25}$
T(j = Cotton)	= (Cotton Price Index)$^{1/3}$: beyond 1976
	= 1.0 up to 1976
$RRIN(j)^2$	$= (RAIN(j)-100) \cdot |(RAIN(j)-100)|$
T(j = Sugarcane)	= 1.0 up to 1976
	$= (1.015^{(year-1976)}$ for later periods
T(j = Tobacco)	= 1.0 up to 1976
	$= (1.01)^{(year-1976)}$: beyond 1976
T(j = Other Pulses)	$= Max[0.; 1.015^{(year-1976)}]$
T(j = Other Oilseeds)	= 1.0 up to 1976
	= 1.015 beyond 1976
TM76	= Max (0.; year-1976)

Fertilizer

1. Total fertilizer in the country:

   $FLZR_t = \exp[4.2983 + 0.1487 \text{ TIME}]$

2. Nitrogen nutrient within total fertilizers:

   $NTRZ_t = 36.5683 + 0.6632 \text{ } FLZR_t$

3. Nitrogen allocated for rice and wheat:

   $NTRW_t = 0.6202 \text{ } NTRZ_t$ (*1)

   i.e., $[S_{11} \text{ } F_{11} + S_{21} \text{ } F_{21} + S_{31} \text{ } F_{31}]$ AREA (Wheat)
   $+ [S_{12} \text{ } F_{12} + S_{22} \text{ } F_{22} + S_{32} \text{ } F_{32}]$ AREA (Rice)
   $= NTRW_t$

4. Nitrogen allocated for other major crops:
   PF (Bajra) $= 0.0205 \text{ } NTRZ_t$ (*2)
   PF (Maize) $= 0.0414 \text{ } NTRZ_t$
   PF (Sugarcane) $= 0.0623 \text{ } NTRZ_t$
   PF (Rape & Mustard) $= 0.0046 \text{ } NTRZ_t$
   PF (Jowar) $= 0.0303 \text{ } NTRZ_t$
   PF (Barley) $= 0.0076 \text{ } NTRZ_t$
   PF (Ragi) $= 0.0108 \text{ } NTRZ_t$
   PF (Tobacco) $= 0.0098 \text{ } NTRZ_t$

Note:

*1: From Sarvekshana (1978) it was observed that 62.02% of the total value of fertilizer consumption over all crops in India was by rice and wheat alone.

AREA(j), PF(j), S_{ij} and F_{ij} are all as defined earlier.

*2: 0.0205 etc., were, again, observed from Sarvekshana (1978), as in the case of rice and wheat.

Note that the 8 crops listed under other major crops, plus rice and wheat, would together account for more than 80% of the total fertilizer nutrients. Groundnut and cotton, as per Sarvekshana (1978), accounted for another 5% each; but the yield regressions of these two crops did not show sensible results with respect to fertilizer variable.

Dairy:

(i) Cattle Stock:

$$LVCTL_t = (LVCTL_{t-1}) (1.003) \text{ :up to 1976}$$

$$= (2.38) \, (0.9) (0.6\text{-TIME } 0.002)NSA_t \text{ :beyond 1976}$$
$$= (TCWA) . (WBWA) . (WAPH) . NSA_t$$

(ii) Buffalo Stock:

$$LVBFL_t = (LVBFL_{t-1}) (1.015) \text{ :all periods}$$

(iii) Total Stock:

$$LVMLK_t = LVCTL_t + LVBFL_t \text{ :all periods}$$

(iv) Milk Output (MILK):
   (a) *Up to 1976:*
   $$MILK_t = 1.0522 \, (- 813.26 + 27.04 \, [\, WPMLK / WPFDG \,]_t + 0.0043 \, LVMLK_t \,)$$
   (b) *After 1976:*
   Cows in milk $= CM_t = \underset{P_{cm}}{(0.4)} \underset{P_{cw}}{(0.3)} . LVCTL_t$
   Buffaloes in milk $= BM_t = \underset{P_{bm}}{[(0.25).(1.006)^{TM71}]} \, LVBFL_t$

(v) $MYC_t = $ Cow milk yield $= 0.00465 \, [1.0136]^{TM71} \left[\dfrac{WPMLK}{WPFDG} \right]^{0.2}$

(vi) $MYB_t = $ Buffalo milk yield $= 0.0093 \, [1.0136]^{TM71} \left[\dfrac{WPMLK}{WPFDG} \right]^{0.2}$

(vii) $Milk_t = [CM_t.MYC_t + BM_t. MYB_t]$

Note:

   TCWA   = Total cattle/work bullock
   WBWA   = Working bullocks/work animals
   WAPH   = Work animals/hectare
   NSA   = Net sown area
   WPMLK = Price index of milk
   WPFDG = Price index of foodgrains
   P_{bm} = Proportion of milk-buffaloes in total stock
   TM71   = Max [0,(year-1970)].
   0.00465 and 0.0093 represent the base year milk yields of cows and buffaloes respectively (tonnes/year/animal).

Livestock Products:

t : time subscript
j = beef, mutton & pork, other meat products, hides & skins, eggs & poultry, wool & hair, other livestock products

$(LSTP)_{jt}$ = Livestock Product Output (jth product in t)
$$= [(LSTP)_{jt-1}] \, (1+g_j): \text{up to year 1979}$$

$$= \left[(LSTP)_{jt-1}\right] (1+g_j) \left[1 + \left\{ \frac{Sinc_{jst}}{Sinc_{10t}} - 1 \right\}.el_j \right]: \text{beyond 1979}$$

where

js : Sector S to which j belongs
el_j: Elasticity, and
$Sinc_{jst} = (SPI_{jst} + SPI_{jst-1})$, and
$SPI_{jst} = (P_{jst-1} / \, P_{jst-2})$
$Sinc_{10,t} = (SPI_{10,t} + SPI_{10,t-1})$, and
$SPI_{10,t} = (P_{10,t-1} / P_{10,t-2})$

Parameters:

j	js	g_j	el_j
Beef	4	0.025	0.5
Mutton and pork	4 & 6	0.0084	0.1
Other meat products	4 & 6	0.025	0.1
Hides and skins	9	0.0038	0.15
Eggs and Poultry	6	0.050	0.1
Wool and hair	9	0.0104	0.2
Other livestock products	9	0.0381	0.2

Fish production
(i) Boats:
$BOAT_t = 1002.68 + 698.06 \, (TIME)$
(ii) Fish Output:
$FISHQ_t = 692.24 + 0.1132 \, (BOAT)_t$: up to 1976
$= FISHQ_{t-1}[1 + \{SinC_6/SinC_{10t}) - 1\} \, 0.15]$:beyond 1976

$Sinc_{6t}$ and $Sinc_{10t}$: average price indexes of Sectors 6 & 10 as defined earlier.

Note: $P_{js,t}$ = Price of sector js in time t
$(SPI)_{js\ t}$ = Sectoral Price Index
SPI_{10}, P_{10} correspond to Sector 10

Agricultural GDP:

Value of Agricultural GDP:
$GDPAG_t = \Sigma(PRAW^*_{it}.Q_{it}) - INNON_t - FEEDLS_t$ (i = 1,9)

Value of Fertilizer Consumption:
$FLZCST_t = 2756 .(PNA)_t (FLSUM)_t$
(Fertilizer Price = Rs. 2756/ton in base year)

Proportion of other Intermediate Consumption:
$OINON_t = 0.012 + 0.0042\ TIME.$

Value of Feeds:
$FEEDLS_t = \Sigma(PRAW^*_{it} . FEED_{it})$

Depreciation:
$DEPR_t = 0.0285\ (GDPAG_t)$

Net Domestic Product Agriculture:
$VANET_t = GDPAG_t - DEPR_t$

$$WAGES_t = 0.201844.VANET_t$$
$$RENT_t = 0.020571.VANET_t$$
$$INTRST_t = 0.039542.VANET_t$$
$$PROFIT_t = 0.001291.VANET_t$$
$$SELFEM_t = 0.736752.VANET_t$$

Note:

Variables have already been explained in the text (Chapter 3 on Technical Description). (See eqn. 60.)

$INNON_t = FLZCST_t + (OINON)_t.VOLAG_t.$
$FLSUM$ = Total fertilizer(tons) consumed.
PNA = Non-agricultual price index.
$FEED_{it}$ = Amount of ith commodity set aside as feed.
$VOLAG_t = \Sigma(PRAW^*_{it} .Q_{it})$ = Value of agricultural output.

Non-agriculture:

1. Demand for Non-agriculture:

$$Y10DAt = \frac{\text{Non - agricultural GDP (Rs. crores)}}{\text{Population (millions)}}$$

$$= -27.3909 + 0.1918\left[\frac{\text{AGGDP}}{\text{POPN}}\right]_t - 4.2370\left[\frac{\text{PNA}^*}{\text{PA}^*}\right]_t$$

$$+0.9560\left[\frac{\text{TGDP}}{\text{POPN}}\right]_{t-1}$$

(See eqn. 42)

where

AGGDP = Agricultural gross domestic product
TGDP = Total gross domestic product
POPN = Population

and

PNA* & PA* = Expected Price Indexes of Non-agriculture and agriculture respectively.

2. Expenditure elasticity for non-agriculture demand:

η (in the equation $Y10DB_t$) = 1.5   (See eqn. 43)

3. Variance of the actual output level:

$V(Q_t) = (6.31107)^2 = 39.8296$ (See eqn. 35)

Demography:

1. Total population:

$POPN_t$ = 1.0226 $POPN_{t-1}$: up to 1990
$POPN_t$ = 1.0220 $POPN_{t-1}$: beyond 1990

2. Proportion of urban population:

$UPPRN_t = 0.1991 \, (1.0159)^{\text{TIME}}$

3. Proportion of rural non-agricultural population in total rural population:

$RNPRN_t = 0.1250 \, (1.0242)^{\text{TIME}}$

Population and Endowment Distribution:

$c = \log C,$

$y = \log Y$

$c = a_1 + a_2 y + v$ where $y \sim N(\mu_y, \sigma_y^2)$, $v \sim N(o, \sigma_v^2)$ and

$c \sim N(\mu_c = a_1 + a_2\mu_y, \; \sigma_c^2 = \sigma_v^2 + a_2^2 \sigma_y^2)$

	a_1	a_2	σ_v^2	σ_y^2
Agriculture	1.36734	0.77814	0.002474	Endogenous
Rural Non-agriculture	1.36734	0.77814	0.002474	0.49246
Urban	1.54073	0.76777	0.000054	0.77538

Distribution of Foodgrains:

1. Net Production of Foodgrains (million tons):

$PDN_t = 0.879\ PRDN(Wheat)_t + 0.924\ PRDN\ (Rice)_t$
$+ 0.779\ PRDN(Gram)_t$
$+ 0.875[PRDN(Bajra)_t + PRDN(Barley)_t$
$+ PRDN(Jowar)_t$
$+ PRDN(Maize)_t + PRDN(Ragi)_t$
$+ PRDN(Other\ Pulses)_t$
$+ PRDN(Sm.millets)_t]$

2. Distribution Proportion:

$[DIST/PDN]_t = 0.337012 - 1.2938\ [(PDN/POPN)_t$
$+ (PDN/POPN)_{t-1}]$
$- 38.036\ [(PDN/POPN)_t - (PDN/POPN)_{t-1}].\ [|\ (PDN/POPN)_t$
$- (PDN/POPN)_{t-1}|\ ]$
$+ 0.005139\ [(GDPNAG/POPN)_t]$

Procurement of foodgrains:

1. Wheat (10^3 tons):

$PROWHT_t = -11034 + 0.3556\ PRDN(wheat)_t$
$+ 10447.9\ [PRPR(wheat)/PRC(wheat)^*]_t$

2. Rice (10^3tons):

$$\text{PRORCE}_t = 164.245\ [\text{DIST}_t - \text{STOK}_{t-1}]$$
$$+ 0.27374\ \text{PRDN}(\text{Rice})_t - 8841.64$$

3. Coarse grains (10^3tons):

$$\text{PROCGR}_t = 0.04[\text{PROWHT}_t + \text{PRORCE}_t]$$

4. Procurement price:

$$\text{PRPR}_{jt} = \text{PRPR}_{jt-1} \cdot \left[1.0 + 0.65 \left[\frac{\text{PI}_{jt-1} - \text{PI}_{jt-3}}{\text{PI}_{jt-1} + \text{PI}_{jt-2}} \right] \right]$$

Processing Margin Coefficients (percent of Raw Prices):

S1   Wheat: 0.06
S2   Rice: $[0.10 + (0.01443\ \text{PNA}_t)/\text{PRAW}_{rice,t}]$
S3   Coarse grains: 0.08
S4   Bovine ovine meat: 0.
S5   Dairy: 0.07
S6   Other meat: 0.
S7   Protein feeds: 0.
S8   Other food agriculture: 0.0033
S9   Non-food agriculture: $0.4998 + 0.3\ (1.035)^{tm76}$
S10 Non-agriculture: 0.

Note:

PRDN(j)   = Production of crop j (million tons)
POPN   = Population (million)
GDPNAG   = Non-agriculture GDP (Rs. crores)
PRPR(j)   = Procurement price of crop j
PRC(j)*   = Expected open market price of crop j
PI_j = Price Index of crop j
DIST and STOK are distribution quantity and total stocks (public) in all grains.

Feed Specifications.

Feed (wheat)$_t$	$= 0.05.\text{PRDN(wheat)}_t$
	$+ 0.025.[\text{PRDN(wheat)}_t - \text{PRDN(wheat)}_{t-1}]$
Feed (rice)$_t$	$= 0.012.\text{PRDN (rice)}_t$
Feed (coarse	
grains)$_t$	$= 0.05. [\text{PRDN(bajra)} + \text{PRDN(jowar)}$
	$+ \text{PRDN(maize)}$
	$+ \text{PRDN(ragi)} + \text{PRDN(small millets)}]_t$
	$+ 0.16.\text{PRDN (barley)}_t$
Feed (protein	
feed)$_t$	$= 0.7.Q_{7t}$
Feed (other food	
agriculture)	$= 0.10.Q_{8t}$

$\text{Feed}(4) = \text{Feed}(5) = \text{Feed}(6) = \text{Feed}(9) = \text{Feed}(10) = 0.$

Note:

tm76	$= \text{Max } [0, (\text{year} - 1976)].$
PRAW$_j$	= Rawprice of commodity j.
PNA$_t$	= Non-agricultural Price Index.
Q$_{it}$	= Output of Sector i.
Feed(k)	= Feed from the output of Sector k.
PRDN(j)	= Production of crop j.

Demand Parameters

Marginal Budget Shares: b_{ji} (i = Commodity sector S1, S2, S3 etc. ; j = Expenditure group)

j/i		S1	S2	S3	S4	S5	S6	S7	S8	S9	S10
Rural	1	0.0154	0.2846	0.2874	0.0059	0.0313	0.0177	—	0.2203	0.0063	0.1312
	2	0.0608	0.2995	0.1502	0.0080	0.0630	0.0240	—	0.2265	0.0078	0.1602
	3	0.0555	0.2196	0.0567	0.0101	0.1404	0.0303	—	0.2202	0.0635	0.2037
	4	0.0644	0.0970	0.0001	0.0077	0.1620	0.0231	—	0.1923	0.1482	0.3052
	5	0.0263	0.0474	0.0056	0.0032	0.0732	0.0094	—	0.1328	0.1201	0.5820
Urban	1	0.0802	0.1748	0.2189	0.0094	0.0473	0.0282	—	0.2700	0.0068	0.1645
	2	0.0352	0.2125	0.0943	0.0105	0.0817	0.0315	—	0.2845	0.0078	0.2420
	3	0.0198	0.1286	0.0281	0.0112	0.1452	0.0335	—	0.2949	0.0196	0.3191
	4	0.0102	0.0376	0.0103	0.0106	0.1573	0.0315	—	0.3031	0.0547	0.3847
	5	0.0024	0.0083	0.0006	0.0061	0.0915	0.0181	—	0.1752	0.0993	0.5986

Demand Parameters *(contd.)*

Committed Coefficients: c_{ji} (i = Commodity sector S1, S2, S3 etc.; j = Expenditure group)

	j/i	S1	S2	S3	S4	S5	S6	S7	S8	S9	S10
Rural	1	7.9248	11.8925	11.0123	0.0134	—	0.0072	—	0.7668	—	1.1361
	2	5.1843	15.1979	32.4981	—	—	—	—	1.9114	—	0.8957
	3	16.5431	41.1875	63.0170	0.2132	—	0.1149	—	4.6432	—	1.8620
	4	38.2786	72.0445	—	0.9926	20.9435	0.5350	—	9.9000	—	2.4410
	5	92.4819	98.0063	—	2.2022	86.6539	1.1869	—	24.4514	15.9587	4.6658
Urban	1	9.8675	3.4069	-0.5498	0.0376	—	0.0223	—	1.2770	—	1.7662
	2	26.6561	8.9309	13.5969	0.0218	—	0.0130	—	3.2677	—	1.5677
	3	36.7433	26.6304	24.9945	0.2434	—	0.1446	—	6.5331	—	1.7618
	4	42.6863	40.0497	19.0698	0.4332	4.0895	0.2574	—	10.7156	—	2.6013
	5	50.5144	38.6388	10.3013	1.8644	42.2192	1.1078	—	44.5079	1.6223	4.8493

Appendix 3.7

CONSTRUCTION OF CROPWISE RAINFALL INDICES

Rainfall indices are necessary to estimate and project gross cropped acreage and yields of various crops, and also total and cropwise gross irrigated acreage in the country.

In this appendix we describe the methodology adopted in constructing the rainfall indices that were used in our econometric estimations described earlier.

S.K.Ray (1977) constructed such a series for the period 1949-50 to 1974-75 for his study on variations in output of Indian crops. We essentially followed the same methodology as he adopted but with minor modifications.

Monthwise data on actual rainfall in millimeters in 35 zones covering all of India were collected from the India Meteorological Department for the years 1975 to 1980. The zonewise data were then aggregated to Statewise figures for these years using the zonal weights given by S.K.Ray (1977) which represent geographical proportions of the zones in a State. Such monthwise, Statewise rainfall figures for the years 1975-1980 were supplemented with the figures given by S.K.Ray (1977) for the years 1949-1975 which were derived from the same data base. Thus, we have Statewise, monthwise rainfall for 31 years.

The details of the zonal classification, correspondence between various zones and States and also the zonal weights given by S.K.Ray (1977) are given in Table 1. Ray does not have separate figures for Haryana and Punjab and has figures only for undivided Punjab (UDP henceforth). We aggregated the figures of Haryana and Punjab (with their geographical or zonal weights as 0.468 and 0.532) to derive those of UDP.

Now, from the Statewise, monthwise rainfall figures, two kinds of rainfall indices for various crops have been constructed for each major State in India: (a) overall rainfall indices taking into account all the months of the crop season, i.e. from the first month of sowing period to the first month of harvesting period of that crop in that State. We have taken this period as a modal period for that crop as we do not have information on the proportions of crops sown in different months in the sowing period. Had we had that we could have taken the period from the first month of the sowing period to the last month of the harvesting period; and (b) sowing period rainfall indices taking into account only the sowing period months of a crop, i.e., from the first month to the last month of the sowing period of that crop in that State. Suppose for a crop c, in a particular State s, the sowing period is March to June and harvesting period is August to October then the two rainfall indices in year t in that State are as follows:

(a) $(\text{Overall Rainfall Index})_{s,c,t} = \dfrac{\displaystyle\sum_{m=\text{March}}^{\text{August}} (\text{Rainfall})_{s,m,t}}{\displaystyle\sum_{m=\text{March}}^{\text{August}} (\hat{\text{Rainfall}})_{s,m}}$

where

$(\hat{\text{Rainfall}})_{s,m} = \displaystyle\sum_{t=1949\text{-}50}^{1979\text{-}80} (\text{Rainfall})_{s,m,t} / 31$

and s = State, t = year, m = month and c = crop;

(b) $(\text{Sowing-period Rainfall Index})_{s,c,t} = \dfrac{\displaystyle\sum_{m=\text{March}}^{\text{June}} (\text{Rainfall})_{s,m,t}}{\displaystyle\sum_{m=\text{March}}^{\text{June}} (\hat{\text{Rainfall}})_{s,m}}$

where s, m, t, c, and $(\hat{\text{Rainfall}})_{s,m}$ are as defined under (a) above.

It may be noted that at the State level, autumn-rice, winter-rice and summer-rice have been treated as three separate crops though finally, at the all-India level, one rainfall index for rice as a whole has been computed as explained later. And similar is the case for kharif-jowar and rabi-jowar.

However, for the less important crops which, in some of the States, are grown in more than one season (for example: ragi in Andhra Pradesh and groundnut in Tamil Nadu) such a distinction has not been made. In such cases, the relevant months for both the seasons of the crop have been taken into account in computing the rainfall indices for these crops for such States.

Thus, the overall and sowing period rainfall indices for various crops in sixteen States have been arrived at. Table 1 gives a list of the crops considered.

In arriving at the all-India overall rainfall indices for the nineteen crops, the Statewise cropwise indices, computed as mentioned above, have been aggregated, except for rice and jowar, with the same weights given by S.K. Ray (1977) which represent Statewise cropwise production levels. These weights were derived by considering "the averages of 1967-71 Statewise productions".

In aggregating for autumn-rice, winter-rice, summer-rice, kharif-jowar and rabi-jowar from State levels to all-India, the corresponding State level productions have been used as weights. These production levels have been averaged out over a period of 1970-71 to 1977-78 before being used as weights.

The fact that we have used different periods as averages for rice and jowar compared to other crops, is not material for the purposes for which we use these indices. Table 2 gives these weights of various States for different crops.

In aggregating for total rice and total jowar at the all-India level from all-India indices of autumn-rice, winter-rice, summer-rice and kharif-jowar and rabi-jowar, corresponding all-India levels of productions have been used as weights. Again, these production levels have been averaged out over a period of 1970-71 to 1977-78 before being used as weights. The all-India overall rainfall indices were then computed.

For aggregating to the all-India level the Statewise cropwise sowing period rainfall indices, we use the same procedure as above, except that Statewise sown areas are used as weights instead of production levels. Moreover, the weights for all the crops are obtained from the data covering the period 1970-71 to 1977-78.

TABLE 1 Zonal weights and State-Zone correspondence

No.	State	Zone No.	Zone weight	Zone coverage
		01	.....	Andaman & Nicobar Islands.
1.	Assam	02	0.390	Arunachal Pradesh
		03	0.397	Assam and Meghalaya
		04	0.213	Nagaland, Manipur, Mizoram and Tripura.
2.	West Bengal	05	0.179	Sub-Himalayan West-Bengal (and Sikkim).
		06	0.821	Gangetic West Bengal.
3.	Orissa	07	1.000	Orissa.

4.	Bihar	08	0.274	Bihar Plateau.
		09	0.726	Bihar Plains.
5.	Uttar Pradesh	10	0.553	East UP.
		11	0.447	West UP Plains.
		12	0.000	West UP Hills.
6.	Haryana	13	1.000	Haryana, Chandigarh and Delhi.
7.	Punjab	14	1.000	Punjab.
8.	Undivided Punjab	13	0.468	Haryana, Chandigarh and Delhi.
		14	0.532	Punjab.
9.	Himachal Pradesh	15	1.000	Himachal Pradesh.
10.	Jammu and Kashmir	16	1.000	Jammu and Kashmir.
11.	Rajasthan	17	0.530	West Rajasthan.
		18	0.470	East Rajasthan.
12.	Madhya Pradesh	19	0.444	West MP.
		20	0.556	East MP.
13.	Gujarat	21	0.480	Gujarat region, Daman, Dadra and Nagar Haveli.
		22	0.520	Saurashtra, Kutch and Diu.
14.	Maharashtra	23	0.049	Konkan and Goa.
		24	0.424	Madhya Maharashtra.
		25	0.264	Marathwada.
		26	0.263	Vidarbha.
15.	Andhra Pradesh	27	0.327	Coastal Andhra Pradesh.
		28	0.400	Telangana.
		29	0.273	Rayala Seema.
16.	Tamil Nadu	30	1.000	Tamil Nadu and Pondicherry.
17.	Karnataka	31	0.031	Coastal Karnataka.
		32	0.604	North Interior Karnataka.
		33	0.365	South Interior Karnataka.
18.	Kerala	34	1.000	Kerala.
		35	...	Lakshadweep.

1.1 List of Crops:

1. Wheat
2. Bajra
3. Rice-autumn
4. Rice-winter
5. Rice-summer
6. Jowar-kharif
7. Jowar-rabi
8. Maize
9. Ragi
10. Barley
11. Small millets
12. Gram
13. Groundnut
14. Sesamum
15. Rapeseed and mustard
16. Sugarcane
17. Tobacco
18. Cotton
19. Jute and mesta
20. Total rice
21. Total jowar

TABLE 2 State weights for various crops

	Wheat	Bajra	Rice autumn	Rice winter	Rice summer	Jowar kharif	Jowar rabi	Maize	Ragi	Barley
1 Assam	0.04	0.00	2.17	7.77	1.40	0.00	0.00	0.37	0.00	0.00
2 West Bengal	1.87	0.00	4.35	22.47	25.05	0.00	0.00	0.72	0.41	1.60
3 Orissa	0.09	0.03	2.24	15.34	8.45	0.24	0.00	0.90	6.88	0.00
4 Bihar	5.81	0.14	1.69	20.18	3.22	0.07	0.00	16.39	5.91	7.02
5 Uttar Pradesh	32.84	12.02	12.64	7.66	0.38	6.85	0.00	21.77	8.56	50.66
6 Undivided Punjab	32.22	13.59	10.62	0.00	0.00	0.69	0.00	14.75	0.00	9.97
7 Himachal Pradesh	1.38	0.00	0.58	0.00	0.00	0.00	0.00	7.47	0.46	1.84
8. Jammu & Kashmir	1.08	0.14	0.00	1.91	0.00	0.00	0.00	4.99	0.00	0.38
9. Rajasthan	7.28	24.23	0.85	0.00	0.00	5.08	0.00	12.41	0.00	22.77
10. Madhya Pradesh	11.00	2.62	18.64	0.00	0.00	21.59	0.48	8.32	0.25	5.49
11. Gujarat	3.63	21.34	2.47	0.00	0.00	5.00	4.65	4.03	2.44	0.07
12. Maharashtra	2.07	11.84	8.87	0.00	0.90	28.32	44.71	0.32	8.81	0.10
13. Andhra Pradesh	0.02	5.06	3.42	14.98	44.42	8.79	23.50	5.25	13.04	0.00
14. Tamil Nadu	0.00	5.33	20.20	5.84	3.25	7.09	5.00	0.19	16.61	0.00
15. Karnataka	0.67	3.66	8.27	1.13	7.06	16.28	21.66	1.02	36.27	0.10
16. Kerala	0.00	0.00	2.97	2.72	5.87	0.00	0.00	0.00	0.36	0.00

TABLE 2 *(Contd.)*

	Small millets	Gram	Ground-nut	Sesa-mum	Rape & mustard	Sugar-cane	Tobacco	Cotton	Jute & mesta
1. Assam	0.16	0.03	0.00	1.06	2.63	1.13	1.98	0.12	18.61
2. West Bengal	0.44	1.51	0.00	1.06	2.19	1.11	2.83	0.00	51.55
3. Orissa	4.10	0.26	1.54	10.21	1.63	1.62	2.83	0.00	7.20
4. Bihar	5.63	2.90	0.06	2.13	3.07	4.75	3.97	0.04	13.32
5. Uttar Pradesh	19.32	26.32	4.86	21.49	69.85	42.32	2.83	0.80	1.66
6. Undivided Punjab	0.00	19.74	3.80	1.06	8.03	9.81	0.00	22.27	0.00
7. Himachal Pradesh	0.98	0.38	0.04	0.41	0.06	0.04	0.00	0.02	0.00
8. Jammu & Kashmir	0.71	0.03	0.02	0.43	1.32	0.02	0.00	0.02	0.00
9. Rajasthan	1.42	22.05	2.17	12.77	7.03	0.56	1.13	3.65	0.00
10. Madhya Pradesh	21.07	21.54	5.36	12.34	3.20	1.18	0.57	5.89	0.41
11. Gujarat	5.85	0.82	24.15	7.25	0.81	1.47	27.85	29.74	0.00
12. Maharashtra	4.76	2.59	12.18	7.45	0.06	10.81	1.25	21.60	1.53
13. Andhra Pradesh	10.12	0.51	19.17	9.79	0.00	9.00	43.34	2.39	5.06
14. Tamil Nadu	20.14	0.10	16.52	7.66	0.00	9.05	6.23	6.73	0.02
15. Karnataka	5.14	1.22	9.74	4.04	0.12	6.74	5.10	6.61	0.64
16. Kerala	0.16	0.00	0.39	0.85	0.00	0.39	0.29	0.12	0.00

Note: All-India weights for rice-autumn, rice-winter, and rice-summer are: 0.456, 0.475, and 0.069 respectively. Similarly jowar, kharif & rabi, are 0.710 and 0.290 respectively. Also see S.K. Ray (1977).

4

Scheme of Analysis and the Reference Scenario

4.1 Need for and Specification of a Reference Scenario

A scenario generated with the help of a model can be characterized by the values of the exogenously specified parameters and the change in the specification of any function that may have been made. To use a model for policy analysis one generates scenarios with and without the policy change being studied. A change in policy may be introduced by changing values of some parameters and/or by altering the specification of some functions. Comparison of the outcome of the two scenarios for the indicators reflecting the various objectives of the society show the impact of the policy change. Such a procedure raises some questions. What should the scenarios look like, and, in particular, what should the before-policy-change scenario, needed to set the stage for policy analysis, be? Also, what indicators should one use to compare the outcomes?

In defining our reference scenario, we were guided by the following considerations:

First, and most important, the model is not a forecasting model and the simulated course of the economy in the reference scenario for the period 1980-2000 should not be viewed as a forecast of the likely actual course of the economy. Second, although in our model, unlike many AGE models in the literature, the values of most of the parameters were econometrically estimated, nevertheless, the values of several others were exogenously specified. Whether these would have been close to the values that would have emerged had they been econometrically estimated as well, is not known. After all, we resorted to exogenous specification in some cases only because econometric estimation was infeasible or led to unacceptable values for one reason or the other. For example, we have specified an incremental capital output ratio of 6.0 while the value assumed by the Planning Commission in the Sixth Plan is 4.7. But there is no strong evidence based on sound econometric analysis to prefer one value to the other. To take another example, we have assumed for simplicity that the foreign trade deficit would be 1.5% of GDP while in fact it has exceeded it in recent years. Since the only purpose served by the base scenario is to provide a bench mark or reference path, relative to which policy changes are to be introduced and their impacts studied, these differences in exogenously specified parameter values need not be serious. In other words, it is our contention that any alternative specification of values of these parameters will change both the base and the policy scenarios in a similar way so that the impact of policies expressed as changes relative to the reference scenario would be the same whichever set of parameter values were used. To a certain extent, this is more an article of faith than an analytically or empirically established fact. For example, if the parameters related policy variables and outcomes, measured in absolute (or logarithmic) way, in a linear fashion, then clearly the above contention is valid as long as policy impact is measured in absolute units in one case and in proportionate terms in the other. Even though our model is non- linear in parameters and variables, as long as the range of variation considered in parameters and exogenous variables indicating policy variables is not too large, the assertion based on linearity will be true by and large. Nevertheless, one has to accept the fact that the policy analysis of the model will not be credible to others, when the assumed paths of exogenous variables and the simulated paths of endogenous variables in the reference scenario (hereafter REF) are too far from common beliefs.

Thus it is convenient to have as reference scenario a business- as-usual scenario in which past policy regimes continue. Even when the policy changes being studied are such that the differences between the scenarios depend on the particular reference scenario selected or on the extent of policy change considered, a business-as-usual reference scenario provides a relevant starting point.

Before turning to the specification of the reference scenario described in this chapter, one other remark needs to be made. Although the same reference scenario serves as a bench mark for most of our policy analysis, in some cases we modify the reference scenario for analyzing others for good reasons. For example, in the standard reference scenario, total fertilizer availability is exogenously projected and, in many years, it is this availability rather than profitability of use that constrains fertilizer application. In considering a policy of substantially increasing the subsidy to fertilizer use, it makes little sense to work with a reference scenario in which even at the unchanged rates of subsidy the farmers would like to use more fertilizer than is available. As such we specify a modified reference scenario in which fertilizer availability is substantially increased for the analysis of fertilizer subsidy policies.

Before describing the reference scenario and the results in the next section we describe the indicators that may be used to compare the results and evaluate the impact of policy change.

4.2   Indicators for Comparison of Scenarios

For each year of simulation in a scenario, all the details for a complete social accounting matrix, the commodity and financial flows are generated. To facilitate comparison one needs to use some aggregate indicators which reflect on economic development, individual well being and social welfare. For these we use the following indicators:

Indicator for economic growth: In spite of all its limitations, gross domestic product GDP at 1970 prices is used as the main indicator for it is widely understood and nothing better is possible to generate. When GDPs of a given year, say 2000, of two different scenarios are compared, depending on the prices used, the outcome may be different. This is shown in Figure 4.1. This index number difficulty has to be kept in mind in using GDP as an indicator.

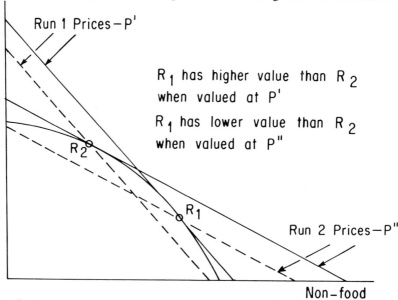

Fig. 4.1   Problem of prices in comparing GDPs.

In addition to aggregate GDP, the sectoral GDPs are also calculated.

Since total rural, urban and agricultural populations do not vary from one scenario to another, per capita GDPs give the same comparison as aggregate GDPs.

Indicator for individual well being: The level of food energy and protein intake per capita by persons in each expenditure class are calculated to assess their nutritional status.

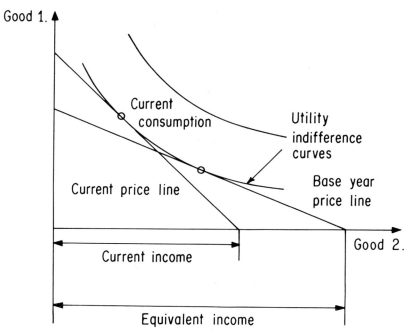

Both incomes at corresponding prices provide equal satisfaction

Fig. 4.2 The notion of equivalent income.

Since consumer behaviour in each expenditure class is characterized by a separate linear expenditure system, the underlying parameters of the Cobb-Douglas utility function for each class are known. Using these and 1970 prices as the base prices, "equivalent income" is calculated. The equivalent income measure for a year is the income required to obtain at the base prices (i.e. 1970 prices) a consumption basket that provides the same utility as provided by the current basket of consumption. The notion is illustrated in Figure 4.2. Formally, equivalent income is defined as follows:

$$E^t = \Sigma P_{io} c_i + \Pi(P_{io} / P_{it})^{b_i} . [\Sigma P_{it} X_{it} - \Sigma P_{it} C_i]$$

where

E^t is equivalent income for period t
P_{it} is price of commodity i in period t
P_{io} is price of commodity i in the base period
c_i, b_i are parameters of the Cobb-Douglas utility function $U = \Pi(X_i - c_i)^{b_i}$, i.e. the committed quantities and marginal budget shares of the associated linear expenditure systems.

Indicators for social welfare: It may be recalled that in the model scenarios, the expenditure class limits are kept constant in terms of equivalent income, and the number of persons that fall in each class are endogenously determined. It should be noted that though the class limits remain constant, average equivalent income in each does vary somewhat.

The welfare impact of alternative policies can be seen by comparing the distribution of the population according to their equivalent incomes, i.e. income needed to achieve the welfare achieved under each policy if consumers were to face 1970 prices. But as the distribution of the population among these expenditure classes shifts from year to year in a policy scenario and for the same year from scenario to scenario, not only the number of persons within a class with fixed limits of real expenditures (i.e. equivalent incomes) changes, but the average real expenditure of persons in each class (and the average for all classes) also shifts somewhat. Thus, both shifts have to be taken into account in comparing the distributions. One of the approaches for such a comparison is due to Willig and Bailey (1981) (hereafter W-B). They show that, given a population of individuals ranked from 1 to n according to their equivalent incomes, m_i^1 and m_i^2, in two distributions (i.e. m_i^j = the expenditure that a person i needs at some base price p_o to achieve the same welfare that he enjoys at prices p and nominal income y in distribution j, j = 1, 2), the first distribution is preferred to the second according to any social welfare function that satisfies the Pareto principle, anonymity and aversion to regressive transfer if and only if

$$\Sigma m_i^1 > \Sigma m_i^2 \text{ over } i = 1, k \text{ and for } k = 1, 2, \ldots n.$$

It should be noted that person i (i.e. the one having the i-th lowest equivalent income) in distribution 1 need not be same as person i in distribution 2. As the authors point out, the above inequality for k = 1 corresponds to a Rawlsian social welfare function (or we may note the Gandhian "Antyodaya" criterion), and for k = n corresponds to the Hicksian compensation criterion. But for a general social welfare function, the inequality has to hold for all k to ensure dominance. Of course, the ranking is not independent of the base price vector p, and this serious limitation has to be kept in mind in interpreting the results.

This procedure is easily extended to take into account grouped data, in which more than one person (in fact all persons within a class) have the same equivalent incomes. We use this criterion to compare social welfare in two scenarios.

4.3. The Reference Scenario – Specification

The reference scenario was simulated with the model for the period 1970-2000. The "historical" period for the model was 1970-77 during which the model was constrained to reproduce the actually observed course of the economy with respect to most of the major endogenous variables as equilibrium values. Policy changes relative to the base scenario were introduced in 1980 and their impacts studied over the period 1980-2000. In the reference scenario, it is assumed that the policies with respect to procurement and public distribution of foodgrains, public consumption and investment, foreign trade and aid, etc., would correspond to those prevalent in the recent past. In particular the following assumptions are made:

(i)   Demographic changes (exogenous): The total population of India is projected to grow at the rate of 2.26% per annum (p.a.) reaching 1048 million persons by 2000 from its value of 674 million in 1980. The proportion of urban population in the total is projected to grow at a rate of 1.6% p.a. so that it becomes 31.45% in 2000 as compared to 22.95% in 1980. The proportion of rural non-agricultural population in the total rural population was projected to grow at a rate of 2.4% p.a. Thus non-agricultural population within rural population becomes 33.33% in 2000.

(ii) Trade deficit is 1.5% of the GDP.

(iii) Trade quotas on different agricultural commodities range from 5% to 15% of domestic supply, i.e. production plus initial stocks.

(iv) Domestic price policy is to try to move gradually closer to the world market prices as described in Chapter 3.

(v)   Procurement and distribution of foodgrains will follow the estimated

equations described in Chapter 3.
(vi) Public consumption and investment will follow historical time trends.

4.4   The Reference Scenario — Results

We present the results of the reference run in some details in order to give
the reader an idea of the level of detail and consistency obtained in the results. The reference scenario serves as a point of comparison for many policy
scenarios. Also, even though the model is not a forecasting model and the
reference scenario is not a forecast, we do compare some results with actual
data for 1980 if only to show that the model is after all a model of India and
that the numbers are in the credible ballpark of common belief.

Our discussion of the results are organized in terms of the following attrib-
utes for the period 1980-2000 which are relevant for policy analysis.

(i)   The nature of results
(ii)   Macro-economic dimensions
(iii) Production,consumption and trade patterns
(iv)   Distribution of consumption expenditure
(v)   Government operation.

The nature of results: As mentioned earlier the model generates for each
year all the details needed for a detailed social accounting matrix showing the
physical and financial flows and their balances.

As an illustration, these are given for the years 1980 and 2000 in Tables
4.1 and 4.2, respectively, showing commodity flow balances, trade balances,
national income and expenditure balances, government expenditure balance as
well as income and expenditure balances for each of the 10 expenditure classes.

Table 4.3 compares the simulated results of 1980 with the actual observed
ones. Considering that the model is not meant to be a forecasting one and
also that normal weather is assumed in the scenario, the results seem to be in
a credible range.

Macro-economic measures: Table 4.4 gives average annual growth rates of
selected variables between 1980 and 2000 for the reference scenario (REF).
In REF agricultural gross domestic product at 1970 prices (GDPA70) grows
at the rate of 2.4% p.a. Non-agricultural gross domestic product (GDPNA70)
and the total gross domestic product (GDP70) grow at 6.4% p.a. and 5.1%
p.a. respectively. In per capita terms the total gross domestic product (GDP)
grows at the rate of 2.8% p.a. Gross domestic investment grows at 7.8% p.a.

TABLE 4.1 Physical and financial flow balances for the year 1980

1. SUPPLY AND DEMAND (Physical units 000 tonnes or 10⁶ US dollar 1970. See appendix 3.1 for units)

Commodity	Production +	Initial stock	= Household consumption + savings	+ Feed	+ Intermediate consumption	+ Public demand consumption	+ Ending stock	+ Net exports
Wheat	33576	9598	29817	1844	—	—	9704	1809
Rice	46645	626	47704	589	—	—	722	-1744
Coarse grains	26269	4064	28349	1677	—	—	4082	-3775
Bovine & Ovine	799	13	791	—	—	—	13	8
Dairy products	31512	512	33897	—	—	—	525	-2398
Other meat products	317	6	317	—	—	—	5	—
Protein feeds	2215	6	—	1551	—	—	7	664
Other food agriculture	20504	397	17071	2050	—	—	441	1338
Non-food agriculture	2297	91	1772	—	503	—	94	19
Non-agriculture	41931	2178	35619	—	3206	4412	2288	-1416
Value at current prices (10⁹ Rs.)	1068.5	+ 55.5	= 944.1	+ 26.5	+55.3	+63.5	+ 57.8	-23.2

TABLE 4.1 (*contd.*)

2. PUBLIC DEMAND (in physical units) and prices (in 10^6 Rs./unit)

Name	Public consumption	Public investment	Private investment	Raw material price	Domestic market price	World market price
Wheat	0	0	0	1.30	1.37	1.22
Rice	0	0	0	1.76	1.98	2.53
Coarse grains	0	0	0	0.98	1.06	0.86
Bovine & ovine	0	0	0	8.01	8.01	9.45
Dairy products	0	0	0	1.88	2.01	1.25
Other meat products	0	0	0	105.47	105.47	68.11
Protein feeds	0	0	0	3.27	3.27	4.28
Other food agriculture	0	0	0	7.98	8.25	13.98
Non-food agriculture	0	0	0	18.38	33.68	13.27
Non-agriculture	8598.7	−4186.7	18846.0	14.38	14.38	19.88
Value at current prices (10^9 Rs.)	123.7	−60.2	271.0	—	—	—

TABLE 4.1 (*contd.*)

3. CLASSWISE INCOME, CONSUMPTION AND SAVINGS (at current prices)

| | Consumer Expenditure limit in 1970 equivalent Rs. | | | | | | | | | |
| | RURAL - Expenditure class | | | | | URBAN - Expenditure class | | | | |
	<216	<336	<516	<900	>900	<216	<336	<516	<900	>900
Population (millions)	163.9	93.4	92.8	94.3	75.0	3.0	12.2	28.9	52.5	58.0
(proportions)	(.315)	(.180)	(.179)	(.181)	(.144)	(.019)	(.079)	(.187)	(.340)	(.375)
Consumer price index	163.6	167.4	172.5	182.9	185.9	170.2	174.4	180.4	187.2	191.5
Per Capita Values										
Income	174.7	444.8	800.3	1551.8	4261.9	212.1	401.3	722.4	1409.0	4208.7
Tax*	-0.0	-0.2	0.1	5.3	43.4	0.5	1.8	8.3	22.7	96.7
Saving	-37.7	-3.5	93.7	377.5	1759.6	-71.1	-63.5	-3.8	212.4	1572.8
Cons. expenditure	212.4	448.4	706.5	1169.0	2457.9	282.4	463.1	717.9	1175.0	2539.2
Food energy intake (Kcal/day)	981.0	1896.0	2474.0	2490.0	3653.0	1085.0	1555.0	1935.0	2332.0	3108.0
Protein intake (gms./day)	27.0	52.0	69.0	75.0	110.0	30.0	42.0	53.0	61.0	75.0
Equivalent income	129.1	266.1	406.7	634.7	1309.0	164.7	264.3	396.7	625.7	1322.1

TABLE 4.1 (*contd.*)

4. GOVERNMENT ACCOUNTS at current prices (billion Rs.)

Initial endowment	+ Inc. tax	+ Trade deficit#	+ Tariffs	+ Procurement tax	= Dist. subsidy	+ Public cons.	+ Public savings	+ End stock
83.0	10.8	14.7	8.4	7.2	2.9	123.7	-60.2	57.8

5. NATIONAL ACCCOUNTS at current prices (billion Rs.)

GDP	+ Trade deficit#	+ Tariffs	= Private cons.	+ Public cons.	+ Savings	+ Stock changes
986.6	14.7	8.4	673.0	123.7	210.8	2.2

*Negative taxes imply subsidies.
#Valued at border prices excluding tariffs.

TABLE 4.2 Physical and financial flow balances for the year 2000

1. SUPPLY AND DEMAND (Physical units 000 tonnes or 10⁶ US dollar 1970. See appendix 3.1 for units)

Commodity	Production	+ Initial stock	= Household consumption + savings	+ Feed	+ Intermediate consumption	+ Public demand	+ Ending stock	+ Net exports
Wheat	86376	12104	67510	4661	—	—	12236	14073
Rice	88389	2628	87041	1117	—	—	2783	76
Coarse grains	34834	4459	38153	2067	—	—	4478	-5404
Bovine & Ovine	1328	22	1314	—	—	—	22	14
Dairy products	58402	943	64307	—	—	—	973	-5935
Other meat products	606	10	621	—	—	—	10	-15
Protein feeds	2994	9	—	2096	—	—	9	898
Other food agriculture	36822	1119	33401	3682	—	—	1176	-318
Non-food agriculture	3347	141	2584	—	732	—	144	28
Non-agriculture	144290	7137	111060	—	13355	22200	7607	-2787
Value at current prices (10⁹ Rs.)	3955.8	+ 183.7	= 3251.9	52.7	284.2	433.7	194.2	-77.2

TABLE 4.2 (*contd.*)

2. PUBLIC DEMAND (in physical units) and prices (in 10⁶ Rs./unit)

Name	Public consumption	Public investment	Private investment	Raw material price	Domestic market price	World market price
Wheat	0	0	0	0.97	1.03	1.27
Rice	0	0	0	1.82	2.07	2.41
Coarse grains	0	0	0	1.15	1.24	1.10
Bovine & ovine	0	0	0	18.87	18.87	9.46
Dairy products	0	0	0	2.84	3.03	1.47
Other meat products	0	0	0	212.36	212.36	69.38
Protein feeds	0	0	0	0.77	0.77	5.33
Other food agriculture	0	0	0	11.44	11.82	13.02
Non-food agriculture	0	0	0	31.85	68.86	12.91
Non-agriculture	30964.0	−8764.7	74421.0	19.54	19.54	20.85
Value at current prices (10⁹ Rs.)	604.9	−171.2	1453.8	—	—	—

TABLE 4.2 (*contd.*)

3. CLASSWISE INCOME, CONSUMPTION AND SAVINGS (at current prices)

| | Consumer expenditure limit in 1970 equivalent Rs. | | | | | | | | | |
| | RURAL - Expenditure class | | | | | URBAN - Expenditure class | | | | |
	<216	<336	<516	<900	>900	<216	<336	<516	<900	>900
Population (millions)	147.6	114.0	136.0	154.9	165.0	1.5	10.6	41.2	109.0	167.3
(proportions)	(.206)	(.159)	(.190)	(.216)	(.230)	(.004)	(.032)	(.125)	(.331)	(.508)
Consumer price index	193.0	196.3	211.0	237.5	254.2	203.3	212.9	232.3	253.5	271.4
Per Capita Values										
Income	229.6	564.6	1086.5	2365.1	7523.3	296.1	572.6	1091.0	2289.3	7842.5
Tax*	-0.7	-3.2	-8.5	25.9	438.0	2.9	11.3	53.5	157.1	769.1
Saving	-32.4	33.2	210.6	782.6	3794.5	-70.7	-38.6	97.7	563.2	3669.4
Cons. expenditure	262.7	534.6	884.4	1557.9	3315.3	364.9	599.8	939.9	1569.0	3405.0
Food energy intake (Kcal/day)	1059.0	2019.0	2673.0	2796.0	3858.0	1252.0	1742.0	2059.0	2375.0	3021.0
Protein intake (gms./day)	29.0	56.0	76.0	86.0	117.0	35.0	48.0	56.0	61.0	72.0
Equivalent income	132.8	261.4	399.1	616.2	1227.3	171.8	272.9	394.8	604.9	1223.6

TABLE 4.2 (contd.)

4. GOVERNMENT ACCOUNTS at current prices (billion Rs.)

Initial endowment	+ Inc. tax	+ Trade deficit*	+ Tariffs	+ Procurement tax	= Dist. subsidy	+ Public cons.	+ Public savings	+ End stock
305.4	222.8	54.7	22.5	28.3	5.9	604.9	– 171.2	194.1

5. NATIONAL ACCOUNTS at current prices (billion Rs.)

GDP	+ Trade Deficit#	+ Tariffs	= Private cons.	+ Public cons.	+ Savings	+ Stock changes
3618.9	54.7	22.5	1798.1	604.9	1282.6	10.5

*Negative taxes imply subsidies.

Valued at border prices excluding tariffs.

TABLE 4.3 Some results of the reference scenario and actual data for the year 1980 (1980-81)

	Observed	Reference scenario
Gross domestic product agriculture (million Rs.)*	200310.0	220337.0
Gross domestic product non-agriculture (million Rs.)*	304950.0	309659.0
Total GDP (million Rs.)*	505260.0	529996.0
Gross domestic fixed capital formation (million Rs.)*	97280.0	109943.0
Gross domestic product agriculture (million Rs.)[+]	411030.0	—
Gross domestic product non-agriculture (million Rs.)[+]	724810.0	—
Total GDP (million Rs.)[+]	1135840.0	—
Gross domestic fixed capital formation (million Rs.)[+]	252170.0	—
Balance of payments[+]	31470.0	14722.0
Price terms of trade (agriculture/non agriculture)	0.86	0.92
Gross cropped area (mln.-hec.)	173.32	172.51
Gross irrigated area (mln.-hec.)	49.58	45.62
Nitrogeneous fertilizers (million tons)	3.68	3.43
Net production of food grains (million tons)	113.39	113.21
Public distribution of foodgrains (million tons)	14.99	16.13

TABLE 4.3 *(contd.)*

		Observed	Reference scenario
Acreage (mln-hec.)			
	Wheat	22.28	21.65
	Rice	40.15	38.93
	Bajra	11.66	12.58
	Jowar	15.81	14.94
	Maize	6.01	6.09
	Gram	6.58	6.94
	Sugarcane	2.67	2.95
	Groundnut	6.80	7.86
Yield (ton/hec.)			
	Wheat	1.63	1.65
	Rice	1.34	1.26
	Bajra	0.46	0.41
	Jowar	0.66	0.62
	Maize	1.16	1.27
	Gram	0.66	0.63
	Sugarcane	57.84	53.40
	Groundnut	0.74	0.79

Irrigated area (mln.-hec.)		
Wheat	15.52	12.66
Rice	16.34	16.45
Bajra	0.64	0.76
Jowar	0.63	0.80
Sugarcane	2.29	2.44
Production		
Wheat	36.3	35.7
Rice	53.8	49.1
Bajra	5.4	5.2
Jowar	10.4	9.3
Maize	7.0	7.7
Sugarcane	154.4	157.5

* At 1970-71 prices; + At current prices

mln.-hec. : Million hectares, Ton/hec: Tons per hectare.

The investment/GDP ratio increases from .207 in 1980 to .345 in 2000. As a result the reference scenario projects a growth rate of the GDP that is higher than the historically observed growth rate.

TABLE 4.4 Average annual growth rates of selected variables between 1960 and 1980 (actuals) and growth rates between 1980 and 2000 in the reference scenario

Variable	Average annual growth rate (%) 1960-1980 (actuals)	Average annual growth rate (%) 1980-2000 (reference scenario)
GDP Agriculture (1970 prices)	1.99	2.4
GDP non-agriculture (1970 prices)	4.80	6.4
Total GDP (1970 prices)	3.49	5.1
Investment (1970 prices)	5.10	7.8
Trade deficit (1970 prices)	3.1*	5.1
Per capita GDP (1970 prices)	1.13	2.8
Production		
Wheat	6.15	4.84
Rice	2.22	3.25
Yield		
Wheat	3.31	2.14
Rice	1.41	1.88
Gross cropped area	0.63	0.8
Gross irrigated area	2.94	3.1
Total fertiliser consumption (Nitrogen)	15.39	6.08

* calculated from current prices using GDP deflator.

Sources for actuals: *Economic Survey 1985/1986 and National Accounts Statistics (various issues)*.

The growth rate of agricultural GDP is comparable to the historical rate and it grows only marginally faster than population. Though the relatively higher than historical growth rate of GDP and a more or less historical growth rate of agricultural GDP might suggest that price of agriculture relative to that of non-agriculture might increase, it does not do so. This is because the pricing policy stipulated for the reference scenario attempts to move domestic prices towards the world market prices. The trade bounds imposed permit some movement towards it and the relative price of agriculture falls. The time path followed is shown in Figure 4.3 whereas the time paths of aggregate and sectoral GDPs are shown in Figure 4.4.

The growth of GDP per capita, average equivalent income and calorie intake per person are shown in Figure 4.5. They show modest improvement with time in the reference scenario.

TABLE 4.5   Average annual growth rates of production and demand over 1980-2000 in the reference scenarrio

Commodity	Production	Area	Yield	Demand
Wheat	4.84	2.64	2.14	4.17
Rice	3.25	1.35	1.88	3.05
Coarse grains	1.42	—	—	1.50
Maize	3.28	0.98	2.27	—
Bajra	2.27	0.60	1.66	—
Jowar	0.27	–2.3	2.62	—
Bovine and Ovine meat	2.57	—	—	2.57
Dairy products	3.13	—	—	3.25
Other meat	3.29	—	—	3.4
Other foods	2.97	—	—	3.41
Non-food agriculture	1.9	—	—	1.9
Non-agriculture	6.37	—	—	5.85

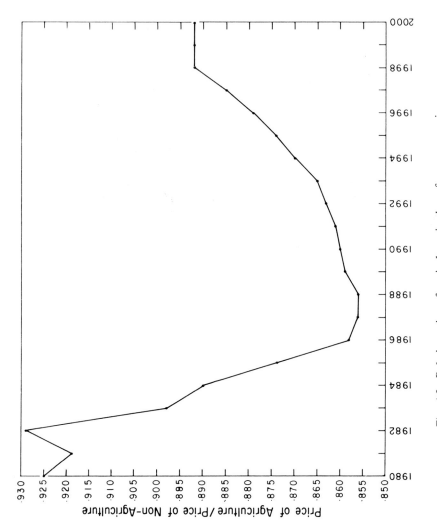

Fig. 4.3   Relative price of agriculture in the reference scenario

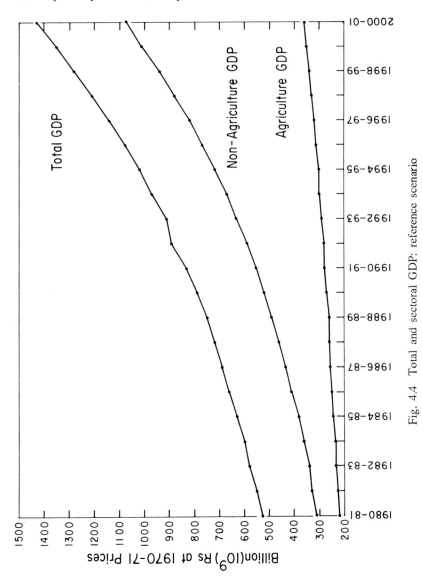

Fig. 4.4 Total and sectoral GDP: reference scenario

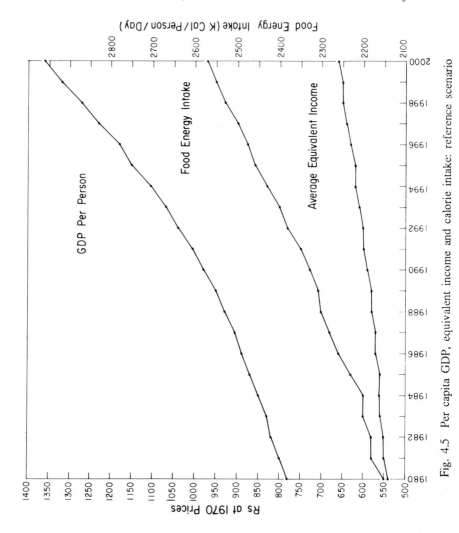

Fig. 4.5 Per capita GDP, equivalent income and calorie intake: reference scenario

Production, consumption and trade patterns: The assumed growth rate of 0.8% in gross cropped area reflects the difficulties in bringing additional land under cultivation and increasing the aggregate crop intensity substantially. However, gross irrigated area (endogenous) grows at 3.1% p.a. because of the fairly rapid growth in investment (see Figure 4.6). Consumption of nitrogenous fertilizers grow at a rate of 6.1% p.a. from 3.4 million tons (mt) in 1980 to 11.2 mt in 2000. By assumption other chemical fertilizers are applied in fixed proportions to nitrogenous nutrients.

Growth in irrigation and fertilizer-use, coupled with a high rate of adoption of high yielding varieties, leads to growth at 4.84% p.a. of wheat production and to 3.25% p.a. of rice production (see Figure 4.7 and Table 4.5). Gross cropped area under wheat grows at a rate of 2.64% while irrigation intensity (in terms of irrigated area as a proportion of total cropped area) grows only at 1.05%. In the case of rice, both cropped area as well as irrigation intensity grow at a rate of about 1.35% p.a. Fertilizer application per hectare of land under wheat and under rice grow at more than 4% p.a. from 47 kilograms to 100 kilograms per hectare in the case of wheat compared to 38 kg to 89 kg. per hectare for rice. Consequently, average wheat yield goes up from 1.65 tons per hectare (tph) in 1980 to 2.52 tph in 2000, implying an annual rate of 2.14%. Average rice yield goes up from 1.26 tph in 1980 to 1.83 tph in 2000, implying a growth rate of only 1.88% p.a.

Performance of other cereal crops is not as impressive as that of wheat and rice. For instance, though the acreages of bajra and maize go up by 12.7% and 21.75% respectively between 1980 and 2000, jowar's acreage goes down substantially by 37%. Though yield per hectare of all three goes up, it is not enough to raise the annual growth rate of the production of all these coarse grains put together to above 1.42% p.a. The growth rate of the output of sector 8 (other food agriculture covering sugarcane, pulses, oilseeds, etc.) is a modest 2.97% p.a. Sector 9 (cotton, jute, tobacco, etc.) records an even lower growth rate of 1.9% p.a. The growth rates of other sectors are shown in Table 4.5. The development of yields is shown in Figure 4.8. The growth rates of yields of many crops show a break at 1986 because by then fertilizer availability stops being a constraint and thereafter dosages are guided by relative prices.

The time paths of production of other sectors are shown in Figures 4.9 to 4.12.

Turning to demand, it turns out that for four out of the nine agricultural sectors, the growth rate in human consumption between 1980 and 2000 is greater than that in production (see Table 4.5). These sectors are coarse grains, dairy, other food and other meat. In the wheat and rice sectors production grows at a faster rate than demand. In non-food agriculture and bovine and ovine meat sectors, production and demand grow at the same rates.

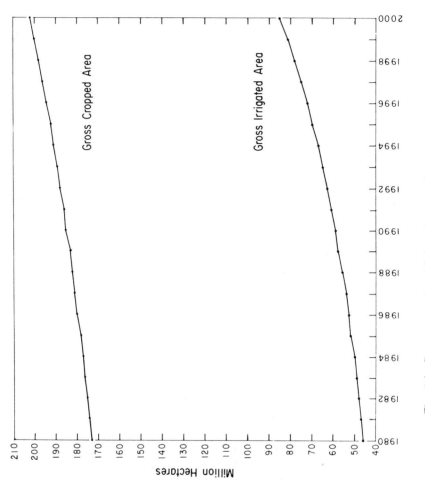

Fig. 4.6 Gross cropped and irrigated area: reference scenario

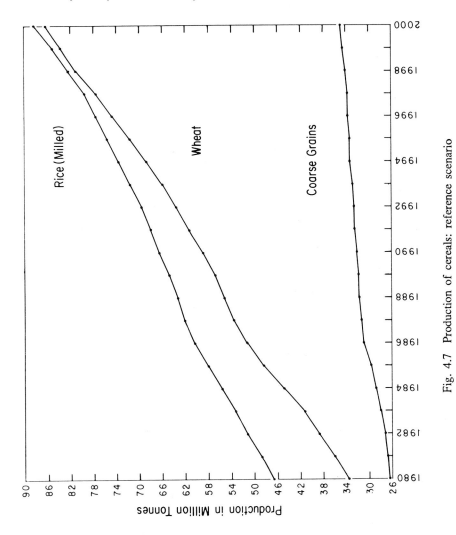

Fig. 4.7 Production of cereals: reference scenario

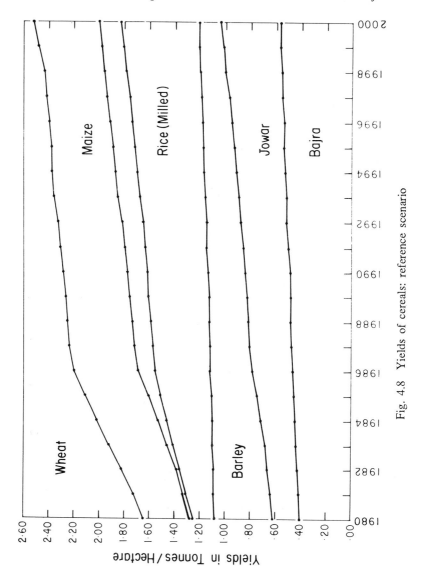

Fig. 4.8 Yields of cereals: reference scenario

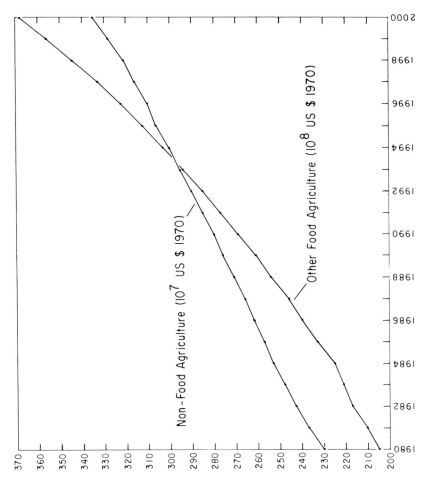

Fig. 4.9 Production of other foods and non-food agricultural products

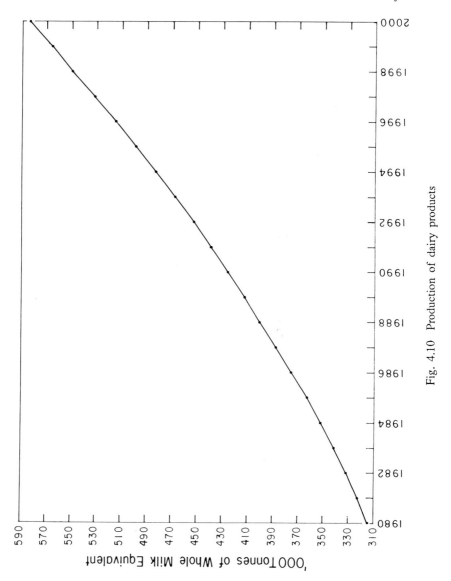

Fig. 4.10 Production of dairy products

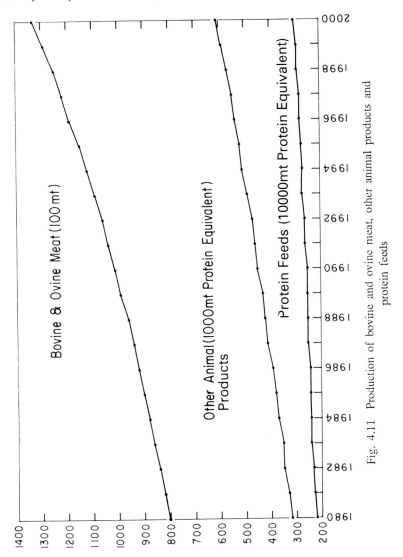

Fig. 4.11 Production of bovine and ovine meat, other animal products and protein feeds

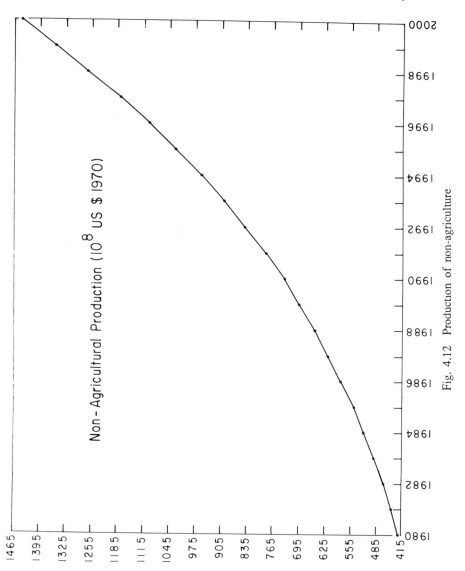

Fig. 4.12 Production of non-agriculture

Recall that in the model target levels of demand along with minimum and maximum demands from exports and stock accumulation are exogenously specified (see Table 4.6). The realized prices, stocks, imports or exports and final demands are all endogenous and mutually dependent. Hence in the case of wheat, with demand not growing as fast as production, stock targets are expected to be realized. In fact, the wheat stocks hit the maximum bound (see Table 4.7). With production still in excess over demand despite a fall in price compared to the target price, there are substantial exports of wheat. Over the years between 1980 and 2000, wheat exports move towards the exogenously specified maximum permissible limit.

The gap between production and demand is not that wide in the case of rice. The same is true with respect to coarse grains and other food agriculture also though here, unlike in the case of rice, production lags behind demand. However, the narrow gaps between production and demand of these three sectors did not prevent the target prices from being realized since neither human consumption demands, nor foreign trade nor stocks hit their respective minimum or maximum bounds. Eventually (by 2000) rice imports go down and even marginal exports take place. In the case of other food sector containing edible oils, pulses, sugar etc. it remains a net importing sector. Coarse grains continue to be imported in large quantities (as much as 12 to 14% of domestic availability) in order to maintain the targets for domestic consumption and stocks.

To sum up if a price policy of gradually moving towards the world prices within the limits of prescribed self-sufficiency bounds is followed, then our model projects large imports of coarse grains, other food items such as edible oils, sugar and pulses, etc., and large exports of wheat and near self-sufficiency in rice.

The sector non-food agriculture contains items traditionally exported by India such as jute, mesta, tobacco, hides and skins, wool and hair, and cotton lint, etc. It is unlikely that India would import these items in the near future. With this view, we constrained the reference scenario so as to preclude substantial imports of these sectoral items without at the same time not precluding large-scale exports. We did this by constraining the domestic demand to lie between 99% (maximum) and 80% (minimum) of total domestic availability. The results indicate that demand will be at the maximum limit throughout the period with stocks held at the minimum level. This in a sense reflects the growing domestic industrial demand for the agricultural raw materials which by our specification have to be met only by domestic production. With the demand and stock limits binding and no imports allowed, the realized price is greater than the target price.

In the case of dairy products, the position is somewhat similar to that of other food agriculture with the difference that target domestic stocks and demand are met within the bounds specified by increasingly relying on imports. Ultimately the upper limit of 10% of the domestic availability on imports is reached. Thus the target price is met for initial but not for later years. In the case of bovine and ovine meat products and other animal products the picture is very much similar to that of non-food agriculture. Here also no imports are allowed. Growing demand particularly for bovine and ovine meat keeps the stocks at their minimum level; and price targets are not met for most of the years.

There is no human demand for protein feeds (sector 7). It is a by-product, mainly consisting of oil-cakes. We exogenously allocated all of its availability to meeting domestic animal-feed and export requirements. All the relevant maximum and minimum bounds are widely set so that price targets are always met.

The tenth sector, non-agriculture, is the numeraire for the model i.e. the prices of all other sectors are expressed relative to the price of this sector. Our model is a real model with no monetary sector. Only relative prices matter in it. The unit of non-agricultural output is million rupees worth of output in base year (1970) prices. Since all target and realized prices of the other commodities are expressed relative to the price of the non- agricultural commodity, the results would be meaningful only if the targeted and realized price of the non-agriculture sector are the same. Put in another way, a failure to realize the target price for the numeraire sector is equivalent to a general deflation or inflation, a phenomenon that is meaningful only in a monetary model. By setting the trade bounds widely so that they are never hit, the target price of the non-agriculture sector is always realized. The results indicate that non-agricultural imports as percentage of the domestic availability goes down over time.

Distribution of consumption expenditure: In the model, the total population is distributed among ten consumer expenditure classes: five rural and five urban. The limits of per capita annual expenditure classes are updated every year based on the prices realized in the previous year and current year's target prices relative to the base year prices. Tables 4.1 and 4.2 give expenditure classwise population proportions within the rural and urban areas separately for 1980 and 2000 respectively. In the rural areas, population shifts from the two poorest expenditure classes to the three higher classes. In the urban areas, population in the lower four expenditure classes go down. By the year 2000, while more than 50% of the urban population belong to the highest expenditure class, in

TABLE 4.6 Bounds and progressive nature of taxation

(a) Consumption bounds as % of domestic availability

					Sectors					
	1	2	3	4	5	6	7	8	9	10
REF										
Maximum	1.15	1.05	1.15	0.99	1.1	1.0	1.1	1.1	0.99	3.00
Minimum	0.85	0.90	0.85	0.90	0.9	0.99	0.01	0.9	0.80	0.01
REFR										
Maximum	1.15	1.05	1.15	1.25	1.25	1.25	1.10	1.3	1.3	3.00
Minimum	0.85	0.90	0.85	0.90	0.90	0.99	0.01	0.9	0.8	0.01

(b) Progression of tax [tax rate = $\theta_j(1-\phi)$]

	RrlCl1	RrlCl2	RrlCl3	RrlCl4	RrlCl5	UrbCl1	UrbCl2	UrbCl3	UrbCl4	UrbCl5
θ_j	0.1	0.2	0.4	0.6	0.9	0.1	0.2	0.5	0.7	1.0

Note: RrlCl1 & UrbCl1 etc. are rural and urban classes.

TABLE 4.7 Target realization in REF

Prices (RP </> TP)			Stocks (NS/FS/XS)			Demand (ND/FD/XD)			Sector
1980	1990	2000	1980	1990	2000	1980	1990	2000	
=	<	<	FS	FS	XS	FD	FD	ND	Wheat (S1)
=	=	=	FS	FS	FS	FD	FD	FD	Rice (S2)
=	=	=	FS	FS	FS	FD	FD	FD	Coarse grains (S3)
>	>	>	NS	NS	NS	XD	XD	XD	B & O meat (S4)
=	>	>	FS	FS	FS	FD	FD	FD	Dairy (S5)
>	>	=	NS	FS	FS	XD	FD	FD	Other meat (S6)
=	=	=	FS	FS	FS	FD	FD	FD	Other food (S8)
>	>	>	NS	NS	NS	XD	XD	XD	Non-food agriculture (S9)

RP: Relaized price.
TP: Target price.
NS: Minimum stock.
FS: Free stock.
XS: Maximum stock.

ND: Minimum demand.
FD: Free demand.
XD: Maximum demand.

(NS < FS < XS).
(ND < FD < XD).

the rural areas only 25% of the population do. Thus, in each area there is a shift of population to higher expenditure groups with the shift more pronounced in urban areas. This shift is associated with a movement in terms of trade between agriculture and non- agriculture: the index of terms of trade (with 1970 as base) falls from 93 in 1980 to 89 in 2000. In fact, the fall is entirely due to the fall in the prices of wheat, rice and coarse grains relative to that of non-agriculture between 1980 and 2000. Though the relative price of other agriculture rises, because of the greater weight of the cereal crops in agricultural terms of trade, the overall terms of trade show a downward movement.

Except for the richest urban expenditure class, the classwise per capita energy intake levels for all the other classes, in rural and urban areas, rise. However, caution is required in comparing the results of different years since population composition in various expenditure classes varies. To compare the two situations one needs to account for both the changes in average welfare in each class and the shift in population between classes. We compute within class average utility level and equivalent real income as an indicator of average welfare in each class. These are used based on a procedure suggested by Elizabeth Bailey and Robert Willig (1981) to compare the two situations represented by the two scenarios. Equivalent income at any time period is the expenditure required to achieve the same utility level as in that time period but at base year (here 1970) prices. These incomes, comparable across different years and across different scenarios, are, by definition, monotone increasing in per capita utility levels. The classwise equivalent incomes are also presented in Tables 4.1 and 4.2. While for the poorest rural and the poorest two urban calsses equivalent incomes per capita go up, for all the rest of the population they go down. The Gini coefficient of the distribution of equivalent incomes (GINIEQY) falls, indicating a more egalitarian distribution in 2000 compared to 1980 by this measure.

Government operations: The government plays a significant role in the Indian economy. In our model this role is depicted in its procurement and distribution of foodgrains, in public investment and consumption and in setting foreign trade and aid policies and in taxing incomes. Its revenue consists of taxes on foreign trade (tariffs), income-taxes levied at progressive rates on non- agricultural income of rural and urban residents, foreign aid (equated with the trade deficit in the model) and the net revenue from procurement and buffer stock operations in foodgrains.

The quantity of publicly distributed foodgrains through urban ration shops increases from 16 mt in 1980 to 45 mt in 2000. In the model there is a ceiling of 135 kilograms per year per urban resident on the amount distributed. The ceiling is binding in the last few years of the period 1980-2000. The total amount distributed as a percentage of total net production of foodgrains rises from 14.25 in 1980 to 20.65 in 2000. The government-held foodgrain stocks change from 12.62% of net production in 1980 to 8.90% in 2000. As noted earlier, India becomes a net exporter of cereals in the final years of the time horizon. Increasing burden of public distribution naturally calls for increasing procurement operations. Wheat (rice) procurement as a percentage of wheat (rice) production rises from 14.6 (22.4) in 1980 to 24.0 (35.0) in 2000. These figures suggest the growing role of government operations in the distribution of foodgrains.

As already mentioned, the trade deficit is fixed for all years at 1.5% of the total gross domestic product in base year prices. Thus the trade deficit also grows at the same rate as real GDP, i.e., 5.1% between 1980 and 2000. As noted above the trade deficit is treated as foreign aid accruing to government. In fact, it contributes the largest share to the government revenue. This is followed by domestic income taxation and tariff revenue. While the growth rate in tariff income between 1980 and 2000 at 5.03% is slightly less than that in the total gross domestic product, the growth rate in tax incomes is substantially higher at 16.33%. Growth of income tax revenues is reflected in the rise in the aggregate tax rate on non-agricultural incomes from 2.3% in 1980 to 9.8% in 2000. With the exogenously specified progression, the tax rates on rural and urban poorest classes varied from 0.23% in 1980 to 0.98% in 2000 and that on the rural richest class varied from 2.07% to 8.82%. The corresponding figures for the urban richest class are 2.3% and 9.8%. The increasing tax rates and the growth of non-agricultural incomes also explain the phenomenal increase in income-tax revenues over time.

Public consumption at 1970 prices grows at a rate of 6.52% p.a. between 1980 and 2000. It is spent entirely on non- agricultural goods. Public investment on the other hand acts to maintain total investment along a target path by saving and investing whatever is needed over and above the amount saved by the private sector. Total investment and agricultural investment grow at the rate of 7.79% p.a. between 1980 and 2000.

It was noted earlier that government is assumed to steer domestic prices over time towards the world market prices subject to meeting trade quotas as specified by its trade policy on certain commodities. The resulting path of the barter terms of trade for agriculture has already been described. The relative price (in terms of non-agriculture) of wheat, rice and coarse grains move respectively from 1.37, 1.98 and 1.06 in 1980 to 1.03, 2.07 and 1.24 in 2000.

4.5   The Reference Scenario: Concluding Summary

In the reference scenario we have stipulated a pricing policy to move gradually, within the stipulated self-sufficiency limits, towards world prices. Also the investment rate goes up from 21 percent of GDP in 1980 to 35 percent of GDP in 2000.

The scenario shows a growth rate that is higher than the historical one. With this, poverty as measured by population in the lowest two classes as a percentage of total population is reduced from nearly 50 percent of the rural population in 1980 to around 36 percent in 2000. However, in absolute terms the number of the poor remains more or less unchanged.

5

Public Distribution Policies

5.1   The Issues

Governments in many developing countries of the world are committed to a policy of subsidized distribution of food to a part or the entire population. In some countries a large and increasing proportion of the government budget is spent on such subsidies. Yet it is almost impossible politically to reduce, let alone eliminate, the subsidies. Attempts to do so have sparked off riots, the most recent such instance being that of Malawi. The forms of subsidization, the type of foodstuffs included, its financing, the extent of population covered, the modes of procuring supplies for the distribution system vary enormously across countries and over time within countries. For example in Sri Lanka a limited quantity of rice was supplied free of charge to the entire population until 1977. Since then, it has been replaced by the issue of food stamps to a subsection of the population. The stamps can be used to pay in part for the purchase of rice in the open market. The costs and benefits attributed to such programs have been controversial. Taylor et al. (1980) provide a survey of the experience with food subsidies in a number of countries. The impact on the welfare of different groups(rural landless and small farmers, rural surplus producers, urban poor and the urban rich) of the introduction of a compulsory procurement at below market price of a graded (by farm size) quantity of food from rural surplus producers for distribution to urban consumers is analyzed theoretically by Saah and Srinivasan (1987). In this chapter, we report the results of simulating the impact of altering the foodgrains procurement and subsidy system as it has been in operation in the recent past in different ways ranging from its complete abolition to its extension to the entire country. The consequences of providing a limited amount of foodgrains free of charge and alternative ways of financing its cost are also analyzed.

It is evident that a food procurement and subsidized distribution system has a number of micro-economic and macro-economic effects as well as the anticipated effects on the level and distribution of food consumption. Taking the macro effects first, depending on the rate of subsidy and the amount distributed, the budgetary impact of the subsidy could be substantial. The revised estimates of the 1984-85 central budget showed an expenditure of Rs.1100 crores accounting for roughly 5% of the tax and non-tax revenues of the central government. In considering any change in the system, one needs to examine how any increase (or decrease) in the subsidy will be financed (absorbed). The alternatives include an increase (decrease) in taxation, reduction (increase) in public investment or public consumption. Different ways of financing the same total subsidy can have different effects on overall growth and on the welfare of different socio-economic groups.

The micro-economic effects largely turn around the incentive effects - whether the procurement at below market price for subsidized distribution will result in a lower market price for the rest of the surplus of producers, thus affecting producer incentives, or, as Dantwala (1967) argued, it will in fact raise it by removing, in effect, poor consumers with elastic demand from the market by supplying them from the public distribution system. Also depending on the extent and direction of the effect on the relative returns to the production of the grains distributed through the public distribution system, the output of other agricultural commodities and, through the terms-of-trade effects, the output of non-agricultural commodities could be affected.

In the late fifties and the sixties, India received external assistance in the form of subsidized imports of foodgrains (and a few other commodities) from the United States under US Public Law 480. Some have argued that, to the extent the availability of PL 480 imports reduced the domestic price of foodgrains below what it would have been in the absence of PL 480, incentives for domestic production of foodgrains were blunted. Also, these imports were paid for in rupees credited to a special account in favour of the USA, the withdrawal from which was governed by procedures agreed upon by the Indian and US governments. Whether the PL 480 rupee deposits had any impact on money supply and thus had macro-economic effects has been debated. Since the analysis in this book does not extend to the monetary sector, issues arising from any future arrangement like the PL 480 payments will not be discussed. However, since PL 480 imports were used primarily to support the public distribution system, the incentive effects of a distribution based on imported grains are pertinent.

The questions that arise from the above discussion and which we address here are the following:

(a)   What has been the impact of the present procurement and distribu-
      tion policy? Or, equivalently, what would be the consequences of
      removing the present policy?
(b)   Should rationing, i.e. subsidized distribution of limited quantity of
      food, be extended to cover also the rural population?
(c)   Should restrictions be imposed on the resale of "rationed" food, as-
      suming that these can be enforced costlessly? Would such restriction
      increase the food energy intake of the poor?
(d)   Is food subsidy preferable to income subsidy?

5.2. Public Distribution System

Before setting out the scenarios for analysis, it is worthwhile to describe briefly
the evolution and features of the Indian public distribution system. The public
distribution system for foodgrains and other essential commodities is a legacy
of the Second World War. During the war and the immediate post-war years,
severe shortages of essential commodities led to formal (statutory) rationing
in metropolitan cities and major urban areas with no private trade allowed in
these commodities, and an informal rationing in the rest of the country. The
commodities covered by the system included at one time or the other the
following: major foodgrains, sugar, kerosene, textiles, refined edible oils including vanaspati (hydrogenated vegetable oil). The areas covered, the quantity distributed, subsidies involved and the modalities of procuring the supplies needed, in particular whether open market sales and purchases were
permitted, etc., have varied over time. As of April 1987, the commodities
covered include cereals, edible oils (refined and hydrogenated) and kerosene.
An open market for these commodities operates as well. Still the system is
largely confined to urban areas. The data on the amounts of cereals distributed through the public distribution system per head of the urban population
during 1951-1985 and, for comparison, per capita availability (domestic production plus net imports minus change in public stocks) of cereals and pulses
in the country as a whole are shown in Table 5.1.

It is clear from Table 5.1 that availability of foodgrains per person has
fluctuated a lot, mostly because of fluctuations in domestic production that
were not altogether offset by changes in net imports.[1] There is a barely per-

---

[1] The availability estimates allow for changes in government stocks of foodgrains.
     To the extent changes in private stocks (with traders, farmers and even consumers)
     are significant, the availability measure is somewhat misleading.

ceptible upward trend in per capita availability — the average for the period 1951-55 being 152.9 kg./year as compared to 166.9 kg./year for the period 1981-85. As can be seen from Table 5.1 this glacial growth in per capita availability is the total effect of a significantly rising availability of cereals and significantly falling trend in the availability of pulses. While there is a large international market for cereals which can be used to augment domestic supplies, there is as yet no such market for pulses. Thus a stagnant output of pulses that could not be augmented by imports in the face of a rising population led to fall in per capita availability of pulses. On the other hand, the amount of grains distributed in the urban areas through ration shops has been steadily increasing. As is to be expected in the years of severe shortfalls in domestic output such as 1965-66 and 1966-67 relatively large amounts were distributed through the ration shops.

The sources of supply for the distribution were obviously two: purchases from domestic producers, and imports. In order to contain the cost of the distribution system to the exchequer, the government procured part of the marketed surplus of foodgrains at below market prices mostly through a system of levies on traders and processors (e.g. rice mills) and, in some years, on producers as well. However, partly to ensure that supplies were available for procurement and partly to reduce the open market prices, various restrictions on the movement of foodgrains from surplus producing areas to urban and other deficit areas were enforced from time to time. Thus inter-state movement of grains on private account were banned until recently. One of the disastrous episodes of such controls was the attempts at monopoly procurement of wheat in the 1974 marketing season.

Until the mid-sixties access to concessional imports of foodgrains (mainly wheat) was available under US Public Law 480. Further, the domestic price of wheat was considerably higher than the landed cost of imports. It is not surprising that the government, as the sole legal importer of foodgrains, used imports as a major source of supply for the public distribution system. Indeed, until the late sixties, that is, until the phenomenal growth in wheat output with the adoption of high yielding varieties associated with the green revolution, imports constituted over 60% of the grains distributed during thirteen of the seventeen years 1951 to 1967.

It is important to note that the system of procurement and the considerations that underline the determination of procurement prices have radically changed since the success of the green revolution, first in wheat and then in rice. To understand the nature of the change involved, it is necessary to discuss briefly the price policy with respect to foodgrains. To begin with, there are a number of distinct prices to consider. These are in roughly increasing

TABLE 5.1 Per capita availability, public distribution and imports of food grains

Year	Per capita availability cereals (Kg/year)	Per capita availability pulses (Kg/year)	Per capita availability Total food grains (Kg/year)	Public distribution urban per capita (Kg/year)	Procurement as % of p.d.	Imports as % of p.d.	Urban population (millions)
1951	122.0	22.1	144.1	129.62	—	60.09	61.64
1952	119.1	21.6	140.7	107.82	51.18	57.74	63.07
1953	127.7	22.9	150.6	71.27	45.43	44.24	64.54
1954	141.7	25.4	167.1	32.56	66.51	38.70	66.04
1955	136.1	25.9	162.0	24.27	7.93	31.28	67.57
Average	129.3	23.6	152.9	73.11	42.76*	46.41	—
1956	131.9	25.7	157.6	30.08	1.92	65.96	69.14
1957	137.0	26.2	163.2	43.11	9.84	118.69	70.75
1958	127.9	21.3	149.2	54.98	13.32	80.65	72.39
1959	143.6	27.3	170.9	69.65	35.08	74.63	74.08
1960	140.6	24.0	164.6	65.17	25.91	103.62	75.80
Average	136.2	24.9	161.1	52.60	17.21	88.71	—
1961	145.9	25.2	171.1	51.32	13.57	87.59	77.56
1962	145.6	22.6	168.2	54.44	11.01	83.23	80.09
1963	140.2	21.8	162.0	62.53	14.48	87.57	82.71
1964	146.4	18.6	165.4	101.39	16.51	72.19	85.41

1965	152.8	22.5	175.3	114.29	39.98	73.80	88.20
Average	146.2	22.1	168.4	76.81	19.11	80.88	—
1966	131.4	17.6	149.0	154.59	28.48	73.23	91.08
1967	132.1	14.5	146.5	140.02	33.86	65.75	94.06
1968	147.5	20.5	168.4	105.22	66.63	55.49	97.13
1969	145.2	17.3	162.5	93.51	68.02	40.77	100.31
1970	147.1	18.9	166.1	85.34	75.90	40.12	103.58
Average	140.7	17.8	158.5	115.74	54.58	55.07	—
1971	152.4	18.7	171.1	73.10	113.30	25.70	106.97
1972	153.0	17.2	170.6	102.61	67.28	-4.37	111.10
1973	138.9	15.0	154.0	98.89	73.79	31.44	115.38
1974	149.8	14.9	164.7	90.04	52.36	47.78	119.83
1975	133.5	14.5	148.1	90.39	84.98	66.99	124.46
Average	145.5	16.1	161.7	91.01	78.34	33.51	—

TABLE 5.1 *(contd.)*

Year	Per capita availability cereals (Kg/year)	Per capita availability pulses (Kg/year)	Per capita availability Total food grains (Kg/year)	Public distribution urban per capita (Kg/year)	Procurement as % of p.d.	Imports as % of p.d.	Urban population (millions)
1976	136.4	18.4	154.8	70.94	140.13	7.31	129.26
1977	141.0	15.8	156.8	87.37	84.14	0.85	134.25
1978	154.2	16.6	170.8	73.01	109.04	−5.89	139.43
1979	157.6	16.3	173.9	80.52	118.70	−1.72	144.80
1980	138.5	11.3	149.8	99.67	74.52	−2.27	150.39
Average	145.5	15.7	161.2	82.30	105.31	−0.34	—
1981	151.9	13.7	165.6	83.30	99.77	5.07	156.19
1982	151.4	14.3	165.7	91.05	104.40	10.70	162.22
1983	144.9	14.4	159.3	96.21	96.67	25.11	168.48
1984	159.2	15.3	174.5	76.24	140.33	17.77	174.98
1985	154.9	14.2	169.1	77.42	142.15	−2.27	181.73
Average	152.5	14.4	166.9	84.84	116.66	11.28	—

Notes:- (1) *Average over 4 years.

(2) Figures under public distribution from 1978 onwards include the quantities released under the Food for Work Programe.

(3) Time series of urban population was worked out based on the urban data given for the years 1951, 1961, 1971 and 1981 in "Census of India 1981 (Series - India) - Paper 2 of 1981"

(4) p.d. : public distribution

order, minimum support prices defined as prices at which the government is willing to buy any amount offered so as to ensure that the open market price does not fall to unremunerative levels in years of surplus; procurement prices, defined as prices at which the government secured a limited quantity for the distribution system; farm harvest prices, defined as the open market prices at which producers sell mostly to traders and processors at harvest time; whole-sale prices, defined as prices charged by wholesale traders at major markets; issue prices, defined as prices at which grain rations in limited quantity are sold to urban consumers; and, finally, retail prices, defined as prices at which consumers can buy grains in the open market from retail sellers. Among these, support, procurement and issue prices are policy-determined. The Agricultural Prices Commission (APC) (renamed later as the Commission for Agricultural Costs and Prices), an autonomous body nominally in the Central Ministry of Agriculture, has been charged with the task of recommending the appropriate levels for these prices, taking into consideration in particular the trends in costs of production. The Central Government announces the price policy based on these recommendations prior to each harvest. Purchases for the public distri-bution system are made both by Central and State Government agencies. State Governments announce their own procurement prices which are often consid-erably higher than those announced by the Central Government.

Until the early seventies the trends in the open market prices were such as to make the announced support prices largely irrelevant and the procurement price involved a certain amount of implicit tax on producers. Whether or not the procurement prices announced by the APC in the past were in fact based on trends in open market prices as argued by Raj Krishna and Chibber (1982), has become moot with the differences between the two having narrowed significantly with the increases in marketed surpluses as the green revolution took hold and expanded. Indeed, procurement prices have taken on the role of support prices and a powerful farm lobby has emerged agitating for ever-increasing procurement prices as well as input subsidies. Government purchases are no longer limited to the needs of the public distribution system; in effect, the Government buys whatever is offered at the announced procurement prices, regardless of the offtake from ration shops. The result has been the accumu-lation of huge stocks (23.6 million tons at the end of December 1986) carried at a significant cost in terms of storage and opportunity cost of resources locked up.

It was mentioned earlier that the public distribution system is largely ur-ban. According to the report of the Committee on Controls and Subsidies (1979) (hereafter RCCS), even though over three-quarters of the 2,39,204 fair price shops were located in rural areas, nearly 60% of the offtake was from urban areas. Once one allows for some of the problems in the definition of what constitutes a rural area and for the fact that the "catchment" area of a rural (urban) shop may include urban (rural) consumers, it is likely that the urban bias of the system in terms of the share in the quantity of grains distributed will go up. The RCCS concluded that "while the public distribution system has been able to meet the requirements of the urban population generally with varying degrees of success, it has not succeeded in reaching foodgrains at a reasonable price to the rural poor". In part this is due to the fact that the poorest sections of the population such as casual labourers in rural areas, migrant construction workers mostly in urban areas and the homeless do not usually have means of acquiring ration cards. In any case, the Committee rightly argues: "If banks and other public agencies can today identify the weaker sections of the population for purposes of concessional finance, there is no reason why the same population cannot be identified for the supply of concessional foodgrains. All heads of households having farms of a marginal size as well as all agricultural labour families could be identified, and issued with ration cards."

One of the avowed objectives of the subsidized public distribution system is to raise the nutrition and health of the poor by enabling them to consume more food than they otherwise would have. Unfortunately, a significant proportion of the population apparently are too poor to buy and consume their entire ration, given their other needs. Leela Gulati (1977) reports that in Kerala ration cards were mortgaged by the poorest (i.e. those consuming the least amount per capita of cereals and cereal substitutes) to others in return for cash loans that they used for medical and other necessary expenses. Presumably, for the lenders the holding of the borrower's ration card meant some assurance against default and that they appropriated the implicit subsidy involved in the purchase of rations. Although the loans were nominally interest-free the implicit interest paid by the borrowers in terms of subsidy forgone can exceed 5.5% per mensem according to Gulati.

There have been allegations of corruption in the operation of the system. It is a demonstrable fact that the grains distributed contain a larger proportion of removable impurities such as small stones than the grains purchased in the open market, so much so that it has been claimed (undoubtedly an exaggeration) that once the weight of the impurities and the cost (in time, if not in direct cash outlay) of removing them are taken, the implicit subsidy in the purchase of rations vanishes! Although quantitative rationing rather than queuing for purchase at the subsidized price was used for allocation of grains in the system, nevertheless, in the past, the erratic availability of supplies in the ration shops led to long queues of purchasers formed in front of the shops when supplies became available. Fortunately, since the number of consumer commodities covered by the system was small, the Eastern European phenomenon of queues, search costs and forced substitution (i.e. purchase of commodities that happened to be available rather than those desired but not available) did not occur to a significant extent. For an interesting analysis of queues, quantity of rations, etc., as allocation mechanisms see Saah and Stiglitz (1986). As procurement prices became in effect support prices, corruption in the purchase of grains for the system has been alleged. It is said that in applying the quality standards such as moisture content, official purchasers extract bribes particularly from the small producers. While the corruption issue is important from the point of view of the political economy of subsidies, controls and rent seeking, for the purposes of this chapter, only the fact that some consumers may be too poor to purchase their rations will figure in the analysis.

5.3. Specifications of Alternative Policies and Scenarios

It will be recalled (Chapter 3) that in the base or reference scenario the quantity of foodgrains distributed to the urban population as a share of the net output of foodgrains in any year was a non-linear function of the level and the change over the previous year of net output per capita of foodgrains and real non-agricultural income per head. A ceiling of 135 kg. per urban resident was set exogenously on the amount distributed to reflect the fact that even in the two historically unprecedented drought years of 1965-66 and 1966-67 only about 150 kg. was distributed. The quantity of foodgrains procured and the implicit tax on procurement were related to outputs of rice and wheat, the trends in wholesale prices of foodgrains, etc. The distribution subsidy on rations to urban consumers was set at 20 percent.

In the first policy scenario, called DPO, both procurement and urban distribution are eliminated while all other policies such as quotas on foreign trade, wedges between domestic and international price, etc., are maintained.

Scenario RUN extends the distribution system to the rural areas as well but limiting the amount distributed per head to the entire Indian population to 100 kg. of wheat. Since the ration of 100 kg. is provided at a subsidy of 20% and since the consumer is not precluded from selling part of the ration in the open market, the ration is equivalent to an income transfer equivalent to the subsidy value of the ration. Of course in the real world there will be some transactions costs incurred by the seller in any resale. For simplicity these have been neglected.

Scenario RUR is the same as scenario RUN in every respect except that the consumer is prohibited from buying the entire 100 kg. of ration and re-selling a part of it. This means that his purchase from the ration shops is the minimum of his consumption of wheat, or 100 kg. Once again, the enforcement of resale restrictions is not costless to the government. But this is neglected in the analysis.

Scenario FRF is the same as scenario RUN except that the subsidy is fully financed by increases in taxation as required relative to REF.

Scenario FRF-X is the same as FRF except that the subsidy is financed by reductions in public investment rather than by change in taxation relative to REF.

In all the above six scenarios, the exogenously imposed quotas on exports and imports were left intact. This meant that in the years and sectors for which the quotas were binding, the realized domestic prices will differ from target domestic prices. Also, the realized domestic prices could differ from scenario to scenario even though the quotas were the same because of the complex interaction between the policy changes introduced by the secnario and the trade and the stock bounds. This interaction may confound the policy impact and the impact of the severity of trade bounds. Three more scenarios were developed which, by dropping the quotas, altogether eliminated this problem; in all the three scenarios the realized domestic prices are the same, equalling their target values.

Scenario RFQ is the same as the reference scenario REF except that there are no trade bounds.

In scenario UDQ, a ration of 100 kg. of wheat is provided to all urban residents at a price subsidy of 20%, with no restriction on resale and no trade quotas being applied at any time on any sector.

In scenario RUQX, the ration of 100 kg. of wheat is provided to rural as well as urban residents, with the subsidy rate unchanged at 20%, and the cost of the additional subsidy compared to UDQ being financed through reduction in public investment. The rate of taxation remains the same as in UDQ and again no trade quotas apply.

5.4. The Results

In interpreting the results, it is worthwhile to keep in mind first certain general considerations about policy change in economies with distortions and, second, the complex interaction between micro, macro and intertemporal effects of such a change in a sequential general equilibrium model.

The theory of the second best has shown that removal of, or changes in, one policy in a less distortionary direction in an economy with several distortionary policies in place may end up accentuating the effects of the unchanged policies. As such, broadly speaking, the efficiency and welfare effects of such a change could be the opposite of what would have occurred, had the changed policy been the only distortionary policy initially present.

We have already pointed out the relevant macro and micro effects of policy change in general terms. Specifically in our model the budgetary impact of any change in policy has static as well as dynamic effects. For example, the elimination of the public distribution system, say, without the elimination of the procurement system, means that, compared to the reference situation when distribution and procurement are present, an incipient budget surplus emerges. The reason is that while the implicit procurement tax is still in place, the distribution subsidy is no longer required. Suppose the implicit budget surplus is eliminated by requiring that it be used to increase public investment. The static effects (as compared to the reference situation) arise mainly from the price changes induced by the additional demand for goods and services arising from larger public investment and the income effects from the elimination of distribution subsidy. The dynamic effects arise from the fact that the additional public investment increases future production capacity of the economy, i.e., it raises the growth rate of the economy. The latter in turn has its welfare effects. This example is sufficient to indicate the flavor of the complexities of interpretation of the results from a model. It is sobering to realize that the model for all its complexity is an abstraction and simplification of reality. Thus in the real world the effects of policy change could be even more complex than in the model. Our hope is that the additional complexities of the real world are not so overwhelming as to reverse the results obtained from the model.

The economy-wide effects of the policy scenarios are considered in terms of real GDP, its break-up in terms of agriculture and non-agriculture, the terms of trade between agriculture and non-agriculture, the overall tax rate, and three aggregate welfare indicators, namely, per capita real GDP, per capita 'equivalent' income, and energy content of per capita food intakes (energy intake hereafter). The distributional effects are evaluated for the ten per capita real consumption expenditure classes (five rural and five urban) in terms of the proportion of population in each class, per capita energy intake in each class, and per capita equivalent income in each class.

Impact of present procurement and distribution policy: By comparing (see Tables 5.2, 5.3 and 5.4) the reference scenario REF with the scenario DPO in which both procurement and urban distribution are abolished, one can study the impact of removing the present procurement and distribution policy. In

DPO, with public investment unchanged, the net budgetary effect of the loss of procurement tax and the gain from not having to subsidize urban distribution results in a slight increase in the aggregate tax rate by 0.91 in the year 1980 and 1.15 in the year 2000. These appear small in the aggregate but, as a proportion of the tax rate in REF, these amount to a substantial 39% and 11% respectively. With total investment unchanged, it is not surprising that the growth of GDP and its components and the aggregate welfare indicators are virtually identical in the two scenarios. However, somewhat more significant distributional effects are seen. The rural classes benefit in DPO from the fact that they no longer have to bear the implicit procurement tax on their agricultural incomes. On the other hand, they have to pay slightly higher taxes on their non-agricultural incomes, the proportion of which in their total income increases over time. On balance, although there is a slight increase in the year 2000 in the proportion of the population in the poorest class compared to REF, the average energy intake and, more comprehensively, the average equivalent income of each class improves. The urban population loses on two counts in DPO: the withdrawal of public distribution on the one hand and the increase in tax rate on the other. Thus the distribution of urban population shifts to the left (towards lower real consumption expenditure classes) and the average energy intake and equivalent income of each urban class is lower in 2000 as compared to REF.

Summarizing, the present procurement and distribution policy makes a net contribution to government revenue (of course, continuing procurement at below market prices and abolishing subsidized distribution will make a larger contribution) and transfers income from the rural to the urban population. The urban welfare is better and rural welfare worse than it would have been without such a policy.

Subsidized ration to both rural and urban populations: In the next policy scenario, RUN, 100 kg. of wheat is given at a subsidized price (or more precisely an income subsidy implied by the price difference between the ration price and market price for 100 kg. of wheat) to every Indian in both rural and urban areas. It is not strictly comparable to REF since a varying amount (subject to a ceiling of 135 kg.) in varying proportions in terms of rice, wheat and coarse grains to every Indian in the urban areas only is distributed in the reference scenario. One can however compare DPO and RUN in that there is neither procurement nor distribution in the former while both are present in the latter. Again (see Table 5.2), with investment unchanged the economy wide indicators except for the average tax rate do not differ much between the runs. The latter is higher in RUN compared to DPO by 1.3 (or 95.7% of the tax rate in REF) in 1980 and lower by 0.7 (or 4.1%) in 2000.

TABLE 5.2 Impact of alternative procurement and distribution systems on selected macroenomic indicators

Variable (units)	Year	Absolute Values Reference Scenario REF	Percentage change over reference scenario		
			No procurement No distribution DPO	Ration to all which can be resold RUN	Ration to all No resale permitted RUR
GDP					
(10^9 rupees	1980	530.0	0	0	0
1970 prices)	2000	1429.0	-0.07	0	0
GDP agriculture					
(10^9 rupees	1980	220.0	0	0	0
1970 prices)	2000	354.0	0	0	0
GDP non-agriculture					
(10^9 rupees	1980	310.0	0	0	0
1970 prices)	2000	1075.0	-0.09	0	0
Total Investment					
(10^9 rupees	1980	110.0	0	0	0
1970 prices)	2000	492.0	0	0	0
Tax rate (%)	1980	2.3	39.0	95.7	-26.1
	2000	9.8	11.2	4.1	1.0

TABLE 5.2 *(contd.)*

Variable (units)		Year	Absolute Values	Percentage change over reference scenario			
			Reference Scenario REF	No procurement No distribution DPO	Ration to all which can be resold RUN	Ration to all No resale permitted RUR
Price index agriculture over price index non-agriculture		1980	0.93	−0.15	1.1	0.14
		2000	0.89	+0.46	0.3	0.70
GDP per capita (10⁹ rupees 1970 prices)		1980	786.0	0	0	0
		2000	1363.0	−0.07	0	0
Food energy calorie intake (Kcal/person/ day)		1980	2162.0	0.42	1.1	1.0
		2000	2569.0	0.45	0.5	0.7
Average equivalent income (AEI)*		1980	544.0	0	0	0.50
		2000	661.0	−0.18	0.1	0.06

*AEI: Income needed at 1970 prices to provide same utility as provided by current consumption at current prices.

TABLE 5.3 Distribution of income and food energy intake in the reference scenario (REF)

	Expenditure classes				
	(1)	(2)	(3)	(4)	(5)
	<216	216-336	336-516	516-900	>900
Rural 1980					
Population	0.316	0.180	0.179	0.182	0.144
Equivalent income	129.0	266.0	407.0	635.0	1309.0
Calorie level	981.0	1896.0	2475.0	2491.0	3653.0
Urban 1980					
Population	0.019	0.079	0.187	0.340	0.375
Equivalent income	165.0	264.0	397.0	626.0	1322.0
Calorie level	1085.0	1556.0	1935.0	2332.0	3108.0
Rural 2000					
Population	0.205	0.159	0.189	0.216	0.231
Equivalent income	133.0	261.0	399.0	616.0	1227.0
Calorie level	1059.0	2019.0	2673.0	2796.0	3858.0
Urban 2000					
Population	0.004	0.032	0.125	0.331	0.508
Equivalent income	172.0	273.0	395.0	605.0	1224.0
Calorie level	1252.0	1742.0	2059.0	2375.0	3021.0

Note : Population is in proportions

TABLE 5.4 Distributional impact of removing present procurement and distribution policy (DPO compared to REF)

	Percentage change over reference scenario Expenditure classes				
	(1)	(2)	(3)	(4)	(5)
Rural 1980					
Population	0.00	0.00	0.00	0.00	0.00
Equivalent income	1.32	1.58	1.57	1.32	0.63
Calorie level	1.33	1.42	1.21	1.00	0.38
Urban 1980					
Population	52.63	7.59	0.00	−2.35	−2.40
Equivalent income	−1.03	0.49	−0.25	−0.54	−0.48
Calorie level	−1.11	0.39	−0.21	−0.39	−0.26
Rural 2000					
Population	1.46	−0.63	−0.53	−0.46	0.00
Equivalent income	2.64	3.52	3.58	2.94	0.53
Calorie level	2.08	2.67	2.69	2.15	0.05
Urban 2000					
Population	75.00	15.63	3.20	−0.91	−1.77
Equivalent income	−1.51	−0.48	−1.06	−1.36	−2.00
Caloric level	−2.64	−1.09	−1.17	−1.18	−1.06

Turning to the distributional impacts in Table 5.5, there are at least three effects on the rural community in RUN compared to DPO: the positive effect of income subsidy, the negative effects of the implicit procurement tax, and the increase in the explicit average tax on non-agricultural incomes. The net effects of the three are: (i) a shift in population away from the poorest class to all the remaining four both in 1980 and in 2000; (ii) a reduction in the average energy intake of all but the poorest class, again in 1980 and 2000; and (iii) a reduction in average equivalent income of all classes but the poorest in 1980 and 2000. A comparison combining the shifts in population between classes and the changes in average equivalent incomes within each class applying the Bailey-Willig methodology is shown in Figure 5.1 (Rural: DPO vs. RUN 2000). For the urban population there is the positive effect of income subsidy, the negative effects of increase in the average tax rate and the effect of change in the relative price of food. The net effect results in (i) a shift in population from the bottom two or three classes to the top two in both 1980 and 2000; (ii) perhaps because the proportionate increase in the average tax rate relative to DPO is substantial in 1980 but negligible in 2000 and also because the food price increases in 1980 but decreases in 2000, the negative effects seem to dominate in 1980 compared to the positive effect of the income subsidy. As such, the average energy intake of all classes go down relative to DPO in 1980 and go up in 2000. The changes in average equivalent incomes are similar except for the poorest class in 1980 which shows no change in its equivalent income. A Bailey-Willig comparison is shown in Figure 5.2 (Urban: DPO vs. RUN 2000).

TABLE 5.5 Distributional impact of ration to all — which can be resold
(RUN compared to DPO)

	Percentage change over DPO Expenditure classes				
	(1)	(2)	(3)	(4)	(5)
Rural 1980					
Population	−11.39	8.33	5.59	3.30	2.78
Equivalent income	4.28	−2.22	−1.67	−1.90	−3.17
Calorie level	4.23	−2.24	−1.56	−1.67	−2.10
Urban 1980					
Population	−31.03	−7.06	0.00	2.11	2.19
Equivalent income	0.00	−1.54	−1.49	−1.74	−3.47
Calorie level	−0.28	−1.66	−1.35	−1.33	−1.87

TABLE 5.5 *(Contd.)*

	Percentage change over DPO Expenditure classes				
	(1)	(2)	(3)	(4)	(5)
Rural 2000					
Population	−7.69	3.80	2.66	1.40	0.87
Equivalent income	1.17	−2.81	−2.85	−2.52	−1.24
Calorie level	1.67	−2.32	−2.22	−1.89	−0.62
Urban 2000					
Population	−14.29	−8.11	−1.55	0.30	1.00
Equivalent income	0.71	0.15	0.56	0.80	1.40
Calorie level	1.48	0.46	0.64	0.72	0.74

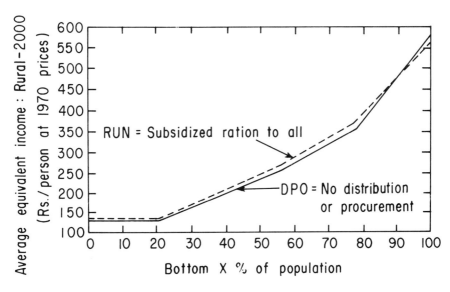

Fig. 5.1 Welfare Comparison — Impact on Rural Populations of Subsidized Ration to All

TABLE 5.6   Distributional impact of susidized ration to all — no resale permitted (RUR compared to RUN)

	Percentage change over RUN Expenditure classes				
	(1)	(2)	(3)	(4)	(5)
Rural 1980					
Population	11.17	−9.08	−4.67	−2.55	0.00
Equivalent income	−4.50	1.56	0.30	1.05	1.60
Calorie level	−4.57	1.47	0.93	3.32	1.15
Urban 1980					
Population	40.85	4.03	−0.66	−1.60	−1.28
Equivalent income	2.87	2.81	2.42	2.76	5.08
Calorie level	3.18	3.35	2.73	2.69	3.03
Rural 2000					
Population	7.26	−5.32	−1.68	−0.52	−0.24
Equivalent income	−3.47	0.77	0.36	1.01	0.51
Calorie level	−3.02	1.16	1.08	2.73	−1.41
Urban 2000					
Population	30.61	5.38	7.23	−0.65	−0.50
Equivalent income	2.32	1.28	0.69	0.53	0.85
Calorie level	3.34	2.27	1.53	1.31	0.93

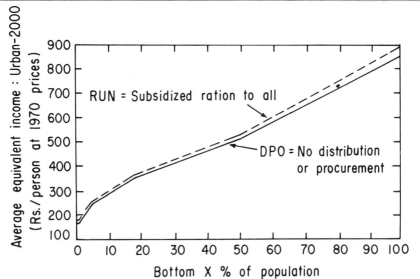

Fig. 5.2   Welfare Comparison — Impact on Urban Populations of Subsidized Ration to All

One can conclude that if additional taxes can be raised giving subsidized food rations to both urban and rural populations, it is better than not having either procurement or any distribution scheme. In the long term it benefits the poor in the rural as well as urban areas. Though there is an adverse short-term impact on the urban poor, a Bailey-Willig comparison for combined rural and urban populations shows subsidized ration for all to be a preferable situation.

Resale restriction on rationed grains: The effect of preventing resale in the open market of a part of the ration provided is to preclude the subsidized ration from becoming an income subsidy. Thus scenario RUR differs from scenario RUN in that, because of the ban on resale (assumed completely effective), the subsidized ration in RUR is no longer equivalent to an income subsidy as in RUN. The impact of this ban is illustrated in a two-commodity (food and non-food) diagram (Figure 5.3) in which a ration equal to R kg. of food is provided at a subsidized price (with non-food as numeraire) equal to the slope of the straight line AB. By construction A'B' and A"B" are parallel to AB and B'C' and B"C" are parallel to BC. The open market price is higher and equals the slope of the straight line BC. Two income consumption curves (Engel curves) corresponding to open-market price, OM, and subsidized price, OS, are also shown.

Consider three individuals with incomes OA, OA' and OA" with OA < OA' < OA". If there is no ban on resale of the ration in the open market, then these three individuals receive an income subsidy equivalent to AE, A'E' and A"E" respectively and since in this case the opportunity cost of food is the market price, the budget constraint for them is represented by the straight lines CE, C'E' and C"E" respectively. Then since OM is the income consumption curve at open market price of food, utility maximization will lead to consume at D_U, D_U' and D_U'' respectively. If resale is banned, the stretch BE (B'E' and B"E") on the budget set is no longer available so that the resale restricted budget constraint becomes the angular ABC (A'B'C' and A"B"C"). It is straightforward then to see that, for the individual with income OA", since D_U'' lies on both the unrestricted and restricted budget sets, it is also the optimal consumption point D_R'' in the restricted case. The individual with income OA' can no longer consume at D_U' and his optimal consumption now moves to D_R' which coincides with B'. Individual with income OA also cannot consume at D_U but his optimal consumption is at D_R to the left of B on the line AB.

It is evident from Figure 5.3 that the richest of the three persons, that is the one with income OA", does not change his consumption of food or non-food with the imposition of the ban on resale, since he was not selling any to begin with. On the middle income person with income OA', the ban has two effects: first, he can no longer sell any part of the ration and realize the ration subsidy as income so that there is an income effect; second, since the shadow implicit relative price of food is the slope of his indifference curve through his consumption point, it falls from the market price at D_U' when there is no ban, to a value above the ration price at D_R' when the ban is imposed, so that there is a substitution effect in favor of food. However, since D_U' and D_R' lie on the same budget line, the substitution effect dominates, so that he consumes more food. The poorest person with income OA suffers loss of income subsidy just as the middle income persons. But in his case the fall in shadow price of food is even steeper; it falls from market price at D_U to ration price at D_R. This places D_R and D_U on different budget lines. Whether he will consume more or less food when a ban on resale of ration is imposed depends on whether the substitution effect dominates or is dominated by the income effect.

The above analysis assumes that all three individuals have the same preferences as represented in the two Engel curves. In our model, the preferences implied by the demand function are not the same across expenditure classes. As such, it is possible that the same ration, say 100 kg. of wheat, sold at the same subsidized price, puts a person from one of the top expenditure classes in a situation such as the one depicted in Figure 5.3 for the person with income OA while it puts a person from a bottom expenditure into the position of a person like the one with income OA". One has to keep this in mind in interpreting the results.*

With investment unchanged as in scenario RUN, with the ban on resale of rations in the scenario RUR there is virtually no change in the macro-indicators between the scenarios. In RUR since some individuals may not buy the entire ration, the implicit ration subsidy to be financed is lower compared to RUN so that the average tax rate is significantly lower (even compared to the REF) in 1980 and insignificantly different in 2000. A comparison of the proportion of each expenditure class in RUN and RUR (Table 5.6) shows that a ban on resale shifts the population distribution to the left. In rural areas, both in 1980 and 2000, population moves from the richer classes to the poorest class. A similar shift is seen in urban areas as well, with population in each of the bottom two classes in 1980 and the bottom three classes in 2000 increasing.

---

* The computational scheme by which the imposition of a ban on resale was implemented in our model is described in Narayana, Parikh and Srinivasan (1984).

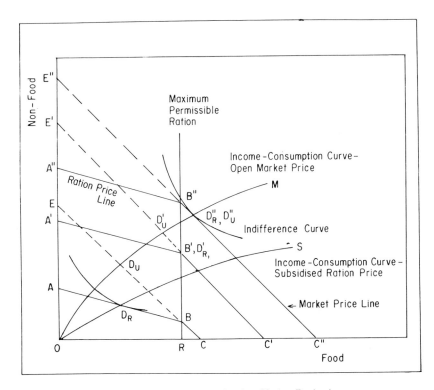

Fig. 5.3 Consumption Choice Under Rationing

The welfare impacts in terms of equivalent incomes and food energy intakes are not obvious from Table 5.6. However, Bailey-Willig comparisons done for rural populations clearly show that resale restriction decreases their welfare both in 1980 and 2000. For urban population such comparisons remain indeterminate. To facilitate welfare comparison for the urban population we made special calculations of equivalent incomes and energy intakes for the RUR scenario corresponding to the same population distribution as observed in the RUN scenario for the year 1980. These calculations given in Table 5.7

show that the poorer classes in the rural and urban areas lose in terms of both equivalent incomes and energy intake. Such calculations for the year 2000 are not easy to make but we expect similar results.

TABLE 5.7 Distributional Impact of subsidized ration to all — no resale permitted (RUR compared to RUN : with same population distribution in 1980)

	Percentage change over RUN Expenditure classes				
	(1)	(2)	(3)	(4)	(5)
Rural 1980					
Population	0	0	0	0	0
Equivalent income	−10.39	−3.61	−1.64	0.49	1.67
Calorie level	−10.62	−3.33	−0.61	2.92	1.22
Urban 1980					
Population	0	0	0	0	0
Equivalent income	−5.86	−2.55	−0.19	1.49	4.53
Calorie level	−6.26	−1.56	0.76	1.85	2.77

One can conclude that when the quantity of ration entitlement is fairly large but the price subsidy is small, as in our scenario RUR, rationing with resale restriction is regressive. The poor get less subsidy than the rich as they are unable to buy the full ration entitlement.

These results also imply that if the total government budget for giving food subsidy is limited, it is better to give large price subsidy on a smaller ration entitlement. More of the poor would then be able to avail themselves of the full subsidy.

It is also interesting to note that what one may think of as the purpose of imposing resale restriction, namely to ensure that the poor eat more, is not served. Resale restriction does not increase food energy intake of the poor compared to when no such restrictions are imposed.

Thus imposition of resale restrictions, even assuming that they can be costlessly enforced, is not a desirable policy.

Impact of free food distribution: The scenario FRF is like scenario RUN except that the ration entitlement of 100 kg. of wheat is given freely. Thus the subsidy is roughly five times as much. Since people are free in both these scenarios to resell the wheat they get, these are really income subsidy runs.

Like RUN, scenario FRF is not strictly comparable to REF and for the same reason except that with investment being the same in the two runs (see Table 5.8), the GDP figures are almost identical in the runs. Of course, the massive food subsidy in FRF leads to an average tax rate 5.87 times that in REF in

1980 and 1.19 times that in 2000. The distribution of the population among expenditure classes (Table 5.9) shifts to the right with population increasing in the top four classes and decreasing in the poorest class in rural areas in 1980 and 2000 and the top two classes gaining population from the other three in urban areas compared to REF.

TABLE 5.8 Impact of free food distribution to all on selected macro-economic indicators

Variable	Year	Percentage change over reference scenario	
		Free food to all	
		Tax rate adjusted FRF	Tax rate fixed FRFX
GDP*	1980	0	0
	2000	0.72	−9.36
GDP agriculture*	1980	0	0
	2000	0.47	−2.50
GDP Non-agriculture*	1980	0	0
	2000	0.81	−11.62
Total investment*	1980	0	−16.71
	2000	1.19	−18.46
Tax rate (%)	1980	486.9	160.87[+]
	2000	19.39	0
Price agriculture/	1980	12.5	18.44
price non agriculture	2000	2.89	4.30
GDP per capita#	1980	0	0
	2000	0.72	−9.36
Food energy caloric intake (Kcal/person/day)	1980	3.63	5.42
	2000	1.59	−1.18
Average equivalent income (AEI)**	1980	−0.44	3.43
	2000	0.46	−2.82

* 10^9 Rs. at 1970 prices.

** AEI: Income needed at 1970 prices to provide the same utility as provided by current consumption at current prices.

\# Rs. at 1970 prices.

\+ Only from 1986 onwards, the reference level taxes could be realized.

Even though urban populations shift rightward the equivalent incomes of all urban classes fall. The high food prices and the higher tax rates (applicable only on non-agricultural incomes) offset the value of the food subsidy. Not only are there 60% fewer persons in rural poorest class, their equivalent incomes are also 15% higher. A Bailey-Willig comparison of equivalent incomes (not shown here) for the combined populations of rural and urban areas shows clear improvement in welfare under the scenario FRF.

Once the government is able to finance free food distribution through additional taxes, such income subsidy is clearly welfare improving.

The fact that the two income subsidy runs are better than the resale restriction scenario, RUR, shows that it is better to give a lump sum income subsidy rather than a subsidy in kind. And the superiority of FRF over RUN shows that it is better to give more subsidy than less.

But the main difficulty in income subsidy programs is that government is unable to raise additional taxes to finance them. The interesting question is what else can adjust and what are the long-term consequences of such adjustment.

TABLE 5.9 Distributional impact of a free food policy (100 kg. of wheat free to all) financed by changes in tax rates (FRF compared to REF)

	Percentage change over reference scenario Expenditure classes				
	(1)	(2)	(3)	(4)	(5)
Rural 1980					
Population	−60.32	44.39	31.84	18.68	12.50
Equivalent income	15.49	−5.98	−1.06	−2.11	−11.28
Calorie level	14.78	−6.80	−2.34	−2.85	−7.77
Urban 1980					
Population	−89.47	−41.77	−5.35	7.94	8.80
Equivalent income	−7.95	−9.31	−11.27	−13.66	−25.01
Calorie level	−9.77	−10.22	−9.97	−10.16	−13.45
Rural 2000					
Population	−38.54	18.87	13.76	6.94	3.90
Equivalent income	15.51	0.00	0.60	−0.45	−4.73
Calorie level	15.20	−1.29	−0.60	−1.86	−4.15
Urban 2000					
Population	−50.00	−21.88	−4.00	1.21	2.17
Equivalent income	−0.29	−0.62	−0.51	−1.47	−5.36
Calorie level	−1.92	−2.01	−1.46	−1.73	−3.08

Does a free food programme at the cost of investment benefit the poor? A more interesting comparison of FRF is with FRFX where the tax is kept at the same level as in REF with the food subsidy financed by a reduction in public and hence total investment (see Tables 5.8, 5.9 and 5.10). As is to be expected, the GDP in 2000 is lower by 10% in FRFX in 2000, with non-agricultural GDP falling by about 12%. Since the same amount of food is supplied free in both the runs, the differences in the distributional consequences are largely due to the slower growth in GDP in FRFX together with the effect of lower taxes. These can be seen by comparing Tables 5.9 and 5.10. Since the policy change is introduced in 1980 and our calculation of population proportions is based on target prices, there is no change in the population distribution in the two runs in 1980. In 2000, the slower growth in FRFX seems to shift the rural population from the top most class to the others except the third class in which the population is virtually unchanged. Similarly, in the urban areas also, there are fewer persons in FRFX in the top most class and more in the other four. The within class average energy intake and equivalent incomes reveal a mixed picture between 1980 and 2000, between classes and between rural and urban areas. Except for the top most class in both areas and the rural poorest when the changes in energy intake and equivalent incomes exceed 5%, all other changes are relatively modest. This suggests that although the inability to finance the food subsidy through taxes reduces growth and worsens income distribution somewhat, with the changes in energy intakes one way or the other being modest relative to the tax-financed scenario FRF, the gains relative to REF are being maintained despite slower growth.

Large reductions in the number of persons in the poorest classes in both rural and urban areas compared to REF in the year 2000 (Table 5.10) indicate that in spite of the slower growth rate, the FRFX scenario is welfare improving compared to REF. A Bailey-Willig comparison for the combined rural and urban populations confirms this. Though one may not consider the reduction in growth rate politically acceptable, particularly when the economy is growing at around 5%, one has to emphasize that even then free food distribution financed at the cost of growth is welfare improving.

Impact of extending subsidized distribution when market prices are maintained: As stated earlier, the scenarios RFQ, UDQ and RUQX without trade quotas were developed to isolate the effects of changes in public distribution uncontaminated by the interaction between binding trade quotas and the changes in public distribution policies. There is very little difference in almost all macro as well as micro indicators between RFQ and UDQ since the only difference between the two lies in some differences in the amount and composition of the grain basket distributed as rations. As there is no resale

TABLE 5.10 Distributional impact of a free food policy (100 kg. of wheat free to all) — tax rate fixed and investment adjusted (FRFX compared to REF)

	Percentage change over reference scenario Expenditure classes				
	(1)	(2)	(3)	(4)	(5)
Rural 1980					
Population	−60.44	44.39	31.84	18.68	12.50
Equivalent income	14.18	−5.94	−0.66	−1.01	−6.94
Calorie level	13.15	−6.91	−1.74	−1.28	−4.87
Urban 1980					
Population	−89.47	−41.77	−5.35	7.94	8.80
Equivalent income	−9.65	−10.48	−10.89	−10.87	−16.00
Calorie level	−11.80	−11.44	−9.72	−8.02	−8.62
Rural 2000					
Population	−34.15	21.38	13.23	9.26	−3.90
Equivalent income	15.59	0.11	0.70	−0.11	−4.82
Calorie level	13.22	−3.02	−2.28	−3.61	−5.52
Urban 2000					
Population	−25.00	12.50	16.00	6.65	−8.66
Equivalent income	−0.87	−1.21	−0.43	−0.76	−4.87
Calorie level	−4.95	−4.48	−2.77	−2.19	−3.11

ban, the ration is equivalent to income subsidies anyway, and as a proportion of the RFQ values, the differences in rations apparently do not result in significant income or expenditure differences.

More interesting is the comparison between the scenarios UDQ and RUQX. In the latter, subsidized ration is extended to rural areas while the tax rates are kept at the same levels as in UDQ and, public investment is reduced to finance the additional subsidy. Interestingly, the reduction in public investment is not substantial and, GDP growth between 1980 and 2000 is affected only marginally. There is a significant reduction in the proportion of population in the poorest class in rural areas and an increase in most of the other classes in 1980 and 2000 in RUQX compared to UDQ. The distribution of the urban population is essentially unchanged. Correspondingly, the food energy intake of the poorest class increases while that of every other class decreases in 1980 and 2000 in rural areas. Once again urban energy intakes are virtually unchanged. The picture with respect to the intra-class average equivalent incomes is similar to that of the average energy intake.

5.5 Conclusions

We can summarize our results as follows:

If the tax rates can be increased substantially for a while, subsidized food distribution can be extended to the entire country rather than restricted to urban areas as at present, without any significant reduction in the rate of GDP growth. Our analysis, using a social welfare measure based on equivalent incomes incorporating aversion to regressive transfer, shows that the extension improves social welfare in a modest way.

One such extension scheme, involving a massive redistributive program giving 100 kg. of wheat free to everyone, financed through higher taxes, results in a substantial reduction of 99 (57) million persons from a reference level of 164 (148) million in 1980 (2000) of the population in the poorest class in rural areas. Their average energy intake and equivalent incomes improve as well. Such a redistributive program is welfare improving even though when it is financed without raising tax rates at the cost of investment it involves a substantial cost in terms of forgone growth. The sacrifice in terms of the slow down in GDP growth is very marginal while the gains, though somewhat reduced, still remain.

The results also give some interesting insights of relevance for the operation of public distribution programs. A program of giving subsidized food imposing a restriction on resale, is regressive when the subsidy rate is small. Such a program does not increase the food energy intake of the poor. Under such restrictions if the budget is limited, it is better to give bigger subsidy on price on a smaller quantity of food rather than a small price subsidy on large quantity of food. It is best to give income subsidy rather than food subsidy.

6

Foreign Trade and Aid Policies

One of the fiercely debated issues in the literature on development economics is the role of foreign trade and aid in the development process, with one side viewing foreign trade as a leading sector ("the engine of growth"), and the other side as a following sector ("the handmaiden of growth"). Much of this debate generated heat rather than light. After all, there can be no denying that voluntary participation in the world economy can only augment a country's production possibilities — exporting part of a country's production in exchange for what is produced elsewhere, is nothing more nor less than adding a technique of transforming domestic resources into desired goods and services, in addition to those available at home. Participation in world capital markets enables a country to augment its investment opportunities.

It is clear that by efficiently exploiting the trading and investment opportunities available in world markets a country can achieve higher levels of real income and possibly (though not necessarily) a faster rate of growth as well. The efficiency of exploitation will depend on the policies pursued. An "outward-oriented" strategy that does not unduly tilt production for sale either in domestic or in foreign markets is likely to be efficient. Such a strategy will minimize the present value of resource costs of meeting present and future final demands. Apart from this analytical argument, competitive pressure from imports in the domestic markets and from rival exporters in foreign markets will place a premium on production efficiency. Although the arguments in favour of an outward development strategy are well known and obvious, many developing countries including India chose an inward-oriented autarkic development strategy with import-substituting industrialization at its core, when they launched their plans for economic development. By now, there is extensive evidence from a large number of countries of the failure of such a strategy either to create a diversified, cost-efficient and rapidly-growing industrial sector or even to alleviate the recurring foreign exchange shortages (Bhagwati

1978; Krueger 1978, 1981 and 1983; Krueger et al., 1981). The Indian experience has been analyzed by Bhagwati and Desai (1970), Bhagwati and Srinivasan (1976) and Ahluwalia (1985). The considerably better performance of a few outward oriented countries, not only in generating efficient and rapid growth but weathering adverse shocks such as the changes in oil prices, is also well documented (Balassa 1981, 1984a, 1984b and 1986).

The role of external capital (private and public) in the development process is also controversial. There are those who view foreign investment by the rich and industrialized North in the poor and non-industrialized South (or lending to the South), as a means of exploitation by the economically powerful of the economically weak. There are others who take such investment as always beneficial to both parties, ignoring the distinction between capital markets and commodity markets, and in particular the problems associated with sovereign lending, and also that in an otherwise distorted economy, foreign investment may be welfare-worsening. In any case, official capital flows from developed countries have declined substantially as a proportion of their GNP. Also, private flows (bank-lending and direct foreign investment) are at a standstill because of the debt crisis of the eighties. Thus the quantitative significance of external finance in total investment in the developing world has diminished despite the role that a larger volume of capital could have played in raising living standards and growth rates in poor countries.

Our Walrasian model, in which only real flows and relative prices matter, cannot obviously deal with financial flows. More important, with its aggregation of all non-agricultural activities (whether producing internationally-traded goods or purely domestic non-traded goods) into one sector producing traded goods, it is not well-equipped to analyze trade policies relating to the industrial sector in which distortions are very serious. However, some broad issues, such as the implications of eliminating all trade barriers (tariff and non-tariff), and of varying the level of foreign trade deficit (viewed as equivalent to real external resource inflow), can be analyzed. This is what we do in this chapter. Before describing the relevant policy scenarios and the results, we present a brief review of India's external transactions (exports, imports, and flows, etc.) and policies towards foreign trade and aid.

6.1   Indian Foreign Trade and Payment Policies

Until 1957, India's foreign payments position was comfortable, with the availability of reserves ('sterling balances') accumulated during the Second World War and with the modest size and import requirements of the First Five

Year Plan (1951-56). Within a year of (the launching of) the substantially larger Second Plan in 1956, with its emphasis on foreign exchange intensive investment in the heavy industries, a foreign exchange crisis of major proportions developed. The import control and foreign exchange allocation regimes, instituted in response to the crisis have governed the external transactions of the Indian economy since then (of course, with some changes in recent years). In brief, the available foreign exchange from exports and foreign aid after deducting the cost of essential imports such as on food, fertilizers, crude oil, and defence needs, was allocated through licenses issued on a strict priority basis to different categories of importers. Public and private sectors were distinguished. The two important criteria for issuing import licenses were essentiality and indigenous unavailability. The latter, in effect, meant that imports were not allowed if a domestic substitute was available, regardless of the cost, quality or timeliness of delivery. Direct imports of non-essential non-food consumer goods were discouraged, though maintenance (raw materials and spare parts) imports for units producing domestic substitutes for such goods were allowed. Transferability between licensees and categories of imports and licenses was restricted. The rigidly restrictive system that prevailed during the Second and Third Plan periods expectedly caused a lot of bureaucratic problems leading to delays, administrative expenses and a lack of coordination among different categories. Besides, as argued by Bhagwati and Srinivasan (BS (1976), henceforth), while the criterion of indigenous availability eliminated competition, the strict licensing procedure for setting up domestic production capacity, which was also initiated during this time, eliminated free entry and efficiency-induced capacity expansion, all of which together eliminated the possibility of cost reduction. One further consequence of such a high-cost inefficient production was a bias against exports. Such a situation prevailed up to May 1966.

The bias against exports in the exchange control regime led to a continuing decline in India's share in world exports further increasing the severity of the foreign exchange constraint. This led to the introduction of a policy of export subsidization in the early 1960s through the grant to exporters of:

(a)   import entitlements (twice the import content of exports subject to a maximum of 75 percent of the f.o.b. value), and

(b)   fiscal concessions such as exemptions from, and/or refunds, of certain direct and indirect taxes like sales tax, custom duties, etc., outright cash subsidies and concessions on rail freight, etc.

The policy of subsidization, though it did not cover many traditional exports, did help in increasing total exports. However, implementation of this policy "was as selective, chaotic and cost-unconscious as the process of automatic protection for import substitution. Thus the subsidization was relatively energetic; but it was not efficient in the neo-classical sense, and as many instances of value-subtraction (at international prices) strongly underlined wasteful in consequence" (BS 1976: 59; see also I.J. Ahluwalia 1985).

The inefficient foreign exchange and investment controls ultimately meant that the domestic resource cost of a unit of foreign exchange saved by discouraging imports, or earned through exports, rose. This meant that the Indian rupee became increasingly overvalued in terms of foreign exchange leading to a large proportion of exports being supported by subsidies at high rates. In part as an attempt to bring some order in the chaotic system the rupee was devalued in June 1966 by 57.5 percent (from Rs.4.76 to Rs.7.50 per US dollar), though as per BS (1976)'s commodity-wise calculations (adjusting for the export subsidies and import entitlements which were removed and for import duties which were reduced simultaneously with the devaluation), the net devaluation for exports and receipts on current account amounted to only 21.6 percent and 22.3 percent respectively. Corresponding figures for imports and payments on current account were 42.3 and 44.8 respectively. It is to be noted that some of these export subsidies and import entitlements (as a replenishment instead of entitlement) were introduced again for promoting exports.

The political and economic effects of the devaluation became controversial. With two consecutive years of severe drought in 1965-66 and 1966-67, prices of almost all commodities went up. Though, at constant prices, income increased slightly, agricultural income went down due to drought. Private investment increased, but public investment remained more or less stagnant; finally, both exports and imports went down. However, non-traditional exports increased during this period while the drought not only resulted in a fall in real income from agriculture but also in a fall in agriculture-based traditional exports. Public investment stagnated during this period for reasons that were not related to devaluation (see Srinivasan and Narayana (1977)). Segregating the drought effects and devaluation effects, BS (1976, p.146) argued that "the devaluation, in so far as it replaced the earlier ad-hoc and selective subsidies on exports, was aimed at rationalizing the indiscriminate and uneconomic way of subsidizing exports".

In the 1970s, the policy perspectives changed towards a greater emphasis on export promotion partly because the cost of further import substitution had increased. In fact, the fervor with which the strategy of import substitution had earlier been advocated regardless of costs now shifted to export planning and promotion, once again with little attention being paid to costs. For example, a report of a study group (NCAER 1969) argued that while efforts should be made to reduce inefficient high costs of domestic production, "exports cannot wait for cost reduction". Since the volume of exports depends basically on their profitability, it further argued that "we should match our prices with the international prices, irrespective of our cost of production" (see NCAER (1969: 128, 130)). Also see other official reports in this context (Parliament's Export Policy Resolution 1970; the Report of the Committee on Export Strategy, 1980s; and the Report of the Import and Export Policies 1978).

The linking of the Indian rupee with the depreciating pound-sterling soon after the collapse of the Brettonwoods system of fixed exchange rates in 1971 (and subsequently to a basket of foreign currencies) brought, in effect, a further mild but not insignificant devaluation which helped exports. Apparently, however, export promotion appears to have been pushed regardless of private and social costs involved. Such a strategy is clearly a prescription for economic trouble. S.K. Verghese (1978), after pointing out that a significant fraction of the increase in the value of India's exports during the 1970s was because of some fortuitous circumstance, questions the real effect of subsidies on exports and doubts whether these effects, if any, are sustainable. After netting out from the value of total exports the values of grants to Bangladesh, and the unanticipated, temporary increases in sugar and silver exports, the growth rate in the net exports, adjusted for either a trade-weighted exchange rate or unit value of exports, turns out to be much lower than the nominal growth rates.* Verghese computed the total value of export subsidies consisting of cash assistance, customs duty drawbacks and opportunity cost of the subsidized export credits and found it to be rising over time, and disproportionate to the relative performance of subsidized over unsubsidized exports. Although one may correctly argue that subsidies in the case of some commodities are necessary correctives for domestic distortions, this is not the case in general. Some commodities were subsidized even though the net increase in foreign exchange earnings by exporting them is zero or even negative! A policy of subsidization, if continued without economically meaningful criteria for the selection of commodities to be subsidized and the rates of subsidy, may again lead to as "chaotic" a situation as was prevailing prior to the 1966 devaluation.** Budgetary expenditures on export promotion now account for

---

*   Indian exports of silver were Rs. 5.6 crores in 1973-74 and Rs. 174.1 crores in 1975-76; total value of exports to Bangladesh was Rs.372.56 crores between 1971-72 and 1975-76; sugar price in 1974 was more than five times what it was in 1970.

**   The import-export policy for 1984-85 announced by the Union Commerce Minister in the Indian Parliament on April 13, 1984 took into account for the first time, the criteria of "net foreign exchange earnings" and "value-addition"; the latter implies a shift towards value-added items from primary commodities.

nearly 6% of the value of exports.

We have plotted in Figure 6.1 the time path of India's exports, imports and exchange rate, whereas in Figure 6.2 are shown capital inflows and balance of payments. Table 6.1 presents data on the changing structure of India's exports and Table 6.2 shows imports and exports of food and fertilizers.

6.2 Foodgrains Imports

Ensuring an adequate domestic availability of foodgrains has always been a major concern of Indian policy makers. Even during the regime of tight import controls, imports of foodgrains remained a priority item. Foodgrains can be imported only by the government. Imports played a major role in maintaining the public food distribution system in pre-green revolution years. But in the fifties and sixties when concessional imports were available from the USA under PL 480 against rupee payments into a blocked account, because of the revenue generated by domestic sales of these imports, foodgrains were imported even in years of adequate domestic production.

Foodgrains imports as a fraction of net production never amounted to more than 9 percent except during the two drought years, 1965-66 and 1966-67, when the imports amounted to 14.1 and 11.7 percent. In these two years the largest ever amounts of 28.6 kg. and 26.1 kg. per capita of foodgrains were publicly distributed.

Concessional imports of foodgrains under PL 480 played multiple roles. It augmented domestic supply without having to spend scarce foreign exchange for imports. It was also a source of revenue for the government. The final impact of these revenues, and the impact on the money supply and price inflation of the deposits made to a special account of the rupee payments for the imports, has been controversial (see Uma Srivastava et al. 1975 and Sundaram 1967, 1970.)

Many economists deemed such food imports to have hurt producer incentives in both the short term and long term, while encouraging consumption. Raj Krishna (1967) attributed the government's failure to increase domestic procurement while production was increasing, to the easy availability of these imports. More important are the long-term implications on production. The econometric analysis of J.S.Mann (1967) based on a simultaneous equations model showed that PL 480 imports depressed prices and production. However, Mann assumed that there were no differences in marketing imported and domestically-produced grains and that the two were perfect substitutes in consumption. Uma Srivastava et al. (1975), reformulated his model without making

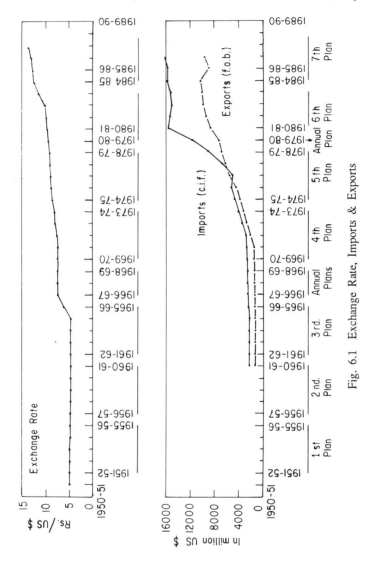

Fig. 6.1   Exchange Rate, Imports & Exports

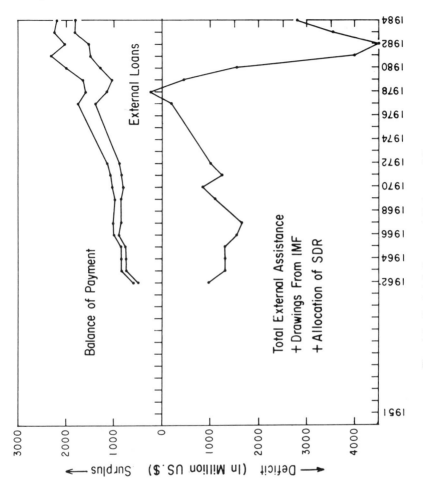

Fig. 6.2 Capital Inflows and Balance of Payments

TABLE 6.1 Exports of traditional commodities (as percentage of total exports)

Year	Cotton yarn and manufactures	Jute yarn and manufactures	Fruits and vegetables and preparations	Leather and leather manufactures	Coir yarn manufactures	Tobacco raw materials manufactures	Coffee and sugar (including molasses)	Tea	Hides skins raw, tanned and dressed	Spices	Total of 1 to 10
	(1)	(2)	(3)	(4)	(5)	(6)	(7)	(8)	(9)	(10)	(11)
1951	22.36	18.96	1.79	3.40	1.79	2.42	0.25	13.0	4.69	3.78	72.44
1956	11.50	19.83	2.60	3.85	1.61	3.77	0.41	18.30	4.88	1.79	68.54
1961	9.38	20.47	3.98	3.78	1.31	4.60	1.59	18.72	5.20	2.51	71.54
1966	7.68	22.59	4.35	3.52	1.32	5.03	2.06	14.19	4.66	2.85	69.25
1971	6.39	12.41	4.26	4.74	0.85	2.14	3.58	9.73	4.98	2.55	51.63

Source : Data on the Indian Economy, Trade Development Authority January 1972.

TABLE 6.2 Imports and Export of food and fertilizers

Year	Wheat Imports (mt.)	Rice Imports (mt.)	Import of other cereals (mt.)	Import of pulses (mt.)	Value cereal imports (m Rs)	Edible Oil seeds (000) ton	Edible Oil seeds m. Rs.	Veg. oil Import (000) ton	Veg. oil Import m.Rs.	Sugar Export (000) ton	Sugar Export m. Rs.	Fish Exports (000) ton	Fertilizer nutrient imports (000) ton
1951	3.063	0.761	0.977	—	2167.9								
1952	2.551	0.734	0.641	—	2090.7								
1953	1.711	0.178	0.146	—	859.5								
1954	0.198	0.628	0.008	-0.002	485.3								
1955	0.440	0.165	-0.009	-0.083	331.1								
1956	1.104	0.287	-0.002	-0.017	563.4								
1957	2.879	0.747	—	-0.006	1623.9								
1958	2.709	0.396	0.111	-0.006	1205.1				16.0	8.0			
1959	3.543	0.295	0.020	-0.007	1414.1				17.8	8.0			
1960	4.376	0.699	0.052	-0.008	1928.4	48.0	54.0	4.0	6.0	267.9	133.0	34	419
1961	3.090	0.384	0.019	-0.007	1295.6	47.0	50.0	-32.0	-50.0	373.3	148.0	24	332
1962	3.249	0.390	—	-0.010	1410.9	48.0	50.0	-87.0	-133.0	478.6	323.0	36	295
1963	4.071	0.480	—	-0.015	1836.0	43.0	45.0	-60.0	-97.0	243.3	191.0	42	290
1964	5.621	0.642	—	-0.011	2662.5	53.0	68.0	43.0	55.0	266.8	116.0	30	302
1965	6.572	0.780	0.095	-0.008	2903.2	39.0	49.0	30.0	46.0	441.2	178.0	38	413
1966	7.827	0.776	1.733	-0.025	5231.3	30.0	46.0	47.0	143.0	216.6	148.0	44	898
1967	6.400	0.448	1.817	-0.006	5321.6	3.0	9.0	-9.0	-25.0	98.7	104.0	50	1486
1968	4.766	0.443	0.478	-0.016	3612.0	-12.0	-61.0	61.0	132.0	94.0	98.0	62	1196
1969	3.090	0.471	0.285	-0.022	2530.1	-6.0	-21.0	59.0	166.0	318.4	257.0	74	881
1970	3.406	0.179	-0.006	-0.032	2075.5	67.0	53.0	57.0	146.0	331.7	315.0	68	629
1971	1.811	0.224	-0.008	-0.017	1234.6								997

TABLE 6.2 (*contd.*)

Year	Wheat Imports (mt.)	Rice Imports (mt.)	Import of other cereals (mt.)	Import of pulses (mt.)	Value cereal imports (m Rs)	Edible Oil seeds (000) ton	Edible Oil seeds m. Rs.	Veg. oil Import (000) ton	Veg. oil Import m.Rs.	Sugar Export (000) ton	Sugar Export m. Rs.	Fish Exports (000) ton	Fertilizer nutrient imports (000) ton
1972	-0.492	0.014	-0.013	-0.007	242.9	16.0	10.0	20.0	21.0	98.8	125.0	76	1194
1973	2.413	-0.018	1.195	-0.003	3195.2	43.0	3.0	103.0	125.0	248.9	422.0	98	1244
1974	4.460	0.006	0.689	0.001	4630.4	-62.0	-267.0	24.0	-159.0	443.4	2042.0	94	1602
1975	7.182	-0.139	0.215	—	10579.0	-83.0	-379.0	-56.0	-148.0	966.1	4390.0	106	1556
1976	6.296	0.164	0.452	0.006	9822.4	-184.0	-765.0	15.0	226.0	843.4	2664.0	124	1051
1977	0.420	0.003	0.051	0.020	781.6	-20.0	-117.0	378.0	1817.0	254.8	5675.0	130	1521
1978	-0.706	-0.139	0.001	0.217	—	80.0	251.0	281.0	1432.0	636.3	1117.0	156	1987
1979	-0.654	-0.331	0.002	0.127	—	13.0	-80.0	651.0	3610.0	656.0	1463.6	184	2005
1980	-0.010	-0.476	0.003	0.133	—	-17.0	-173.0	948.0	6551.0	64.0	260.5	149	2759

Note : Fertilizer (nutrient) imports correspond to financial years, i.e. 1960-61 figure is shown against 1960 and so on.

TABLE 6.3 Interaction of imports with government's domestic operations: All foodgrains

Year	PL-480 imports (mt) Wheat	Rice	Milo	Corn	Total	Per Capita (kg/yr)	Total foodgrains imports Total (mt)	Per capita (kg/yr)	Availability Total (mt)	Per capita (kg/yr)	Public Distribution Total (mt.)	per capita (kg/yr)	Population (millions)	Percapita Procurement all foodgrains (kg/yr)	Public Stocks foodgrains (mt.)
1951							4.801	13.22	52.346	144.1	7.99	22.0	363.26	10.54	—
1952							3.926	10.63	51.961	140.7	6.80	18.41	369.30	9.42	1.95
1953							2.035	5.42	56.579	150.6	4.60	12.24	375.69	5.32	1.47
1954							0.832	2.18	63.915	167.1	2.15	5.62	382.50	3.74	1.67
1955							0.513	1.32	63.156	162.0	1.64	4.21	389.85	0.33	0.92
1956	0.15	—	—	—	0.15	0.38	1.372	3.45	62.642	157.6	2.08	5.23	397.47	0.10	0.32
1957	2.51	0.20	—	0.03	2.71	6.68	3.620	8.93	66.164	163.2	3.05	7.52	405.42	0.74	1.18
1958	1.90	—	0.09	—	2.02	4.88	3.210	7.75	61.779	149.2	3.98	9.61	414.07	1.28	0.91
1959	3.18	—	0.01	0.01	3.20	7.56	3.851	9.10	72.312	170.9	5.16	12.20	423.12	4.28	1.40
1960	4.04	0.26	0.03	0.02	4.35	10.06	5.119	11.83	71.196	164.6	4.94	11.42	432.54	2.96	2.80
1961	2.12	0.19	0.02	—	2.33	5.27	3.486	7.88	75.686	171.1	3.98	9.00	442.35	1.22	2.64
1962	2.70	0.19	—	—	2.89	6.39	3.629	8.02	76.081	168.2	4.36	9.64	452.32	1.06	2.28
1963	3.90	0.30	—	—	4.20	9.09	4.536	9.82	74.846	162.0	5.18	11.21	462.01	1.62	2.26
1964	5.25	0.33	—	—	5.58	11.82	6.252	13.24	78.107	165.4	8.66	18.34	472.23	3.03	1.02
1965	5.93	0.29	0.10	—	6.32	13.10	7.439	15.42	84.572	175.3	10.08	20.89	482.44	8.35	2.08
1966	6.48	—	1.73	0.01	8.22	16.67	10.311	20.91	73.478	149.0	14.08	28.55	493.14	8.13	2.22
1967	4.02	—	1.82	—	5.84	11.58	8.659	17.17	73.871	146.5	13.17	26.12	504.24	8.84	1.96
1968	3.61	—	0.47	0.02	4.10	7.95	5.671	11.00	86.807	168.4	10.22	19.83	515.48	13.19	3.99
1969	2.16	0.10	0.30	—	2.56	4.86	3.824	7.26	85.623	162.5	9.38	17.80	526.91	12.11	4.45
1970	2.45	—	—	—	2.45	4.55	3.547	6.58	89.494	166.1	8.84	16.41	538.80	12.48	5.57

Table 6.3 *(Contd.)*

| Year | PL-480 imports (mt) | | | | | | Total foodgrains imports | | Availability | | Public Distribution | | Population (millions) | Percapita Procurement all foodgrains (kg/yr) | Public Stocks foodgrains (mt.) |
	Wheat	Rice	Milo	Corn	Total	Per Capita (kg/yr)	Total (mt)	Per capita (kg/yr)	Total (mt)	Per captia (kg/yr)	Total (mt.)	per capita (kg/yr)			
1971	1.21	—	—	—	1.21	2.20	2.010	3.65	94.311	171.1	7.82	14.19	551.20	16.07	8.14
1972	—	—	—	—	—	—	-0.498	-0.88	96.218	170.6	11.40	20.23	563.5	13.60	3.44
1973	—	—	—	—	—	—	3.587	6.23	88.794	154.0	11.41	19.81	575.9	14.63	3.13
1974	0.79	—	—	—	0.79	1.31	5.156	8.76	97.142	164.7	10.79	18.34	588.3	9.60	2.73
1975	0.41	0.10	—	—	0.51	0.83	7.536	12.54	89.325	148.1	11.25	18.73	600.8	15.92	8.29
1976	—	—	—	—	—	—	6.918	11.28	102.080	166.4	9.17	14.95	613.3	20.96	19.03
1977	—	—	—	—	—	—	0.494	0.79	99.391	157.6	11.73	18.74	625.8	15.94	17.41
1978	—	—	—	—	—	—	-0.627	-0.98	110.225	170.9	10.18	15.95	638.4	17.38	17.16
1979	—	—	—	—	—	—	-0.856	-1.31	114.199	173.2	11.66	17.91	651.0	21.27	17.52
1980	—	—	—	—	—	—	-0.350	-0.53	101.418	150.4	14.99	22.59	663.6	16.84	11.74
1981	—	—	—	—	—	—	0.777	1.14	114.865	167.9	13.11	19.16	684.1	18.90	

these assumptions. Their results indicated that increasing PL 480 imports depress cereal prices and increase demand and concessional distribution. They found that each kilogram of PL 480 imports depressed production of cereals by 0.027841 kg. per capita over a 14 year period. Our model is well suited for the analysis of incentive effects in a general equilibrium context unlike the partial and sectoral econometric models.

K.N. Raj (1966) and later N.K. Chandra (1975) argued that the food imports could have been eliminated had the foodgrains been distributed equitably on the basis of energy requirements. However, as Bhagwati and Chakravarty (1969) (BC 1969 , henceforth) pointed out, under such a scheme the unsatisfied excess demand of the rich for foodgrains would have spilled over into the consumption of other commodities such as tea and textiles, thereby reducing the export surplus of these commodities and foreign exchange earnings. Thus, eliminating foodgrains imports may not save much foreign exchange. This argument once again points to the need for taking into account the general equilibrium effects of major policy changes as we do in our model.

The USA imposed certain conditions on PL 480 imports including the mode of shipment to be used (K.C.S. Acharya 1983). Two of the more important conditions were: the recipient country had to import a minimum specified quantity of the grains on a commercial basis (sometimes from the US itself) and the recipient country had to "take all possible measures to prevent the export of any commodity of either domestic or foreign origin which is the same as, or like, the commodities financed under this agreement during the export limitation period ..." (K.C.S. Acharya 1983: 86). While the prices of the PL 480 imports had consistently been higher than those of commercial imports, from 1967 onwards, even the advantage of payment in local currency tapered off with a gradual transition to payment in hard currency. The only remaining attraction was that a long-term credit at low interest rates was available for PL 480 imports. In any case, large scale PL 480 imports were discontinued in 1972.

With the introduction of high yielding variety seeds in 1965, the green revolution was ushered in, first in wheat and then in rice. Irrigated area also expanded. Consequently the production of wheat nearly quadrupled in the 21 year period 1964-65 to 1985-86 and rice production increased by 170%. Domestic procurement began to take on the role of a price-support operation. By the year 1978, foodgrains imports, which supported the public distribution, were completely eliminated. With public stocks at a level of nearly 18 million tons in 1979, 15 million tons of foodgrains were distributed without importing any in the drought year 1979-80 in which the total output of foodgrains fell by 17% from its peak in the previous year. The satisfactory

growth of foodgrains production was not matched by other agricultural commodities. In part, the output of foodgrains increased by gaining area from other
crops. Sugar was exported in large amounts in the 1970s only to be followed
by imports in the eighties. Vegetable oil imports have increased phenomenally,
accounting for nearly 5% of the total value of imports in 1984-85 as compared to 1.5% in 1970-71. The import-substitution effort, while substantial in
the case of foodgrains, has been relatively insignificant in the agricultural sector
as a whole, compared to the industrial sector.

For stabilizing food consumption levels, one can procure foodgrains domestically and operate buffer stocks. Alternatively, one could import in years of
domestic production shortfall and export in years of excess production relative to consumption. The choice is between operating stocks of foodgrains and
"stocks" of foreign exchange. While storage costs and losses associated with
buffer stocks could be sizeable, foreign exchange reserves do not deteriorate
or get eaten by rodents, and can even earn some returns if invested properly.
See Reutlinger (1978) for a partial equilibrium analysis of this issue. However, world markets can be unstable, and India may not be able to import
large quantities without driving up import prices. Yet access to the world
market does expand the number of options available for meeting domestic
consumption objectives.

While imports use and exports earn foreign exchange and have balance of
payments implications, raising domestic production through subsidies and
acquiring stocks through raising the procurement price have implications for
the government budget.Imports increase the domestic availability of foodgrains,
while increasing procurement prices to acquire more of a given output for
public distribution, does not. Obviously, the issue is a rather complex one,
involving not only the government budget but also social costs and benefits
since the incidence of alternative policies on the welfare of different consumer
groups (e.g. per capita expenditure classes) and producer groups (e.g. size
classes of land ownership) can be different and has to be aggregated. Nevertheless, as Bhagwati and Chakravarty (1969) pointed out, fundamentally
"whether self-sufficiency in foodgrains is an acceptable objective of short term
or long term agricultural policy is itself an issue which must be assessed in
the light of a general equilibrium analysis of the entire economic position,
including aid-flow sensitivity to alternative policies instead of being regarded
as axiomatic". This, in fact, we do with our model. In Table 6.3, we present
the data on concessional and non-concessional imports of foodgrains and some
relevant data on public distribution.

6.3. Foreign Aid

Early development models, such as the celebrated two-gap model of Hollis Chenery and Michael Bruno (1979), emphasized the dual role played by external resources in development, in augmenting the capacity to finance imports, including capital equipment and other development goods, and in enabling more resources to be invested than available from domestic savings. A savings gap arises if the investment needed to attain the target growth in output, exceeds domestic savings. A trade gap arises if the value of imports needed to sustain the investment exceeds the foreign exchange available from exports and foreign aid. There are some unrealistic rigidities assumed in the model e.g., a fixed capital-output ratio and fixed import requirements per unit of capacity creation. Also, it completely neglects price adjustment, i.e., as a means of alleviating, if not eliminating, the disequilibrium revealed by the existence of one gap or the other. Even then, the model does highlight an important point; namely, the marginal productivity of external resources will be higher when the economy is foreign-exchange-constrained than when it is savings-constrained.

In the two-gap model, foreign exchange from exports and that from external assistance are perfect substitutes for each other. In the real world, external aid, particularly bilateral aid from one government to another, comes with some strings attached, such as commodity-tying (i.e., aid can be used to buy only a specified set of commodities), source tying (i.e., aid can be used to buy only from the donor country), project tying (i.e., aid can be used for purchases related to a specific set of projects) and all possible combinations of the three types of tying. It goes without saying that any form of tying reduces the marginal productivity of aid. For example, unless the donor country is not the cheapest source for aid-financed imports, it will not impose source tying. This in turn, means that, for the recipient country, such imports cost more compared to the cheapest source. Unless there is some grant component in external aid, tied aid will not be worth the same as an equal amount of foreign exchange earned through exports. On the other hand, a unit of foreign exchange made available through aid, enables more domestic resources to be released from the production of import substitutes, than the resources needed to earn a unit of foreign exchange through exports, if the economy's import-substitution has imparted significant bias against exports. That is, a unit of foreign exchange through aid is more valuable than a unit of foreign exchange through exports. Thus, given the cost of tying, either the concessional component of aid or the excess cost of import-substitution has to be sufficiently large to make tied aid acceptable over acquiring the same imported commodity through a reallocation of domestic resources towards exports. The concessional component of aid can be assessed by comparing aid received with the present value of repayments at the social rate of discount, taking into account any grace period that may be associated with aid.

In Table 6.4, data relating to foreign aid and public gross capital formation are given. It is seen that, over the years, external assistance has become quite a small fraction of public investment.

TABLE 6.4 Public investment and total external assistance
(Rs. crores: current prices)

Year	Public GDCF	Public GDFCF	Total external assistance
1950-51	259	224	—
1951-52	303	262	78.7
1952-53	256	281	42.0
1953-54	292	327	18.2
1954-55	436	394	9.6
1955-56	499	533	37.1
1956-57	666	615	112.6
1957-58	833	643	253.6
1958-59	815	701	325.8
1959-60	900	884	283.4
1960-61	1141	1054	399.2
1961-62	1147	1107	331.5
1962-63	1445	1312	433.5
1963-64	1681	1562	568.7
1964-65	1948	1824	710.0
1965-66	2216	2046	757.4
1966-67	2135	2046	1131.4
1967-68	2332	2012	1195.6
1968-69	2168	2111	902.6
1969-70	2259	2190	856.3
1970-71	2773	2394	791.4
1971-72	3165	2802	834.1
1972-73	3607	3619	666.2
1973-74	4814	4009	1035.7
1974-75	5664	4272	1314.3
1975-76	7677	5600	1840.5
1976-77	8508	7058	1598.9
1977-78	7408	7672	1290.0
1978-79	9999	9144	1265.8

Source: National Accounts Statistics (CSO) and Economic Surveys of Government of India;
Bhagwati and Srinivasan (1976).

Note: Gross Domestic Fixed Capital Formation (GDFCF) = Gross Domestic Capital Formation (GDCF) - Change in stocks.

6.4   The Scenarios

Before turning to the scenarios, it is worth recalling in brief some important features of the way in which foreign trade and aid policies have been incorporated in our model, and of the particular policies embodied in the reference scenario. The full details have already been discussed in Chapter 4.

First, the traditional distinctions between balance of trade, balance of payments in the current account and capital account are not maintained in the model. The balance on all items of the current account and capital account are aggregated into a single figure called, somewhat misleadingly, the trade deficit. This is expressed in terms of the numeraire of the model, namely, sector 10. In the reference scenario the trade deficit is exogenously set at 1.5% of GDP. Since one of the capital items, viz., foreign aid is part of the trade deficit the way we have defined it, variation in aid is translated into an equivalent variation in the trade deficit.

Second, for simplicity, the entire foreign trade sector is treated as a public sector operation. This means that the foreign capital inflow corresponding to the trade accrues to the government. Since all commodities are internationally-traded in our model, any difference between the domestic price and the world price of a commodity is a tariff or subsidy on its traded volume, thus generating revenues or expenditure on subsidies. This means that, the effects of policy changes on domestic prices and hence, on the government budget have to be taken into account.

Third, we have in effect set trade quotas, i.e., maximum and minimum bounds on traded volumes. A variation in a quota which continues to be binding, or which becomes binding (not binding), even if it was not (was) to begin with will have domestic price effects. Thus, changes in quotas are instruments of trade policy which have price (and as before government budget) effects. The precise way in which effective trade bounds are set is already described in Chapter 3.

Fourth, we steer the target price for any period t of a commodity towards its world price over a period from its realized domestic price in period t-1. If the world price is realized as the domestic price in year t-1 then this procedure will set the world price as the target price. Of course, this target will be realized as a domestic price in year t so that the target for year t + 1 also becomes the world price provided that the bounds on trade volumes and stocks are not binding in period t. Also, by setting the bounds on trade volumes fairly wide and setting world prices as target prices, one ensures this happens. Indeed, this is how we implemented a free trade policy in our model. We now turn to the policy scenarios other than the standard reference scenario REF.

FRT: Free trade scenario. Target and realized domestic prices equal world prices.

SFR: A scenario in which the trade deficit is set at zero from 1990 on. This could be termed the self-reliance scenario as the nation entirely meets its import bill with its export earnings. Investment is maintained as in REF with the average tax rate adjusting to the loss of revenue from foreign aid.

REFR: Same as REF except that the effective bounds on trade widened somewhat (see Table 4.6). This scenario serves as a reference scenario for the following two scenarios in which foreign capital is increased substantially.

LANR: A liberal aid scenario in which the trade deficit is set at 6% of the GDP as contrasted with 1.5% in REFR. The entire additional aid (4.5% of the GDP) is invested in the non-agricultural sector. This is in addition to the investment behavior specified in the REFR. The tax rate adjusts to absorb the impact of additional revenue from foreign aid. This scenario could be termed an externally-financed growth.

LATR: Same as LANR but additional aid is invested in both agricultural and non-agricultural sectors in the same way as in REFR. Once again the tax rate adjusts to absorb the impact of additional revenue from foreign aid.

LATRX: Same as LATR but the average tax rate is fixed at its REFR values. Additional aid is invested in both sectors. This is simulated as a scenario in which the government does not relax its efforts at domestic savings mobilization when extra aid is available.

6.5   The Results

In comparing the results, we look at the macro-economic indicators, the patterns of trade, and the distributional implications for the various scenarios, in terms of the distribution of the population according to per capita expenditure classes, the average equivalent income and the average food energy intake within each class.

Impact of agricultural trade liberalization: The average improves but the poor are worse off with agricultural trade liberalization.

A comparison of the free trade scenario FRT with REF reveals several interesting features (see Table 6.5). To begin with, the terms of trade for agriculture (P_a/P_{na}) is much more favorable to agriculture in REF than in FRT in 1980, as well as in 2000. This suggests that the set of tariffs and implicit trade quotas in REF significantly protect the agricultural sector as a whole, relative to non-agriculture, against external competition. The apparently paradoxical consequence that removal of trade distortions by following free trade results in a lower real GDP, real agricultural GDP and real non-agricultural GDP can be due to two possibilities. First, a fall in agricultural incomes may lower demand for non-agriculture whose capacity utilization can go down; secondly, the valuation of inputs and outputs at the tariff-inclusive prices of 1970 gives a distorted picture of GDP in the free trade scenario. On the other hand, a comparison of average equivalent income, which is a better indicator of real income changes, shows that free trade leads to a real income increase of 7.13% in 1980 and 5.31% in 2000. Since in REF itself, domestic prices approach world prices by 2000, the smaller increase in real income in 2000 is not surprising. In our two scenarios, world prices are the same, that is, India's move to free trade as in FRT does not change world prices. In fact, however, were India to shift to free trade, world prices would change at least for those few commodities in which India has a significant share in world markets and the impact on India would be different from what we see in FRT as compared to REF. Results of a simultaneous move to free trade in agriculture by all the less developed countries, reported by Parikh et al. (1987), show that the increase in the average equivalent income for India is somewhat smaller than in FRT.

A comparison of the pattern of trade (see Table 6.6) between REF and FRT confirms that agriculture is protected in the former: imports of non-agricultural goods fall significantly in FRT both in 1980 and in 2000 as compared to REF, and imports of bovine and ovine meats and dairy products rise significantly.

In looking at the distributional impact of free trade (see Table 6.7), it has to be kept in mind that the neo-classical proposition that free trade is Pareto-superior (compared to restricted trade) for a price-taking open economy, is based on the possibility of making lump-sum transfers between individuals so that gainers from free trade can compensate the losers and still have some gains. In our free trade scenario, lump-sum transfers are not introduced and, as such, even though the average equivalent income of the economy as a whole goes up with free trade, it does not mean that every class will gain.

It appears that in rural areas the initial effect in 1980 of free trade is to shift the population from the bottom two classes to the top three. By the year 2000, however, while the richest class continues to gain population (relative to REF), the middle three classes lose population while the poorest class has more people in it. In urban areas, the richest class gains population from all

TABLE 6.5   Impact of alternative trade policies on selected
macro-economic indicators

Variable		Reference scenario	Percentage change over reference scenario		
		REF	Free trade FRT	Self reliance SFR	Relaxed trade bounds REFR
GDP*	1980	529.996	0	0	−0.07
	2000	1429.075	−4.69	−0.53	−2.37
GDP Agriculture*	1980	220.337	0	0	−0.16
	2000	353.902	−5.48	−0.48	−3.58
GDP Non agriculture*	1980	309.659	0	0	−0.007
	2000	1075.173	−4.42	−0.54	−1.97
Total investment*	1980	109.943	−4.04	0	−0.29
	2000	492.422	−8.60	−0.99	−5.17
Tax rate (%)	1980	2.3	−475.21	0	−5.21
	2000	9.8	−26.63	24.08	−9.79
Price-index ratio agriculture/ nonagriculture	1980	0.9252	−14.06	0	−2.65
	2000	0.8922	−22.68	−2.28	−16.49
GDP per capita#	1980	786.28	0.37	0	−0.07
	2000	1363.28	−4.69	−0.53	−2.37
Food energy calorie intake (Kcal/person/day)	1980	2162.0	3.33	0	−0.60
	2000	2569.0	−4.39	−1.12	−2.21
Average equivalent income (AEI)**	1980	543.71	7.12	0	0.77
	2000	661.08	5.30	−2.44	3.57
Trade deficit*	1980	7.924	1.18	0	0.56
	2000	21.599	−4.04	−100.0	−1.74

*   109 rupees at 1970 prices.
\#   Rupeees at 1970 prices.
** Income needed at 1970 prices to provide same utility provided by current consumption at current prices.

TABLE 6.6 Net exports under alternative trade policies

Sector	Year	Reference scenario REF	Free trade FRT	Self reliance SFR	Relaxed trade bounds REFR
1. Wheat (million	1980	1.8	−1.5	1.8	1.9
tonnes)	2000	14.07	21.4	13.8	13.6
2. Rice (million	1980	−1.7	−3.07	−1.7	−1.2
tonnes)	2000	0.07	2.06	0.9	2.7
3. Coarse grains	1980	−3.7	−5.1	−3.7	−3.3
(million tonnes)	2000	−5.4	−3.4	−5.5	−3.6
4. Bovine and ovine	1980	7.1	14.7	8.1	−27.06
meat (thousand tonnes[a])	2000	13.1	−397.03	13.4	−303.8
5. Dairy (thousand	1980	−2397.9	−10945.0	−2397.9	−2231.0
tonnes[b])	2000	−5934.5	−22113.0	−5902.7	−14367.0
6. Other animal	1980	0	−45.38	0	−11.6
products (thousand tonnes[c])	2000	−15.37	−139.24	−16.90	-149.8
7. Protein feeds	1980	664.4	668.9	664.4	661.2
(thousand tonnes)	2000	898.1	825.05	892.5	853.06
8. Other foods	1980	1338.4	2434.8	1338.4	1399.8
(million 1970 US$[d])	2000	−318.1	−1085.6	495.8	−544.9
9. Non-food	1980	18.8	−736.1	18.8	−179.1
agriculture (million 1970 US$[d])	2000	27.5	−1867.6	27.3	−781.5
10. Non-agriculture	1980	−1416.4	−799.9	−1416.4	−1362.6
(Million 1970 US$[d])	2000	−2786.8	−92.7	−749.1	−1178.8

a Carcass weight.
b Fresh milk equivalent.
c Protein equivalent.
d Using an exchange rate of Rs. 7.50 per dollar.

TABLE 6.7 Distributional impact of free trade, FRT

	Percentage change over reference scenario, REF				
	Expenditure classes with per capita equivalent income at 1970 prices				
	<216	216-336	336-516	516-900	>900
Rural 1980					
Population	−9.8	−1.1	1.7	1.1	18.7
Equivalent income	−6.8	−9.7	−8.8	−7.9	3.1
Calorie level	1.1	−1.7	−3.7	−4.5	3.1
Urban 1980					
Population	−36.8	−25.3	−13.9	−1.2	15.2
Equivalent income	−6.0	−6.3	−3.2	−0.6	10.0
Calorie level	5.2	1.7	0.7	−0.3	3.0
Rural 2000					
Population	20.0	−1.3	−13.2	−16.7	10.0
Equivalent income	−9.0	−8.5	−8.1	−5.9	4.4
Calorie level	−9.7	−10.2	−10.9	−12.2	−1.8
Urban 2000					
Population	0	−12.5	−14.4	−9.4	10.4
Equivalent income	0.8	−0.2	2.0	3.2	10.9
Calorie level	−1.6	−2.0	−0.6	0.2	5.3

the other classes in 1980 and in 2000. In terms of equivalent income, all but the richest class in rural areas in 1980 and 2000, and in urban areas in 1980, lose. In 2000, every urban class, except class 2, gains, while the latter loses a negligible amount compared to REF.

Comparing the self-reliance scenario with REF (Table 6.5), the differences in macro-economic indicators for 2000 are negligible. This is to be expected because investment was left essentially unchanged while eliminating the trade deficit from 1990 on. The move to self-reliance does not change the trade pattern (Table 6.6), except that sector 8 (other food agriculture) becomes a net exporter in SFR as compared to being a net importer in REF. Apart from this sector, the only sector in which the change in trade volume is sizeable, is non-agriculture, with imports cut drastically as compared to REF. The distributional effects (Table 6.8), are quantitatively small. Population shifts (in 2000)to the poorest and the richest class from the others in rural areas, and to the richest class from all others except the poorest two, in which it is unchanged, in urban areas. The average equivalent income of the richest class in rural areas goes down by about 3% with the incomes of the other classes essentially unchanged. Every class in urban areas loses some equivalent income,

TABLE 6.8 Distributional impact of self-reliance, SFR

| | Percentage change over reference scenario, REF | | | | |
| | Expenditure classes with per capita equivalent income at 1970 prices | | | | |
	<216	216-336	336-516	516-900	>900
Rural 1980					
Population	0	0	0	0	0
Equivalent income	0	0	0	0	0
Calorie level	0	0	0	0	0
Urban 1980					
Population	0	0	0	0	0
Equivalent income	0	0	0	0	0
Calorie level	0	0	0	0	0
Rural 2000					
Population	1.4	0	−1.1	−1.4	0.9
Equivalent income	−0.2	0	0.1	−0.3	−2.8
Calorie level	0.1	0.3	0.1	−0.2	−1.8
Urban 2000					
Population	0	0	−1.6	−0.6	0.6
Equivalent income	−0.3	−0.6	−1.2	−2.2	−4.9
Calorie level	0.2	−0.3	−1.0	−1.6	−2.5

the loss being 1.2%, 2.1% and 4.9% in the third, fourth and fifth class respectively. Applying the Willig-Bailey criterion, there is some deterioration in social welfare in SFR compared to REF. The quantitatively modest changes induced by the elimination of the trade deficit is to be expected, since aid as a proportion of investment or GDP is small in the model, and in the Indian economy, so that its elimination does not cause significant effects.

It may be noted that this self-reliance scenario is only a zero trade deficit scenario and not an autarchy scenario. Moreover, with one aggregated non-agriculture sector, imports are fully substitutable in the model by domestic production. Thus the impact of self-reliance will be somewhat muted in the model. None the less the model results are not surprising, for Indian economy gets relatively very little net aid.

Larger aid for investment: The scenarios, with relaxed bounds on trade, were simulated essentially to allow a greater scope for efficient utilization of additional aid, the idea being that with the bounds as in the standard reference run, extra aid may be used to import those commodities for which the bounds are relatively wide, rather than commodities that would be imported had there been relatively free trade, i.e., commodities in which the economy has no comparative advantage. Indeed, a comparison of REF with REFR (see Tables 6.5 and 6.6) shows significant changes in trade volumes and trade policies. For example, while non-food agriculture is an export sector in REF both in 1980 and 2000, it is an import sector in both years in REFR. As it is to be expected, the trade patterns in REFR are almost as the trade pattern in FRT, the free trade run, which is consistent with the comparative advantage argument given above. Since REFR was simulated primarily as a basis of comparison with LANR, LATR and LTRX we need not compare REFR with REF in detail.

Turning to LANR, with aid quadrupled and all the additional aid invested in non-agriculture, the real non-agricultural GDP (the total GDP) in 2000 is about 18.2% (13.9%) higher, compared to REFR (Table 6.9)

The only change in the trade pattern (see Table 6.10) is that a marginal amount of rice is imported in the year 2000, rather than exported, as in REFR. Trade volumes change significantly in three sectors. Exports of other food agriculture increases in 1980 and it is imported in a larger volume in 2000. Imports of non-agricultural commodities increase substantially both in 1980 and in 2000. Imports of dairy products decline in 1980 and rise marginally in 2000. On the one hand, the government revenue increases with additional aid flowing into its coffers. On the other, the additional aid changes the trade volumes and the trade pattern in some sectors, thereby affecting the revenues from trade taxes and subsidies. The net effect is a decrease (increase) in total revenues and hence, an increase (decrease) in the tax rate in 1980 (2000) in LANR compared to REFR. Domestic terms of trade of agriculture improve in 2000.

The distributional impact (Table 6.11) of additional aid in LANR is beneficial. In 2000 there are fewer people in the poorest class in rural areas and more in the richest class. The equivalent incomes are also higher for all classes. In 2000, the urban population shifts to the highest income class from all other classes and the equivalent incomes are also higher. Thus, a Bailey-Willig comparison shows welfare improvement in 2000 for both the rural and the urban populations. In 1980, however, there is a small loss in equivalent incomes of the richer classes in both rural and urban areas, resulting from a higher tax rate (which was 2% in 1980 in REFR and becomes 5% in LANR). The increase in tax rate caused by the change in tariff revenues is the result of the changed structure of trade.

Change in sectoral allocation pattern of additional investment: Since LATR differs from LANR only in that a part, rather than all, of the additional investment from foreign aid goes to the non-agricultural sectors, it is to be expected that real agricultural GDP is higher, and non-agricultural GDP lower,

TABLE 6.9 Impact of increased capital inflow on selected macro- economic indicators

Variable	Year	Percentage change over reference run with relaxed trade bounds, REFR		
		Additional aid for non-agriculture LANR	Additional aid for investment LATR	Additional aid for investment with tax rates fixed LATRX
GDP*	1980	0	0	0
	2000	13.9	11.2	10.2
GDP agriculture*	1980	0	0	0
	2000	0.7	4.3	4.2
GDP non-agriculture*	1980	0	0	0
	2000	18.2	13.4	12.1
Total investment*	1980	20.9	20.9	15.1
	2000	31.0	26.7	30.1
Tax rate	1980	129.4	107.8	0
	2000	−43.4	−35.2	0
Price-index ratio (aricultural/non-agricultural)	1980	0	0	0
	2000	11.4	5.6	2.5
GDP per capita*	1980	0	0	0
	2000	13.3	11.2	10.3
Food energy calorie intake (Kcal/person/day)	1980	−0.6	−0.6	0
	2000	5.9	5.8	3.7
Average equiva-lent income	1980	−1.56	−1.56	0
	2000	11.5	9.0	5.0
Trade deficit*	1980	300.0	300.0	300.0
	2000	352.9	343.5	340.1

* At 1970 prices.

TABLE 6.10   Net exports

Sector	Year	Additional aid for non-agri cultural investment LANR	Additional aid for investment LATR	Additional aid for investment with tax rates fixed LATRX
1. Wheat	1980	2.07	2.07	1.96
	2000	13.68	14.27	14.30
2. Rice	1980	−1.12	−1.12	−1.29
	2000	−3.38	5.37	7.68
3. Coarse grain	1980	−3.35	−3.35	−3.39
	2000	−4.96	−3.84	−3.26
4. Bovine and ovine meat	1980	−18.07	−18.07	−27.06
	2000	−316.46	−314.12	−310.79
5. Dairy	1980	−1693.95	−1693.95	−2230.44
	2000	−14736.21	−14714.39	−14587.88
6. Other animal products	1980	−9.60	−9.60	−11.68
	2000	−151.23	−151.09	−150.79
7. Protein feed	1980	661.27	661.27	661.27
	2000	862.59	905.43	903.78
8. Other foods	1980	1641.06	1641.06	1399.84
	2000	−5011.80	−2768.09	−1255.01
9. Non-food agriculture	1980	−141.26	−141.26	−179.15
	2000	−803.60	−808.20	−801.60
10. Non-agri- culture	1980	−3848.19	−3848.19	−3578.27
	2000	−6639.64	−8781.11	−9891.13

in LATR compared to LANR. Aggregate GDP is also lower because the capital-output ratio in agriculture is higher (see Table 6.9). The pattern and volume of trade (except in the case of rice in 2000) and the tax rates are not significantly different for LANR and LATR. However, the domestic terms of trade of agriculture are, as expected, far lower than their corresponding value in LANR and slightly higher than that in REFR.

TABLE 6.11 Distributional impact of additional aid for non-agricultural investment, LANR

| | Percentage change over relaxed trade bounds reference scenario, REFR | | | | |
| | Expenditure classes with per capita equivalent income at 1970 prices | | | | |
	<216	216-336	336-516	516-900	>900
Rural 1980					
Population	0.2	0.2	0.2	−0.1	0.1
Equivalent income	0	0	0	−0.4	−1.7
Calorie level	0	0	0	−0.3	−1.0
Urban 1980					
Population	2.6	−0.8	0.2	0.1	0.1
Equivalent income	−0.2	−0.4	−1.1	−1.9	−3.8
Calorie level	−0.2	−0.4	−0.9	−1.3	−2.0
Rural 2000					
Population	−5.7	1.6	3.3	−1.7	3.1
Equivalent income	3.7	3.1	2.8	2.4	9.8
Calorie level	4.4	3.0	2.8	1.2	6.0
Urban 2000					
Population	−37.5	−26.8	−16.1	−6.8	8.6
Equivalent income	0.9	1.3	2.3	3.9	12.5
Calorie level	0.6	1.4	2.2	3.2	6.6

A comparison of LATR with REFR shows, as expected, that agricultural and non-agricultural GDP are higher in the former. The tax rate in LATR is higher (lower) compared to REFR in 1980 (2000). Also, terms of trade of agriculture improves a bit in 2000 in LATR. The trade pattern in LATR is the same as in REFR for both years. Most of the additional aid in LATR is used for larger imports of non-agricultural products. In the case of other food, there is a reversal of trade pattern between 1980 and 2000 in both scenarios, with exports (imports) being higher in LATR in 1980 (2000). The distributional effects in LATR are similar to the impact in LANR (compare Tables 6.11 and 6.12). However, LANR with a higher GDP, shows slightly higher welfare than LATR.

These scenarios, LANR and LATR, show that the sectoral allocation of the additional investment is important. In LANR in which all the additional investment goes for non-agriculture we get a better growth rate than in LATR in which the investment allocation follows the mechanism of the model.

Larger aid with fixed tax rate: In LATR the tax rate in 1980 increases because of a loss in tariff revenue consequent upon a change in the trade pattern, when much more aid is suddenly introduced. In LATRX, the tax rate is kept at the level of REFR and the loss in tariff revenue is allowed to lower investment in the economy. Thus, LATRX shows a lower growth compared to LATR (Table 6.9). Also, as can be expected, the distributional impact in 1980 which showed a loss in welfare for LATR compared to REFR (Table 6.13) shows no change in welfare for LATRX compared to REFR.

TABLE 6.12 Distributional impact of additional aid for investment, LATR

| | Percentage change over relaxed trade bounds reference scenario, REFR | | | | |
| | Expenditure classes with per capita equivalent income at 1970 prices | | | | |
	<216	216-336	336-516	516-900	>900
Rural 1980					
Population	0	0	0	0	0
Equivalent income	0	0	0	−0.4	−1.8
Calorie level	0	0	0	−0.3	−1.0
Urban 1980					
Population	0	0	0	0	0
Equivalent income	−0.2	−0.4	−1.1	−1.9	−3.8
Calorie level	−0.2	−0.4	−0.9	−1.3	−2.0
Rural 2000					
Population	−6.8	0	2.9	0	4.5
Equivalent income	2.6	1.8	1.3	1.2	7.0
Calorie level	3.2	2.6	2.5	2.8	5.9
Urban 2000					
Population	−25.0	−21.4	−12.8	−5.2	6.9
Equivalent income	0.8	1.0	1.7	2.9	9.2
Calorie level	1.8	2.0	2.4	3.0	5.1

TABLE 6.13 Distributional impact of additional aid for investment with tax rate fixed, LATRX

| | Percentage change over relaxed trade bounds reference scenario, REFR | | | | |
| | Expenditure classes with per capita equivalent income at 1970 prices | | | | |
	<216	216-336	336-516	516-900	>900
Rural 1980					
Population	0.2	0.2	0.2	−0.1	0.1
Equivalent income	0	0	0	0	0
Calorie level	0	0	0	0	0
Urban 1980					
Population	2.6	−0.6	0.2	0.1	0.1
Equivalent income	0	0	0	0	0
Calorie level	0	0	0	0	0
Rural 2000					
Population	−5.3	−0.4	1.2	−1.2	5.2
Equivalent income	1.6	1.0	0.8	0.4	2.7
Calorie level	2.1	2.0	2.0	2.4	3.0
Urban 2000					
Population	−32.5	−22.9	−14.0	−5.7	7.3
Equivalent income	0.5	0.4	0.2	0.2	2.6
Calorie level	1.8	1.4	1.0	0.9	1.6

This scenario indicates that when aid is given to a country, not all of it may be invested. Some part of it may be needed for compensating some of the consequences of the aid.

Concluding comments: We can now summarize our conclusions from this analysis:

Agricultural trade liberalization increases the average equivalent income but makes the poor worse off. The gains in the average equivalent income are not very large. In fact, the gains would be smaller than shown here were the impact on world prices of liberalization by India accounted for, as it was not done here. Thus, agricultural trade liberalization without compensating transfers to the poor cannot be considered a good policy.

A self-reliance strategy of no net capital inflow does not make difference as the net aid received by India is insignificant. There is a small adverse impact on poverty and welfare. However, this result of no great importance of "self-reliance" should be qualified, in that the model has only one non-agriculture sector and imports are fully substitutable by domestic production. One should not, therefore, conclude that such self-reliance is a desirable policy. This is evident as much more aid helps in substantially stepping up the growth rate, reducing poverty and increasing welfare. Also, the effectiveness in the use of aid matters. Moreover, a large inflow of aid may require an adjustment in other policies as well, and planning the use of such aid should account for it.

7

Rural Works Programs

7.1 Why a Rural Works Program?

Three-fourths of India's 750 million people live in rural areas and more than a third of them are poor. The majority of the rural poor are either landless agricultural workers or marginal and small farmers whose landholdings are inadequate to provide full and productive employment for their family members. The incidence of unemployment, particularly in the slack agricultural seasons, is substantial among these groups (see Srinivasan 1965 , Parthasarathy 1978 , Vyas and Mathai 1978 and Visaria 1981). It is unlikely that agriculture, with a growth rate of less than 3%, can absorb those who are unemployed over most of the year and the natural increase in rural labor force at a wage adequate to put them above the poverty line. It is in this context that rural public works programs evolved to employ the rural poor, particularly during slack seasons, and provide them with stable incomes. The rural works thus created are expected to contribute to the growth of the economy directly or indirectly, through the creation of assets such as roads, irrigation works, schools, etc.

The belief that public works can alleviate poverty and unemployment has been questioned on the ground that the incidence of unemployment among the poor is not significant and that, in any case, agricultural growth by itself can generate sufficient employment to eradicate poverty and rural unemployment. Dantwala (1979), Lakdawala (1977), Sinha (1981) et al. have argued that, on the one hand, based on empirical analysis, poverty and unemployment are not related. On the other hand, Parthasarathy (1978), Sau (1978), Visaria (1981) have all argued to the contrary. Sundaram and Tendulkar (1983) find that if one takes an appropriately defined measure of unemployment, poverty and unemployment are indeed related. Their analysis of the data from the 27th round of the National Sample Survey shows that poverty and unemployment are unrelated, given the usual status definition of unemployment (i.e., the so-called chronic unemployment), which means that an individual has to be unemployed most of the year to be classified as unemployed. This is not surprising since the poor cannot afford the luxury of being chronically unemployed! On the other hand, if unemployment is measured by the proportion of days one is unemployed but willing to work, poverty is significantly related with it. The consensus seems to be that a positive association between poverty and unemployment exists. This is a necessary condition for RWP to contribute to poverty alleviation.

The available evidence regarding the relation between agricultural growth and unemployment is also conflicting. Vaidyanathan (1978) analyzed data from several districts and found that though in general labor input per hectare and yield per hectare are positively related, the relation does not always hold. It is stronger across districts than within districts. This is as one may expect since the variance in labor costs within district is likely to be less than the variance between districts and so the variations in yield within a district may depend on the quality of land and the intensity of chemical inputs. Bardhan (1978) also reported a positive association between human labor input and cultivated acreage in the Hooghly district of West Bengal, whereas Mehra's (1976) study dealing with individual crops concluded the opposite. Rural employment elasticities with respect to output per hectare, estimated by Majumdar et al. (1977), were in the range of −0.95 to −0.97 for all regions, −1.86 for developed regions, and anywhere between 0.33 to −0.70 for underdeveloped regions. Vyas and Mathai (1978), analyzing state-wise data for the years 1969 to 1971, did not find any significant correlation between the gross output per hectare and the number of agricultural laborers per hectare. Noting that the proportion of workers engaged in agriculture in relation to the total work force was 72.1, 71.2 and 72.1 percent in 1951, 1961 and 1971, respectively, they argued that even if there were a large-scale increase in resource allocation towards agriculture, the labor absorption in Indian agriculture would be limited. Alagh, Bhalla and Bhaduri (1978) analyzed data of 281 districts and concluded that in 100 high growth districts, "fast growing agricultural output was also sucking workers into agriculture at a rapid rate". But evidence for the reverse process of workers being pushed out of agriculture in negative or low-growth districts, was not found.

Although agricultural growth contributes to a modest extent to the growth of employment opportunities, as Alagh et al. (1978) note, regions with poor agricultural growth also tend to be poor with respect to non-agricultural development. One cannot, therefore, associate the incidence of high unemployment necessarily with poor agricultural growth. Thus, off-farm public works programs in rural areas can be useful in providing needed additional employment to the underemployed rural poor, particularly in off-peak periods. This would provide them stable incomes and help alleviate poverty. Some would argue that rural employment programs are likely to be more cost effective than other avenues for alleviating poverty in a reasonable period of time. For instance, on the one hand, absorbing a sufficient number of the rural poor outside of agriculture in remunerative employment is unlikely if past trade and investment policies continue. This is because such policies have resulted in the slow growth of the urban non-agricultural sector and the high and increasing capital intensity of its manufacturing component.*

On the other hand, rural industrialization in India has yet to generate momentum. Unlike a purely redistributive program, rural works programs (RWP) offer certain additional benefits. By creating productive assets in rural areas, they directly or indirectly contribute to the growth of the economy. To the extent the operation of such programs enables identification and targeting of the poor, they may be cost effective, even when the assets created through RWP are not as productive as similar assets created through other programs. By augmenting the demand for rural labor in the off-peak season and guaranteeing employment in the RWP to those offering themselves for employment, an effective minimum wage for off-peak employment is established through RWP. In contrast, legislated minimum wages either are evaded or result in a loss of employment if enforced.

7.2 Rural Works Programs in India: The Experience

Rural works programs are only a part of a larger set of rural development programs constituting area development, resource development, works, training and rural credit programs. Some of these programs started as early as in 1969-70. A very brief history of these programs follows:

1. *The Small Farmer Development Agency (SFDA):* A credit program initiated by the Government of India (GOI) in 1969-70.
2. *Agency for the Development of Marginal Farmers and Agricultural Laborers (MFAL):* A land-productivity improvement program initiated by the GOI in 1969-70. Activities related to agriculture, like dairy farming, animal husbandry, etc., were also pursued. MFAL was later merged with SFDA.

---

* We do not go into the controversial issue of whether rural-urban migration would call for massive investment in urban infrastructure to serve the migrants.

3. *Drought-Prone Area Program (DPAP):* Taken up during the Fourth Five Year Plan (1969-74), this integrated area development program (IADP) aimed at "optimum utilization of land, water and livestock resources, restoration of ecological balance and stabilization of the income of the people, particularly the weaker sections".

4. *Crash Scheme for Rural Employment (CSRE):* Launched in the early 1970s, the program aims at employment generation and creation of durable assets. Departments of Rural Development of the central government as well as of the state governments financed the program and Block Development Offices and Panchayat Raj organizations implemented it.

5. *Employment Guarantee Scheme (EGS):* Initiated by the Government of Maharashtra in 1972-73, this scheme aimed to provide work to unemployed, unskilled laborers in rural areas. This was one of the more successful rural works programs.

6. *Food for Work Program (FFW):* Initiated in 1977, this program had several novel features to it. While it had the same objectives as other employment programs, namely, the provision of employment and the creation of durable community assets in rural areas, it paid a part of the wages in foodgrains. This was motivated partly by the desire to use rapidly accumulating foodgrain stocks in the hands of the government and partly in the expectation that it would lead to an improvement in the nutritional status of the workers as compared to payment of wages in cash. This expectation will be realized if one can assume that (i) the workers have a higher marginal propensity to consume food from wages received in the form of foodgrains rather than in cash, (ii) foodgrains can be distributed at no higher cost than cash wages and (iii) the impact on rural food prices would be insignificant if the wages are given in the form of food.

7. *Antyodaya:* Another rural development program initiated by the Government of Rajasthan in 1977.

8. *Operation Barga (OB):* Essentially a land-redistribution program to identify and register all the names of share-croppers. It was launched by the Government of West Bengal in 1978.

Detailed review of some of these programs are available in the Mid-Term Appraisal of the Sixth Five Year Plan, Planning Commission (1983).

All these programs, whether initiated by the Central Government or the State Governments, or both, share the fundamental objective of poverty elimination mainly through employment creation. Over time, some of these were merged with others or were modified or renamed and by the time of the Sixth Five

Year Plan (1980-85) these programs stood as follows:

1. Resources and Incomes Development Programs (Integrated Rural Development Program - IRDP).
2. Special Area Development Programs :
    (i) Drought-Prone Area Program (DPAP)
    (ii) Desert Development Program (DDP).
3. Works Programs for the creation of supplementary, employment opportunities :
    National Rural Employment Program (NREP): A restructured form of the Food for Work Program.
4. Training Program :
    National Scheme of Training of Rural Youth for Self-Employment (TRYSEM).

The NREP is the main focus of this chapter. It envisages the generation of 300 to 400 million man-days (mmd) of employment per year. The actual employment generated was 420.81 mmd in 1980-81, 354.52 mmd in 1981-82, and 337.83 mmd in 1982-83. Of the total planned outlay of Rs.9800 million on NREP during the Sixth Plan, Rs.9143 million have been spent in four years. Plan targets are expected to be achieved. Table 7.1 gives details of the nature of assets created under this program during 1981-82 and 1982-83. However, "a number of problems have been encountered in the implementation of this program; these relate to (a) supply and distribution of foodgrains, (b) time taken in preparation of a shelf of projects in different states, (c) unavailability of technical manuals/guidebooks in local languages for facilitating the task of Block staff, (d) difficulties in local resource mobilization, and (e) durability of assets and their maintenance" (Planning Commission 1983).

Besides running into these, and probably many other problems involving leakages, employment programs faced skepticism from many economists over their efficiency in alleviating rural poverty. Among them, particular mention may be made of Guhan (1980) and Dantwala (1978). We briefly note some of their criticisms.

Dantwala (1978) argued that "the public works approach to unemployment would make sense if it is so organized that there will be progressively less and less reliance on it, so that ultimately it becomes redundant. Its role should be accepted as transitional and deliberate efforts should be made to rehabilitate those engaged on public works within the mainstream of the economic systems."

Guhan (1980) pointed out that the budget allocation for NREP would create employment to the extent of only 6 to 8 percent of a total demand of 5000 to

7500 mmd. And if leakages of the system are taken into account, "the actual impact of this programme on rural employment will be quite minimal". However, he was not in favor of larger budget allocations. Based on his study

TABLE 7.1

Sl. No.	Nature of assets	Unit	1981-82	1982-83
(1)	(2)	(3)	(4)	(5)
1.	Area covered under afforestation, social forestry works and govt. lands	Hect.	103319	63492
2.	Drinking water wells, community irrigation wells, group housing and land development for scheduled castes and tribes	No.	90423	155635
3.	Construction of village tanks	No.	13709	12777
4.	Minor irrigation works including those related to flood protection drainage and anti-waterlogging works, construction of intermediate and main drains, field channels and leveling in the common area of irrigation projects	Hect.	105640	106244
5.	Soil and water conservation and land reclamation	Hect.	136964	36190
6.	Rural road construction/ improvement	Km.	73010	93335
7.	School and Balwadi buildings Panchayat ghars, community centres, drinking water wells, drinking water sources for wild animals, cattle ponds, pinjra-poles, gaushalas, community poultry and piggery houses, bathing and washing platforms, etc.	No.	21302	62267
8.	Other works	No.	7276	20171

Source: Planning Commission (1983).

in Tamil Nadu, he dubbed the whole process as a "Tughlaqian enterprise" since to cover all these millions of households would involve the creation of an enormous administrative machinery. In his view, land-redistribution is necessary to make supplementary programs effective. Ironically, Guhan did not discuss the political and administrative effort needed to carry out effective land distribution.

However, there are other studies that suggest that the employment schemes have not all failed everywhere in India. Indeed, some have met their broad objectives of providing gainful supplementary employment to those who need it. MHJ (1980), Reynolds and Sundar (1977), Bagchee (1984) and Dandekar and Sathe (1980), among others, have reported positive results.

Many of the evaluations of RWP have confined themselves to an empirical investigation, mainly descriptive, of specific projects and programs. Few, if any, systematic theoretical analyses of RWPs, that account for their macro-economic consequences and trade-offs, have been attempted. Our purpose here is to evaluate some of the costs and benefits arising out of a nation-wide rural works program taking account of the general equilibrium consequences of RWPs. For this purpose, we shall use our AGRI Model.

7.3 The Issues

The fundamental question is not whether development (or growth) and redistributive objectives can be attained through RWP but, simply, how effective they are in meeting these objectives.

Clearly, those who are willing to work more at the wages offered by RWP but do not otherwise get such work, for reasons to be explored below, get additional employment and do benefit in the short run. Yet, depending upon the way the programs are financed, the long-term consequences could be different. The argument, that resources could be raised by reducing waste or improving efficiency of the public sector, does not apply since waste and inefficiency ought to be eliminated whether or not the saved resources are used in a RWP. If the government is able to raise the resources needed for RWPs, through additional taxation so that the level of investment in the country, excluding the investment under RWPs, is maintained, then the total current consumption would be reduced, but the long term growth of the economy would not be affected. Part of the fall in total current consumption may come from a fall in public consumption and the rest from a tax-induced reduction in private consumption. The productivity of the assets created by RWPs adds to the future income stream of the economy. Indeed, if the government finances RWPs through a reduction in investment, then the effect on the future growth of the economy would depend upon the productivity of the assets created by the RWPs relative to the productivity of assets that would have been created by these resources otherwise.

The social cost-benefit ratio of RWPs as poverty-alleviating instruments is significantly influenced by the productivity of the assets created by the RWPs. The productivity would depend, among other things, on how well the projects are prepared, selected and executed. A poorly-prepared project will increase its ultimate cost. A poorly-selected project, in the sense of having a lower return than the social marginal rate of return in the economy will drain resources from elsewhere in the economy. A badly-executed work will unduly reduce the working life of the assets created. Thus poor preparation, selection and execution of an RWP project inflate its cost compared to other public and private investments.

Apart from these, leakages, through inefficiency and corruption (in addition to the leakages customary in any public investment program) in executing such widely distributed investment programs as RWPs, would affect the cost of the assets created as well as the wages that accrue to the poor rural target groups. Of course, the materials stolen from RWPs such as cement do not leak away from the economy to the extent that such stolen goods are used effectively by the thieves but they nevertheless defeat the purpose of RWPs by reducing their scale and efficiency. Since, in some studies, substantial leakages of wages away from the target groups have been reported, the presumably effective targeting possibilities of RWPs have to be balanced against other less easily-targeted redistributive measures that are not prone to leakages.

The net benefits of RWPs are influenced by how well the rural labor market functions in the peak and off-peak agricultural seasons. To begin with, if the market functions in the ideal textbook fashion, with labor demand arising from producers and supply from labor force participants who take wages (or wage structure, if more than one type of labor is involved) and all other relevant prices as given *and the market clears*, then an RWP will attract no labor, if it offers a real wage below the prevailing market clearing wage prior to its introduction. Put another way, the equilibrium wage in this model is endogenous, and RWPs, by adding to the demand for labor, will raise it. Since at the new equilibrium wage the labor for an RWP will come partly from the release of labor from other uses and in part from additional labor supply, whether or not the RWP should be undertaken has to be determined by comparing the social value of the output of the RWP with the social value of the output loss in the rest of the economy because of a division of labor.

Since the rationale for an RWP is that it employs part of the labor force at periods in which there is no alternative employment for it, the competitive market clearance model is inappropriate. On the other hand, non-clearance of the labor market, i.e., why wages do not adjust to clear the market, has to be explained, if unemployment exists at the going wage. A number of explanations are available. A popular one is to assert that an effectively enforced minimum wage above the market clearance wage results in unemployment. But, in the Indian context, there is no evidence that the legislated minimum wage has been effectively enforced. Another explanation is based on the efficiency wage theory, it being assumed that the labor, in efficiency units, the employer obtains per unit of labor he hires (measured in man days) is a function of the wage rate per man day. The function has the property that the cost per efficiency unit is minimum at a unique wage rate. This would mean that the wage rate cannot fall below this cost minimizing wage rate. If the supply of labor at this wage is below the demand for labor, then the equilibrium wage will be above the critical minimum wage and we will be back in the market clearance world. However, if it exceeds the demand, clearly there will be unemployment. Since, by assumption, the wage rate cannot fall, market clearance through wage adjustment is impossible. A number of economists have analyzed this model and attempted to provide a foundation for the wage-productivity relationship, such as through an alleged nutrition-work effort relationship or through a trade-off between the loss of output from shifting the work by the employer and the cost of monitoring him so as to prevent it. (Leibenstein 1957 , Bliss and Stern 1978 , Dasgupta and Ray 1986).

The Indian rural labor market has been studied by a number of scholars (Bardhan 1984 , Rudra 1981 , Indira Rajaraman 1984). There is ample evidence in these studies, that the labor market (if it could be termed a market at all), is highly segmented, with wage rates differing even for labor involved in narrowly defined agricultural operations across villages that are geographically close to each other, the differences being too large to be accounted for by transportation costs or barriers to rapid dissemination of market information. One explanation offered for this phenomenon is that, each individual village (for reasons that are left unstated or unconvincing) is a closed economy and, further, the distribution of assets (particularly land) is such that a non-competitive framework is needed to analyze the interaction of demand for labor from oligopsonistic large landlords and the supply of labor from an essentially price taking mass of landless workers and small landholders. In addition, circumstances in some areas may provide incentives for the interlinking of labor, land and credit transactions; the power of such incentives may vary from village to village, with the result that inter-village differences in wage rates (or, for that matter, in crop shares or interest rates) by themselves do not convey much information about the labor markets.

RWPs can clearly play a useful role in favor of workers in situations of oligopsonistic labor markets by reducing, if not eliminating, the oligopoly power and rents of the employers. Even if oligopsony was absent, RWPs executed at the same time over a large area may integrate otherwise segmented markets and improve efficiency. In situations of interlinked markets, it is not necessarily the case that intervention in one market, namely, the labor market through an RWP, will benefit the workers, for the reason that employers may be able to alter the other terms of an interlinked contract to offset the effect of labor market intervention. Yet, if the program is of sufficient size and is also a part of a well-designed set of policy interventions in credit and land markets, their joint effect may be to eliminate incentives for interlinking and to improve workers' welfare. Of course, RWPs are clearly beneficial in situations where unemployment exists in equilibrium.

The impact of RWPs on rural employment and wages can be seen from a simple characterization of the rural labor market that may correspond roughly to Indian conditions. In Figure 7.1, two labor demand curves, PP' and QQ' correspond to peak and off-peak seasons, respectively. The labor supply curves for peak and off- peak seasons may be interdependent and different. Also, participation in the labor force may itself depend on prospects for employment and the supply curve may be affected by the introduction of RWPs. Yet, for simplicity of exposition, the same supply curve is assumed for both seasons. The off-peak wage level is OA below which wages cannot fall for any of the reasons discussed earlier. AU is the total labor supply at the wage OA. Employment level is AB and excess supply of labor at wage OA is BU. Wage earnings are given by OABC. If the RWP offers limited employment at the same wage as the off-peak, as shown in Figure 7.2a, the labor demand curve now becomes QBDR'. As long as the additional employment generated does not exceed the available excess labor supply BU, there is no change in agricultural wages and employment. The wage earners earn an additional income corresponding to BDEC. On the other hand, if the wage rate offered by the RWP exceeds the prevailing wage OA, there may be a reduction in agricultural labor employed, depending on the additional employment offered by the RWP relative to the initial excess supply.

In Figure 7.2b, the RWP wage rate is higher than the prevailing wage rate but the employment offered by the RWP is limited. The labor demand curve after the RWP is initiated is QSRR'. The additional employment offered by the RWP is not sufficient to absorb all those who offer themselves for employment at the higher wages, and jobs will have to be allocated among

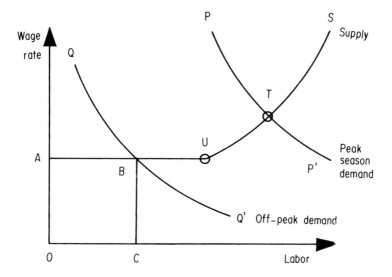

Fig. 7.1   The rural labor market

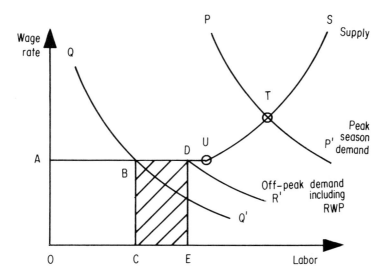

Fig. 7.2a   RWP – Offers limited employment at the initial wage

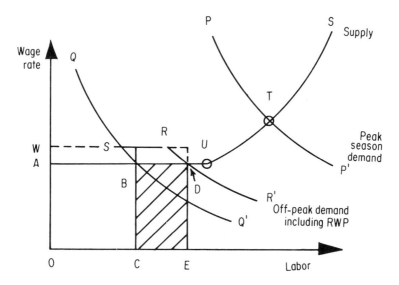

Fig. 7.2b RWP – Offers limited employment at a higher than the initial wage

applicants in some way, for example on a first-come-first-serve basis. The total employment is AD and the employment in agriculture will be unaffected at AB with the agricultural wage continuing at the institutional minimum level OA.

If the RWP is initiated as an employment guarantee scheme, then it will set the rural wage rate. As seen in Figure 7.2c, the labor demand curve is now QSDR'. Equilibrium wage is OW offered by the RWP. Agricultural employment is reduced from AB to WS. However, agricultural wage income OWSF may increase rather than fall if the labor demand curve is sufficiently inelastic. Agricultural output is reduced as a consequence of the reduction in agricultural employment.

Since RWPs are primarily meant to reduce unemployment during the off-peak season, we can assume for analytical simplicity that cases 7.2a and 7.2b are the relevant ones. RWPs then do not affect agricultural employment and output.

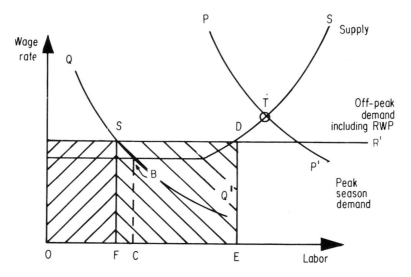

Fig. 7.2c   RWP – Assured employment at a higher than the initial wage, i.e.,
an employment guarantee scheme

To summarize, the following specific questions arise regarding RWPs:

(1) What are the impacts of different levels of RWPs on poverty reduction
    and on economic growth in the short and long runs? How do they
    depend on the Government's ability to mobilize needed resources?
(2) How are these benefits and costs affected by poor selection, prepara-
    tion and execution of RWPs?
(3) As a purely targeting scheme for redistribution, are RWPs cost effec-
    tive?

We address these questions with the help of the AGRI Model.

7.4   Specification of Rural Works Program Scenarios

It will be recalled that there are ten (five rural and five urban) per capita
consumer expenditure classes and ten commodity sectors in the model. We
assume that only the poorest two expenditure classes (consisting of agricultural and non- agricultural households) in rural areas are the target groups to
be covered under rural works programs. An average quantity of 'r' kilograms
of foodgrains per year per person in these two expenditure classes is distributed to participants as wages under the RWP.

In most of our analysis, 'r' is exogenously fixed at 100. However, the per capita quantity 'r_1', of foodgrains distributed to the poorer of the two classes, class 1, is fixed at 125 kg. In a few runs r is fixed at 50 in which case r_1 is set at 62.5.

The amount r_2 distributed per capita to class 2, given r and r_1, would be:

$$r_2 = (rp - r_1 p_1) / p_2$$

where p, p_1, p_2 and r, r_1, r_2 are respectively the population and amounts distributed to the two classes, class 1 and class 2. Though r and r_1 remain constant at 100 and 125, r_2 varies over time depending on p_1 and p_2.

The constancy of r_1, given the same nominal wage rate of the RWP for persons from both classes, implies that the number of days a person from the poorest class is employed under the RWP remains constant but the number of days a person from class 2 is employed changes, depending on the population of the class, p_2.

Though the composition of the basket of foodgrains in terms of rice, wheat and coarse grains to be used for wage payments is, in principle, a policy decision, we have assumed that the basket consists only of wheat. This simplifies comparisons of different scenarios and would not change the nature of the results. Obviously, the wage cost of the RWP is the value of the total foodgrains thus distributed. We compute the wage bill at the target (or open market) prices.

The wage bill is, however, only a part of the cost of investment activity under the RWP. Additionally, some complementary non-agricultural tools and implements, construction materials such as cement, lime or bitumen, as well as transportation services, are needed for digging irrigation channels or building earth works for road construction, and so on. We assumed that the cost of complementary non-agricultural goods is one-half of the wage bill in value terms. This was indeed the norm for the Sixth Plan employment programs. In physical units, the complementary demand for non-agriculture = 0.5 (wage bill)/P(10), where P(10) is the price of the tenth sector (non-agriculture).

The amount of 125 kg. of wheat distributed per person per year for the poorest class is selected as wage on the following considerations. For a family of five, provision of 125 kg. of wheat per person at Rs. 2.0 per kg. would cost Rs. 1250 per year. At an annual employment of 200 person-days per year per family, this implies a wage rate of Rs. 6.25 per person per day. This is marginally higher than the implied wage rate in the RWP of the Sixth Plan. It is proposed to generate 2000 million person-days of employment over the plan with a total outlay of Rs. 16,000 million, of which a third is for the non-wage component of the RWP, implying an average wage rate of Rs. 5.33 per person per day.

The total investment in the economy under the RWP in our scenarios is thus equal to one and a half times its wage bill. This investment may be put in place in either the agriculture or the non-agriculture sector or shared by both. We assume that these two sectors share such investment equally.

Various inefficiencies and leakages can and do in fact occur in the RWPs. For analytical purposes, these can be grouped into two types with distinctly different consequences. The first relates to the effectiveness of the investment generated under the RWPs. Additional output from the RWP investment may be less than what can be obtained from investing the same expenditure in other activities. This kind of inefficiency affects the growth of the economy. The second one relates to a failure of targeting: the actual beneficiaries of the RWP are not the target groups (i.e., the population in the two poorest rural classes) but middle-men belonging to richer classes. Such unintended diversion of benefits to non-target groups affects the degree to which the primary objective of the removal of poverty is realized. Of course, such leakages would also have their own secondary implications on total consumption, savings and investment in the economy by the non-target groups.

In this model, inefficiencies of the first kind are reflected in three alternative levels of 1, 0.5 and 0 of effectiveness of RWP investment relative to the economy-wide average. At one extreme a level of 1 corresponds to well-planned and well-executed programs. At the other extreme, a level of 0 corresponds to a totally infructuous investment. A level of 0.5 is between the two extremes. Thus an investment expenditure of 1.5W where W is the wage bill, leads to an effective investment of $e(1.5W)$ where e could take one of three alternative values: 1, 0.5 and 0.

We also incorporated a characterization of possible targeting failure in the sense that only 50 percent of the wage bill reaches the targeted two poorest rural classes and the remaining 50 per cent of W goes to the other three rural classes in proportion to their populations.

Thus, the following set of scenarios is generated:

(A) *Reference Scenarios:* Contains no specific redistributive policies except the continuation of public distribution of foodgrains to urban groups only.

(B) *Rural Works Scenarios:* The policy of rural works programs denoted by RW, is made operative from the year 1980 onwards. With the combination of two targeting failure levels (with failure (0.5) and without failure (1), denoted by t) and three investment effectiveness levels (denoted by e), six alternative scenarios designated as RW-t-e arise.

To make the RW runs comparable and somewhat easy to interpret, prices are maintained at the same levels in all these runs as in the reference run in corresponding years by removing all export and import quotas and imposing a tariff equal to the difference between the domestic price in the reference run and the world market price.

Moreover, in most of the variants, it is assumed that the government is unable to raise taxes further and that the RWPs are financed by reducing other public investments. A few runs, however, were also made where investment rates were maintained and tax rates increased to finance the RWPs. The fixed tax rate runs are identified with a letter 'X' in their designation.

The scenarios are listed below grouped according to the issue addressed by them:

Issue addressed	Run desig-nation	Per person quantity of wheat distri-buted as wages	Target-ing effec-tive-ness	Invest-ment effec-tive-ness	Tax rates - free or fixed
	RWQ-t-e	Q	t	e	
1. Impact of the	RW50-1-1	50kg	1.0	1.0	free
size of RWP	RW100-1-1	100kg	1.0	1.0	free
and mode	RW50-1-1X	50kg	1.0	1.0	fixed
of financing	RW100-1-1X	100kg	1.0	1.0	fixed
2. Impact of	RW100-1-1X	100kg	1.0	1.0	fixed
targeting	RW100-.5-1X	100kg	0.5	1.0	fixed
failures and	RW100-1-.5X	100kg	1.0	0.5	fixed
investment	RW100-.5-.5X	100kg	0.5	0.5	fixed
inefficiencies	RW100-1-0X	100kg	1.0	0	fixed
	RW100-.5-0X	100kg	0.5	0	fixed

(C) *Free Food Scenario*: In order to compare an RWP with a generalized food subsidy program which does not attempt to distinguish between various income groups, in this scenario 40 kg. of wheat per person was given free to the entire population. The figure of 40 kg. was chosen as it involved roughly the same level of government expenditure as the RWP in which 100 kg. of wheat is distributed so that the long-term impact on growth would be comparable. This run in which tax rates were also fixed to the reference run levels is designated as FF40X.

7.5   The Results

The impact on the growth of the economy and on the welfare of the rural poor can be seen from Table 7.2. The growth indicator is the growth in gross domestic product at 1970 prices (GDP 70). The welfare indicators include the GDP 70 per capita, the energy intake in kilo calorie per capita per day (cal/capita) and the average equivalent income per capita (EQY/capita). The equivalent income of a person is the minimum expenditure needed at 1970 prices to achieve the utility he enjoys in the year 2000. In the table, results for the year 2000 are given as percentage changes in values of various variables in different scenarios from their reference run values.

TABLE 7.2 Impact on growth and rural poor of rural works programs

	Percent change from reference run—Year 2000							
Scenarios	GDP70 per capita	Difference in GDP70 growth rate 1980–2000	AVR EQY/ capita	Cal./ Capita	Rural poor			
					Poorest class		Two poorest classes	
					EQY/ capita	Cal./ capita	EQY/ capita	Cal./ capita
With additional Taxation:								
RW100-1-1	3.5	0.22	2.2	5.7	67	70	39	40
RW50-1-1	1.8	0.13	1.1	2.9	34	35	19	20
With fixed tax rates:								
RW50-1-1X	−2.3	0	−0.1	2.4	33	35	19	20
RW100-1-1X	−4.6	−0.25	−0.2	4.7	67	70	39	40
RW100-1-.5X	−8.5	−0.47	−2.6	3.8	67	70	39	40
RW100-1-0X	−13.2	−0.73	−5.4	2.6	67	70	39	40
RW100-.5-1X	−3.7	−0.20	0	3.0	33	40	19	20
RW100-.5-.5X	−7.3	−0.40	−2.0	2.1	33	40	19	20
RW100-.5-0X	−11.8	−0.66	−4.7	1.0	33	40	19	20
FF40X	−4.2	−0.23	−0.8	1.3	11	11	10	10

GDP70=Gross domestic product at 1970-71 prices
EQY : Equivalent Income
AVR : Average

7.6   Impact on Growth and Hunger

It is obvious from the results for RW100-1-1 that, if rural works programs can be financed through additional taxation, and if they could be carried out without investment inefficiencies and targeting failures, then not only the rural poor improve their welfare substantially but the economy grows faster. The GDP per capita in 2000 is 3.5 percent higher amounting to an increase of 0.22 percent per year in the GDP growth rate over 1980-2000. The poorest rural class improves its calorie intake by 70 percent to a level which virtually eliminates hunger.

7.7   Impact of the Size of the Program

These effects are roughly halved when the size of the rural works program is halved in RW50-1-1 compared to RW100-1-1. The impact of the size of the program for the year 2000 is plotted in Figure 7.3. The gain in GDP, as well as the gain in the average equivalent income are approximately linearly related to the size of the program.

The additional tax effort needed can be seen from Table 7.3 which gives the tax rate on the non-agricultural income of the urban richest class. The tax rates applicable to the non-agricultural incomes of the other urban and rural classes follow as per the θ_j (j: expenditure class) given in Appendix 3.3.

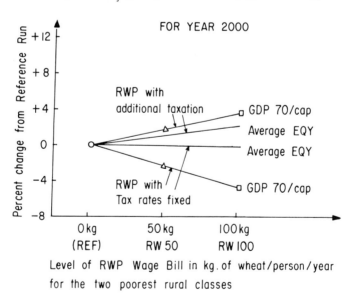

Fig. 7.3 Size of RWP and growth

TABLE 7.3 Tax rates on non-agricultural income

Scenario	1980	1985	1990	1995	2000
Reference	.04	.04	.06	.08	.12
RW100-1-1	.17	.11	.10	.11	.14
RW50-1-1	.10	.07	.08	.10	.13

The tax rate in Table 7.3 can be interpreted as a combination of direct and indirect taxes. It excludes corporate taxes and tariffs on foreign trade.

The additional tax effort in 1980, with the introduction of RWPs is substantial as compared to the reference run. In the reference run in 1980, taxes on non-agricultural income generate revenue of less than 2 percent of the GDP and to finance a RWP at the level of 100 kg. of wheat per person, this tax revenue has to be raised to around 8 percent of GDP. The political feasibility of such an effort, let alone its administrative feasibility, is doubtful. Nevertheless, such a RWP would be effective in drastically reducing poverty and hunger.

A RWP at a lower level of 50 kg. per person has still a substantial impact (nearly half as much as that of RW100-1-1), while reducing the tax effort in 1980 from 8 percent of GDP to about 5.

Though the tax efforts needed in 1980 for financing the RWPs are substantially higher than in the reference run, as the economy grows, the difference in tax rates reduces by the year 2000 to around 1 percent of the GDP. This means that a serious financing problem arises only in the initial years. If foreign grants are available for a limited period, RWPs can be initiated without straining the tax effort. If foreign grants are not forthcoming and a tax effort is not feasible, RWPs may be introduced at a modest level and gradually stepped up, thereby keeping the needed tax effort within modest limits.

7.8 RWP without Additional Taxes or Aid

What are the impacts of RWPs financed not by raising taxes or foreign grants but by reducing other investments? They can be seen from the runs designated X. As can be expected, the impact is primarily to reduce the GDP rate of growth. Thus, in RW100- 1-1X in the year 2000, the GDP per capita is 4.6 percent lower than in the reference run whereas in RW100-1-1, it is 3.5 percent higher. However, it may be noted that the impact on the rural poor is not much different in the two RWP runs. In fact, in the various RWP runs, the improvement in the equivalent incomes and in the calorie intakes of the rural poor depends mainly on the size of the programs.

It should also be noted that, though the per capita GDP at 1970 prices is reduced by 4.6 percent in 2000 in RW100-1-1X, (compared to the reference run), the fall in the average equivalent income is only 0.2 percent. This is also seen in Figure 7.3 in which the average equivalent income line is nearly horizontal even when tax rates are fixed. It seems, then, that financing RWPs through reductions in other investment does not significantly reduce the growth in the equivalent income per capita.

7.9   Effect of Targeting Failure and Investment Inefficiencies

When the RWP wages do not reach the targeted groups, (the two poorest rural classes) and a part of it gets distributed to the other rural classes, the improvement in the welfare of the poor as indicated by the equivalent income and calorie intakes gets correspondingly reduced. Thus in RW100-.5-1X, where only 50 percent of the wages reaches the target group, the improvement in the welfare of the poor is half as much, compared to RW100-1-1X.

However, the fall in the growth of the GDP is less in RW100-.5-1X compared to RW100-1-1X. This is because the leakages go to comparatively richer classes who pay taxes at a higher rate and also save at a higher rate, so that, with the same tax rates government revenues are larger and the reduction in other investment is smaller.

The impact of investment inefficiencies, as can be expected, falls mainly on growth and not on the welfare of the poor.

Figures 7.4 and 7.5 show these impacts on the GDP per capita and on the trade-offs between the GDP per capita and the welfare of the poor in the various tax-fixed runs.

7.10   RWP as a Mechanism for Targeted Redistribution

In the worst case for growth, RW100-1-0X, in which RWPs create totally useless assets, the GDP per capita in the year 2000 is 13 percent lower than in the reference run. However, the rural poor are better off. Even though in the free-food run where 40 kg. of wheat is distributed to everyone without any targeting whatsoever, the impact on growth is similar to RW100-1-1X. However, as is to be expected the distributional impacts on the rural poor are much better in the latter. This is seen in Table 7.2 and Figure 7.6 in which the growth and distributional effects of the two runs are compared.

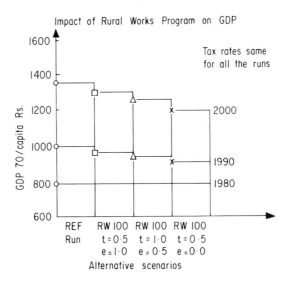

Fig. 7.4 RWP, leakages, investment effectiveness and GDP per capita

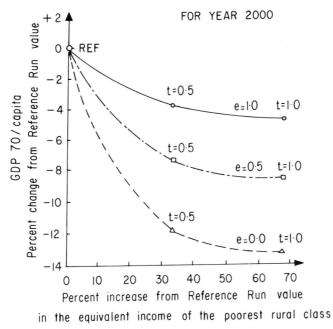

Fig. 7.5 Growth, welfare and RWP leakages and effectiveness

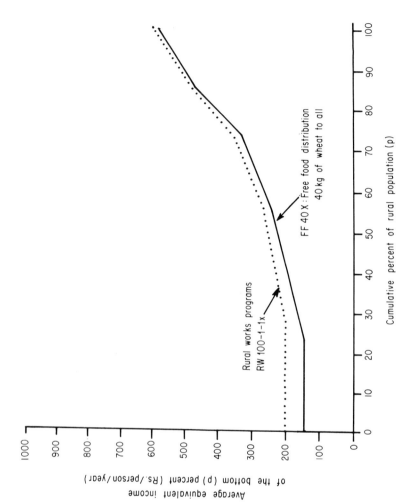

In Figure 7.6, we have plotted the per capita equivalent income for cumulative percentages from the bottom. Thus the X axis shows the percentage of rural population and the Y axis shows the average per capita equivalent income of the bottom x percent. It can be shown that because the curve corresponding to RW100-1-1X is above that of FF40X, social welfare as per the criterion developed by Willig and Bailey (1981) is higher in the former. This criterion ranks income distribution according to any social welfare function that satisfies the Pareto principle, anonymity and aversion to regressive transfer.

7.11 Conclusions

Rural Works Programs are effective instruments for virtually eliminating hunger at a modest cost in terms of growth if they can be well planned and executed.

RWPs create a demand for perhaps the only endowment the rural poor have – unskilled labor. They increase their earnings. In the absence of any radical redistribution of rural assets (particularly agricultural land) and without creating additional demand for unskilled labor, the possibilities of improving incomes of the rural poor in India's mixed economy are very limited.

It may be suggested that by making rural unskilled labor less dependent on the rural land-owning rich, RWPs may loosen the social and economic power of the latter. An anticipation of this happening may lead the rural rich to oppose them. However, RWPs also improve rural infrastructure, thereby increasing productivity of land, which may be sufficiently attractive to the rural rich to blunt their opposition.

The effectiveness of planning and execution determines the success of RWPs. That RWPs were not effectively executed in the past is not an argument against RWPs per se, but only an argument for creating a design and implementation mechanism with less incentives for the diversion of resources to other uses. For instance, the participation of the rural poor in formulating RWPs may help. In any case, it is likely that the efforts and the resources needed to plan and execute RWPs effectively will be modest compared to designing and implementing alternative policies with similar impact on the rural poor.

8

Terms of Trade Policies

8.1 The Issues

Agricultural producers respond rationally to incentives within their operating constraints. This is supported by many empirical studies of supply responses of farmers to price incentives.

Agricultural prices affect profits from agricultural production and therefore can be expected to stimulate higher production when they increase. Many studies of farmers' supply responses relate to individual commodities. Response elasticities, based on studies that do not take into account, in an appropriate way, competition with other crops for inputs and factors, are biased. The few estimates of sector level supply responses that are available show, a relatively modest response of sectoral output to prices. This is understandable in the short term, as farmers may be constrained by the total resource availability and some resources cannot be flexibly shifted between sectors because of their specificity. In the long run, however, resources may be augmented and higher prices and profitability may stimulate investment into agriculture and research that lead to resource enhancement. Also, there is much greater flexibility in allocating new investments. However, both in the short run and in the long run, the magnitude of response depends on the extent to which resources are sector-specific. Thus within agriculture resources may be substitutable and shiftable across crops; resources employed in non-agriculture (other than capital) may not be shiftable to agriculture. Our model of India constitutes a tool to explore sector level responses in the short and long runs.

A higher relative price of agriculture also implies a lower relative price of investment goods which come mainly from the non-agricultural sector and this will lead to higher real aggregate investment in the economy. On the other hand, the specific policy instruments used to improve the agricultural terms of trade may adversely affect the growth of the economy. For example, if domestic terms of trade are changed through changes in import tariff, then revenues from tariffs are changed as well. If other taxes are adjusted to maintain a budget balance so that public savings in the economy are unchanged, then there is no change in investment either. However, if other taxes are not adjusted, a budget balance requires a change in public consumption expenditure and/or investment. The net impact of a higher agricultural price on growth would then depend on the combined effect of a lower price of investment goods and changes in investment.

Higher agricultural prices will lower the food consumption of the poor unless there is a compensating change in their incomes. The income of rural consumers, including the poor who earn their income from agriculture, may rise with higher agricultural prices but this would not be the case for consumers who have no agricultural incomes.

The analytical and policy issues that arise are:

(1) The supply response of agriculture to prices in the short run and in the long run.
(2) The impact on the growth of the economy of changes in the barter terms of trade between agriculture and non-agriculture.
(3) The welfare impact of changes in agricultural prices.

8.2   The Scenarios

In the model, supply responses and consumer decisions depend on relative prices. Since lowering the price of non-agriculture is equivalent to raising the relative price of each agricultural product by the same proportion, the various terms of trade scenarios are generated by this device.

Formally, the retail price targets are set as follows:

$$P_{i,t}^{*s} = P_{i,t}^{ref} \text{ for agricultural commodities i = 1, ..., 9.}$$

$$P_{i,t}^{*s} = a^s \cdot P_{i,t}^{ref} \text{ for non-agriculture, i = 10}$$

where

$P_{i,t}^{*s}$ = target price in scenario s, for commodity i, time period t
$P_{i,t}^{ref}$ = target price in the reference scenario for commodity i, time period t; and
a^s = scenario(s) specific parameter

Producer prices are less than retail prices to the extent of the cost of processing and trade margins. The values of these margins depend on the price of non-agriculture. Since processing and trade margins vary for different agricultural commodities, relative retail prices differ from relative producer prices. None the less, the price ratio between agriculture and non-agriculture, P_a/P_{na}, changes in a similar fashion for both consumers and producers.

The policy changes are introduced in 1980 and are continued till 2000. Moreover, trade quotas are removed so that all price targets are realized through an adjustment in trade flows.

The following scenarios were generated:

(1) REF: Reference scenario in which the price policy is to move domestic prices gradually towards the world market prices between 1980 and 2000.

(2) TT.5: Non-agricultural price multiplied by 0.5 so that the agricultural to non-agricultural price ratio, P_{ag}/P_{non-ag}, is twice as much in each year as in REF ($a^s = 0.5$).

(3) TT.7: Non-agricultural price is multiplied by 0.7 so that P_{ag}/P_{non-ag} is now 1.43 times its value in each year as in REF ($a^s = 0.7$).

(4) TT1.2: Non-agricultural price multiplied by 1.2 so that P_{ag}/P_{non-ag} is lower and is 0.833 times in each year as in REF.

In all the above scenarios the associated changes in government revenues from tariffs because of changes in trade pattern are absorbed by appropriate changes in the average tax rate.

(5) TT.7X: Prices set the same way as in TT.7, but tax rates are fixed at the realized tax rates in REF. Public investment and hence total investment adjust to maintain budget balance.

The simulated supply responses refer to the relative price variation of 0.83 to 2.0 across scenarios.

8.3 The Results

8.3.1 Impact on Growth

Some of the important macro-economic indicators are shown in Table 8.1 for 1985 and 2000.

It is striking that as relative prices of agriculture are increased, as in scenarios TT.5 and TT.7, real GDP from agriculture and non-agriculture sectors increase the latter by a greater proportion relative to REF. This results mainly from the larger real investment made possible by the lower price of non-agriculture.

TABLE 8.1 Macro economic impact of changes in agricultural terms of trade

Indicator	Absolute values	Scenario Ratio to reference run value			
	REF	TT.5	TT.7	TT1.2	TT.7X
1. P_{ag}/P_{na}					
1985	0.86	2.35	1.56	0.80	1.57
2000	0.74	2.70	1.65	0.77	1.66
2. GDP (10^9 Rs.1970)					
1985	654.0	1.10	1.05	0.98	0.99
2000	1391.0	1.37	1.14	0.97	0.92
3. GDP agriculture (10^9 Rs.1970)					
1985	247.0	1.11	1.05	0.98	1.03
2000	337.0	1.24	1.10	0.97	1.03
4. GDP non-agriculture (10^9 Rs.1970)					
1985	407.0	1.10	1.04	0.98	0.96
2000	1054.0	1.42	1.16	0.97	0.88
5. Price index of non-agriculture (1970 = 1)					
1985	2.19	0.50	0.70	1.20	0.70
2000	2.61	0.50	0.70	1.20	0.70
6. Investment (10^9 Rs.1970)					
1980	110.0	1.41	1.18	0.93	0.85
1985	152.0	1.53	1.22	0.92	0.82
2000	465.0	1.70	1.25	0.93	0.82

The desired domestic prices in each of the policy scenarios are realized by imposing suitable ad valorem tariff on the world prices. Thus, when the domestic relative prices are changed, in different scenarios, the government's tariff revenue changes for two reasons. First, when the domestic price of a commodity is increased (decreased), it leads to changes in production and consumption in an opposite direction so that net exports increase (decrease). Second, the difference between the world price and the domestic price, the implicit tariff, changes. When the government is unable to raise tax rates to bring about budget balance, then something else will have to adjust. In the TT.7X scenario we have assumed that the level of public investment and hence total investment adjusts.

In the TT.7 scenario when terms of trade changes are introduced in 1980, the government's tariff revenue falls by 10 percent of the targeted investment level compared to REF. In TT.7 this deficit is made good by raising the tax rate and the investment level is maintained. In the TT.7X case, on the other hand, investment is lower by 15 percent in 1980 and by 18 percent in 2000. Thus, the stimulating effect of the lower price of investment goods is more than offset by the loss in public investment leading to a lower real GDP in TT.7X relative to REF. While non-agricultural GDP falls relative to REF and by increasing amounts because of the shortfall in investment, agricultural GDP rises since the stimulating effect of more favorable terms of trade more than offsets the negative investment effect. Of course, agricultural GDP rises by a smaller proportion relative to REF in TT.7X as compared to TT.7. Thus, if achieving improved terms of trade for agriculture involves the use of a policy instrument that affects budget balance adversely, and if higher levels of taxation are not feasible for political or administrative reasons, growth will suffer.

8.3.2   Supply Responses at the Sectoral Level

The aggregate sector level supply response can be assessed by comparing the real agricultural GDP and relative price of agriculture in the TT.5, TT.7 and TT1.2 scenarios with those in the REF scenario. These response curves for 1985, 1990, 1995 and 2000 are plotted in Figure 8.1. We take the real value added in agriculture as an indicator of sector supply rather than gross value of output. For a sector level response, with input prices also changing across scenarios, the value added notion is the appropriate indicator of output and is easier to interpret.

The price index of agriculture is the current year deflator of agricultural GDP. The response curves in Figure 8.1 show a rather low price elasticity of supply of around 0.1 and 0.15 for small changes in prices and even lower values for larger changes in prices.

Figure 8.1 also shows that in the later years, the supply responses are larger than over earlier periods. This is as expected: the supply response at a point in time results from changes in variable inputs such as fertilizers in response to changes in prices.

However, the response of output to changes in variable inputs depends on the marginal productivity of the latter which depend not only on the levels of their use but more importantly, on the level of fixed inputs (such as irrigation capital and technology). As the stock of fixed inputs increases and the technology (primarily yields' response to fertilizer) improves the marginal productivity curves for variable inputs shift outward. This shift of the curves compensates for any tendency towards diminishing returns along a curve since fixed and variable inputs are substitutes.

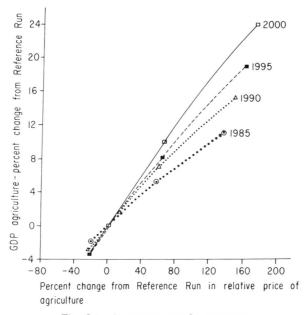

Fig. 8.1 Aggregate supply response

The notion of supply response underlying Figure 8.1 is elaborated in Figure 8.2. where ABCD is the initial production possibility curve. Prices in the reference scenario are represented by the slope of the line PP and the output is at B. Changes in agricultural capital stocks due to investments till period t, shift the production possibility curve outward to ERF. Given ERF optimal production will be at R under PP. In a different scenario, with prices corresponding to the slope of P'P', the production changes from B to C in the initial year. This indicates an increase in agriculture output of $k(Y_o)$. However, with more favorable prices P'P' for agriculture, more investment in agriculture takes place (than in the scenario with prices PP) till period t which further shifts the production possibility curve to STU in period t.

Production levels in period t under price P'P' will be at T and the increase in output compared to under prices PP will be $k(Y_t)$. Our supply response for the year o is obtained by relating $k(Y_o)$ in the year o and $k(Y_t)$ in the year t to changes in the relative prices implied by the slopes of PP and P'P'.

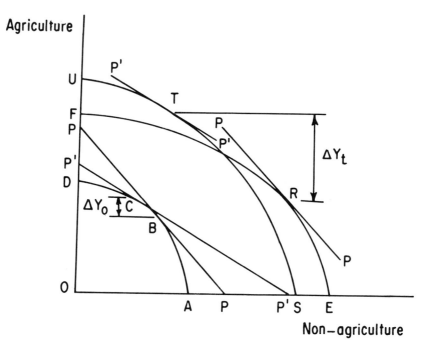

Fig. 8.2 Changing production possibilities – impact of relative prices

8.3.3   Impact on Welfare

Changes in agricultural terms of trade have significant effects on income and consumption distribution in the economy. In Table 8.2 the effect on some welfare indicators is presented. Though with higher relative prices of agriculture compared to REF, real GDP (valued at constant 1970 prices) increases, the average equivalent incomes are lower. In TT.5 when relative prices are doubled the average equivalent income is lower by 28 percent in 1985 and by 17 percent in 2000. Even for TT.7, in which relative prices are increased by about 50 percent, the fall in equivalent income is 10 percent in 1985 and 3 percent in 2000. The equivalent incomes, however, increase in TT1.2 in which relative prices shift against agriculture by about 20 percent. Equivalent incomes in this case improve by 2 percent.

TABLE 8.2 Impact on welfare due to changes in agriculture terms of trade

Indicator		Scenario				
	Absolute values	Ratio to reference run value				
	REF	TT.5	TT.7	TT1.2	TT.7X	
1. Equivalent income	(Rs./person)					
1985	575	0.72	0.90	1.02	0.97	
2000	711	0.83	0.97	1.02	0.90	
2. Energy intake/capita	(Kcal/day)					
1985	2200	0.85	0.94	1.01	0.96	
2000	2430	0.93	0.99	1.01	0.95	
3. Rural/urban income parity	(Ratio)					
1985	0.51	1.75	1.32	0.88	1.38	
2000	0.48	1.51	1.22	0.92	1.36	
4. Rural poorest*						
a. persons	(Million)					
1985	172	0.80	0.89	1.05	0.91	
2000	174	0.66	0.85	1.07	0.90	
b. equivalent income	(Rs./person)					
1985	127	1.11	1.07	0.95	1.07	
2000	125	1.22	1.12	0.92	1.11	
5. Urban poorest*						
a. persons	(Million)					
1985	3	3.1	1.94	0.73	2.42	
2000	2	1.35	1.09	0.55	2.55	
b. equivalent income	(Rs./person)					
1985 167	0.92	0.97	1.01	0.98		
2000	172	0.96	0.99	1.01	0.98	

* Those with per capita consumption expenditure below what is equivalent to Rs. 216 per person per year at 1970 prices.

Several points have to be kept in mind in interpreting these results. First, the trend in the national average equivalent incomes is the weighted average of the trends of the average equivalent incomes of the ten rural and urban expenditure classes, and the trends of classwise equivalent incomes may move in different directions. Second, if the relative price in REF in the initial years differs significantly from world prices in one direction, say, it is higher, then reducing it through policy will reduce distortions provided the reduction is not too much while increasing it will increase distortions. Third, the pricing policy in REF brings the domestic prices closer to the world prices so that the degree of "price distortion" reduces over time. Thus, large changes in the relative price of agriculture introduced in our various scenarios compared to REF may introduce distortion in the later years by a significant amount.

Turning now to the effects on the welfare of different groups: rural population gains and the income parity between rural and urban incomes improve. The rural poorest clearly gain when relative prices of agricultural commodities increase. Thus in TT.7 there are 11 to 15 percent fewer people in the poorest rural class (20 to 25 million persons) and also the equivalent income of this class is 7 to 12 percent higher.

The welfare of urban poor on the other hand is adversely affected by higher agricultural prices. The equivalent income of the poorest class is 3 per cent lower in TT.7 in 1985. Although the number of persons in this class increases substantially (by 95%), the absolute numbers involved are exceedingly small as a proportion of the urban population. Urban poor gain and rural poor lose when agricultural terms of trade worsen by about 20 percent in the TT1.2 run.

Welfare comparisons using the Bailey-Willig (B-W) criteria are summarized in Table 8.3. None of the scenarios leads to an improvement by the B-W social welfare criterion for the total population.

TABLE 8.3 Social welfare comparison with reference scenario for the year 2000

	TT1.2	TT.7	TT.7X
	Relative price of agriculture lowered	Relative price of agriculture increased	Relative price of agriculture increased
	Tax adjusted	Tax adjusted	Investment adjusted
Rural population	Worse off	Better off	Poor better off Rich indeterminate
Urban population	Better off	Worse off	Worse off
Total population	Poor worse off Rich indeterminate	Poor better off Rich worse off	Poor better off Rich worse off

Note: "Poor better off" in this table implies that the bottom 50% or more are better off and that the Bailey-Willig curve for the scenario is above the curve for the reference scenario for the poor.

8.4 Concluding Remarks

The results indicate that none of the changes in the terms of trade compared to REF through policy leads to an unambiguous improvement in all indicators. Two critical assumptions made in these scenarios may explain this outcome.

First, as pointed out earlier, domestic prices gradually shift towards world prices in REF. Increases in domestic prices of agriculture through policy lead to changes in tariff and tax rates which reduce government revenues. This, in turn, reduces investment. The growth reduction associated with the fall in investment may outweigh any favorable effect of the price change.

Second, although average agricultural income changes with time and across scenarios, by assumption, the variance in the rural agriculture income distribution does not change. One may interpret this loosely to mean that the shares of each factor including labor in agricultural output remain constant and that factor prices adjust fully to agricultural output prices. Thus, even landless agricultural laborers gain fully from increases in agricultural prices. Were this not the case, increase in the relative price of agriculture could have perhaps adversely affected the rural poor.

9

Fertilizer Subsidy

9.1 The Issues

Many LDC governments wish to ensure that urban consumers get "cheap" food. If they intervene by maintaining relatively low consumer and producer prices, producer incentives are diminished. This affects food production and ultimately tends to raise food prices or at least the expenditure on subsidies. Alternatively, low food prices for consumers can be maintained by lowering the market price through imports.

In order to compensate for the production disincentive of low product prices, some LDC governments subsidize agricultural inputs. Irrigation water, electricity rates for farmers and fertilizer prices can all be subsidized. We wish to explore the impacts of fertilizer price subsidy on the economy. Once again, the impacts on producer decisions, yield levels and cropping patterns on product prices, on consumers and on government budgets can all be important. Also, the manner of financing subsidy can affect the outcomes.

When fertilizers are in short supply relative to demand at the prevailing prices, lowering of fertilizer prices obviously cannot increase its use and merely acts as an income transfer. In effect the mechanism by which the limited supplies of fertilizers are allocated among farmers determines the distribution of the income transfer. If the interest is in the impact of subsidy per se and not in its use as an income transfer mechanism, we have to ensure that in designing fertilizer price subsidy scenarios, fertilizer availability is increased sufficiently to eliminate excess demand and the need for rationing.

Of course, farmers' decisions on fertilizer use in many LDCs may be constrained not just by relative prices but also by credit availability and their perception of risks. Lowering of fertilizer prices reduces credit needs and also may reduce the risk associated with their use. Even when the expected output is the same, lower outlay on inputs lowers maximum possible loss. Thus, lower fertilizer prices would reduce risk and promote faster adoption of fertilizer use (and new technology) by farmers. We do not incorporate these diffusion processes directly in our model. However, one may argue that credit and risk problems should be addressed by other instruments (such as a credit subsidy to poor farmers or risk insurance), and that these considerations should not be mixed up in the analysis of fertilizer price subsidy.

One should, moreover, note that a fertilizer price subsidy to the extent that it is a promotional device to encourage faster diffusion of fertilizer use, should be viewed as a short-term measure that will terminate once all farmers are convinced of the profitability of using fertilizers. It is in principle different from a strategy of a fertilizer price subsidy to compensate farmers for low food prices.

When fertilizer is subsidized, the subsidy can be financed by raising taxes or by reducing other public expenditures. If we assume that all possibilities of reducing waste expenditures or for raising taxes have already been exhausted (as they should be in any case), the only option for financing the fertilizer subsidy is through reduction of public investments. Then the short-run benefits resulting from use of larger amounts of fertilizer would be offset in the long run by reduced public investments. The effects would, of course, depend on the level of subsidy involved.

9.2. The Scenarios

In order to simplify comparisons and to concentrate on the effects of changes in fertilizer prices, the same path of output prices is maintained in all alternative scenarios. This is done by letting imports and exports bear the burden of adjustment. This also affects government revenue from tariffs and its budget and investible surplus.

The policy (fertilizer price subsidy) is introduced in 1980 and is continued till 2000. The following scenarios are generated:

1. REFF: A reference run where fertilizer availability is exogenously projected as a time trend. As noted above, this scenario differs from the standard reference scenario REF.
2. FRA: Fertilizer availability is not constrained by the time trend but its price is not subsidized. This serves as a base run for assessing the impact of a fertilizer price subsidy.
3. FR.5: Fertilizer availability constraint removed and fertilizer price is subsidized to the extent of 50 percent. The investment rate is maintained and tax rate adjusts to finance fertilizer subsidy.

4. FR.5X: Same as FR.5 except that the tax rate in each year is maintained at the level of the tax rate realized in FRA run for that year and total investment adjusts.
5. FR.7X: Same as FR.5X except that the fertilizer subsidy is reduced to 30 percent and total investment adjusts.
6. FR1.5X: Same as FR.5X except that fertilizer is taxed at the rate of 50 percent on fertilizers and the revenue from the fertilizer tax is invested.

9.3 Some Important Characteristics of the Model and the Specifications of Fertilizer Subsidy

Before we turn to the results it would be useful to emphasize certain characteristics of the model which should be kept in mind in interpreting the results.

Total fertilizer availability is exogenously specified in terms of nitrogen. Phosphorus and potassic fertilizer are assumed to be applied in fixed proportion to nitrogenous fertilizers.

Of the available fertilizers, two-thirds are set aside for application to wheat and rice. The allocation to high yielding varieties (HYV), irrigated or rainfed cultivations of rice and wheat is made within this availability to maximize profits. If the profit maximizing dosages lead to a quantity that is less than the amount of fertilizer set aside for these crops, the smaller amount is applied, and the total quantity of fertilizer available for other crops is reduced by the same proportion.

Fertilizer is allocated to each of the other major crops as a fixed proportion of the quantity of fertilizer for use in all these crops. These proportions are based on their values for 1971 (Sarvekshana (1978)), the only year for which cropwise fertilizer data were available from a large sample. Again actual dosage is set as the profit-maximizing dosage or that based on available amounts whichever is lower.

The fertilizer subsidy was introduced into the model as follows:

(1) Fertilizer availability was increased so that from 1981 its availability was no longer constraining.
(2) Fertilizer price, for calculating profit-maximizing dosages was the subsidy (or tax) inclusive price.
(3) Farmers' income entitlements were increased (decreased) by the value of the total fertilizer subsidy (tax) by a transfer from (to) the government. The total value of subsidies (taxes) were in proportion to farmers' use of fertilizer.

9.4 The Results

Macro-economic indicators for selected years are shown in Table 9.1 for the various scenarios. The policy is introduced in 1980 and 1981 is the first year in which fertilizer availability is not binding. Thus fertilizer use is affected by fertilizer prices from 1981 till 2000 in all the scenarios.

In FRA, fertilizer availability is increased compared to the reference scenario REFF, but it is not subsidized. In the initial years, the GDP is higher in FRA than in REFF. However, as can be seen in Table 9.1, the difference is marginal and by the year 2000, the GDPs are nearly equal in the two scenarios. This is not surprising, for in REFF itself the fertilizer availability is binding only till 1986. In Table 9.2, the shadow price of fertilizer, its market price, and the quantity used in the two runs are shown.

The impact of subsidizing fertilizer is to reduce GDP agriculture measured at 1970 prices where value added in agriculture is calculated by costing fertilizer (compared to its FRA value) without subsidy. Why this is so can be seen in Figure 9.1. In Figure 9.1 YY' shows agricultural output as a function of fertilizer use. If the same output prices are used to evaluate the vector of outputs as fertilizer use is changed, it can be taken to be the value of agricultural output or revenue function. The cost of input, assumed to be a linear function of fertilizer, is shown by OT. At A, where the slope of 'YY' is the same as that of line OT, the GDP-agriculture is maximized and the corresponding fertilier use will be OC. Now when a subsidy on fertilizer price changes the line OT to OS, the optimal production point will be D with fertilizer use OG. The GDP agriculture will be DE at old prices and EF will be the value of fertilizer subsidy. Though private profit or benefit DF is larger than AB, social benefit, i.e., the constant price GDP, DE, is smaller than AB. This is another way of saying that an input subsidy is a distortion if its initial price is its social opportunity cost. Thus when fertilizer price is reduced to 50 percent as in FR.5 and FR.5X scenarios, GDP agriculture in 1981 is about 0.5 percent lower than in FRA, whereas GDP non-agriculture is more or less unchanged in 1981. The same reasoning explains why GDP agriculture at 1970 prices is above its FRA value when fertilizer is taxed.

Of course, the GDP agriculture inclusive of fertilizer subsidy is higher in the FR.5 run than in FRA in 1981 as it should be.

However, the cost of the fertilizer subsidy has to be borne by someone in the economy. In these scenarios, the cost is borne by the government. In the FR.5 scenario, the government maintains the investment/GDP rates at their values in the FRA scenario and raises taxes on non-agricultural incomes to finance the fertilizer susbidy. As fertilizer price subsidy distorts the economy,

TABLE 9.1 Macro-economic impact of fertilizer subsidy

	REFF	FRA fertilizer availability increased	FR.5 fertilizer price 50% of FRA Prices	FR.5X fertilizer price 50% and tax rates same as in FRA	FR.7X fertilizer price 70% and tax rates same as in FRA	FR1.5X fertilizer price 150% and tax rates same as in FRA
GDP (10^9 1970 RS.)						
1981	554.2	557.4	556.3	554.6	555.8	559.9
2000	1421.8	1422.4	1413.3	1349.3	1381.9	1473.3
GDP AGR* (10^9 1970 RS.)						
1981	225.7	229.0	227.8	227.1	228.0	230.4
2000	340.3	340.3	337.6	333.0	335.7	345.0
GDP NON-AGR (10^9 1970 RS.)						
1981	328.4	328.5	328.5	327.4	327.8	329.6
2000	1081.5	1081.1	1075.7	1016.3	1045.6	1128.3
INVESTMENT (10^9 1970 RS.)						
1981	121.7	122.4	122.1	109.0	114.7	133.2
2000	500.4	500.7	497.5	445.6	469.7	538.4
TARIFF RECEIPTS (10^9 1970 RS.)						
1981	7.9	7.1	7.3	6.4	6.7	7.8
2000	8.7	8.6	9.0	8.4	8.5	7.7

FERTILIZER SUBSIDY (10⁹ 1970 RS.)						
1981	0	0	11.8	11.8	6.8	-9.3
2000	0	0	17.8	17.4	10.1	-12.0
FERTILIZER USE (10³ tons N)						
1981	3950.0	7730.0	8580.0	8520.0	8200.0	6808.0
2000	11050.0	11050.0	12740.0	12430.0	11910.0	8723.0
VALUE OF AGR. Output (10 current Rs.)						
1981	489.8	514.3	516.3	514.8	514.7	512.5
2000	969.2	969.2	973.6	960.2	964.6	969.1
SHADOW PRICE OF FERTILISER (CURRENT RS./TON OF N**)						
1981	18843.0	5291.0	2645.0	2645.0	3704.0	7937.0
2000	7157.0	7157.0	3578.0	3578.0	5010.0	10736.0

N : Nitrogenous nutrients

* GDP agriculture at 1970 prices and does not include fertilizer subsidy or tax.

** and associated P_2O_5 and K_2O.

TABLE 9.2   Consumption, market and shadow prices of fertilizer

Year	Market price	REFF Reference scenario		FRA Increased fertilizer availability	
		Shadow price	Total nitrogen use	Shadow price	Total nitrogen use
	Rs/tonne*	Rs/tonne*	'000 tonnes	Rs./tonne	'000 tonnes
1980	5135	20396	3430	14765	5030
1981	5291	18843	3950	5291	7730
1982	5460	17410	4550	5460	7830
1985	5909	10346	6980	5909	8280
1986	6041	7418	8060	6041	8400
1987	6164	6164	8650	6164	8540
2000	7157	7157	11060	7157	11050

*   Rs./tonne of nitrogen (and associated P2O5 and K2O) in 1970 prices.

there is a reduction in GDP and as a consequence the investments are reduced, even though the government adjusts taxes to maintain the same investment to GDP rates. As a consequence the GDP in the year 2000 in FR.5 is lower than in FRA by about 9 billion rupees which is only about 0.6 percent of GDP.

When, however, fertilizer subsidy is financed by reducing investment and the time path of tax rates on non-agricultural incomes is constrained to be the same as that in the FRA run (the various X scenarios), the long term consequences of fertilizer subsidy income become more dramatic. The GDP in the year 2000 is now as much as 5 percent smaller in the 50 percent subsidy run FR.5X compared to its FRA run value. Even GDP-agriculture is lower by 2 percent (but is higher by 1.4 percent once the subsidy is included).

The cost of the fertilizer subsidy in FR.5X is Rs. 11.8 billion in 1981, whereas the investment in 1981 of Rs. 109 billion is lower by Rs. 13.4 billion (9.4 percent) compared to FRA. The reduction in investment exceeds the cost of fertilizer subsidy because of lower GDP, lower trade deficit (which is proportional to GDP) and lower tariff receipts consequent upon changes in the pattern of trade because of the changes in agricultural production structure, in FR.5X. The reduction in investment in FR.5X is 9.4 percent in 1981 and 11 percent in 2000. Thus, a reduction of investment of around 10 percent every year cumulates to a 5 percent lower GDP in 2000, or a fall of 0.3 percent in

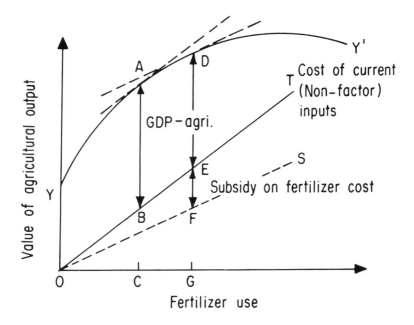

Fig. 9.1 Impact of fertilizer subsidy

the annual growth rate of GDP over 1980 to 2000.

The FR.7X run, in which the fertilizer subsidy is 30 percent and is financed by adjusting investment the results are similar to the FR.5X scenario.

Similarly in FR1.5X when fertilizer is taxed by 50 percent and the tax income is used to augment investment above the investment determined by the specified investment/GDP relationship, the effects are similar but in the opposite direction. The GDP in 2000 is higher by about 3.7 percent compared to the FRA run.

In Figure 9.2, the shadow price of nitrogen is plotted against the total nitrogen used. Since nitrogen use is constrained by availability in some years and profitability in others, one can take these points to be on different demand curves. The demand for nitrogen shifts outward over the years as more land is cultivated, more area is irrigated, and as more land is devoted to the high yielding varieties. The demand will also depend on the price of agricultural outputs and not just on the price of fertilizers. Since in different scenarios the time path of output prices is kept the same through adjustment of trade flows, the points from different scenarios for a given year may be connected to obtain a "demand" curve for fertilizer. Though this is not strictly a demand curve as the areas and other factors are different in the various scenarios, the effects of these differences are likely to be small in 1981 as the policy changes are introduced only in 1980. Thus the curve for 1981 may be closer to the "true demand" curve than the one for 2000.

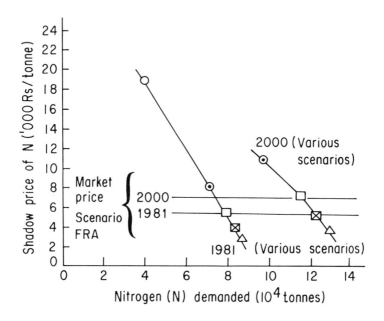

Fig. 9.2　Fertilizer demand

Figure 9.2 indicates that at the market price the fertilizer use in the FRA scenario in 1981 is already high and even a 50 percent reduction in price increases fertilizer use by only 11.0 percent, giving a price elasticity of -0.2.

In Figure 9.3, the value of agricultural output in 1981 at current prices is plotted against the quantity of fertilizer used in different scenarios. Though the points from different scenarios are not strictly comparable, for 1981 the curve connecting these points not differ much from the "true" curve, and one probably gets an "order of magnitude" of output response to fertilizers. The curve indicates the relatively very small contribution of fertilizer to the value of aggregate agricultural output in India. The response is small and the curve is almost flat. When fertilizer use increases from 4.0 million tonnes to 8.6 million tonnes the value of agricultural output increases by Rs. 26 billion from

Rs. 490 billion to Rs.516 billion. Though small, as expected, the increase is larger than the value of additional fertilizer used. The points for 2000 from the various scenarios do not constitute a smooth curve because the different levels of development of irrigation, and area under HYVs affect fertilizer use and the output responds differently to changes in fertilizer use in the runs. The shift in the points from 1981 to 2000 indicates the results of expansion of irrigation, technical progress and changes in prices over the twenty years.

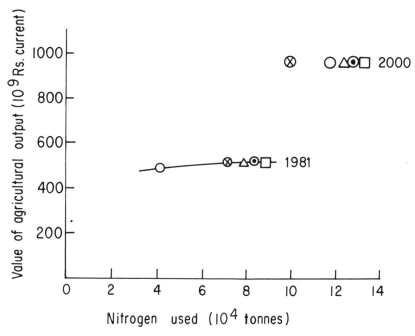

Fig. 9.3 Agricultural output and fertilizer use

The small response of the value of agricultural production to large increases in fertilizer use in a given year shows that the cost of raising agricultural output through fertilizer price subsidy will be substantial. Moreover, there are limits to which output can be so increased.

However, for individual crops, fertilizer subsidy and consequent increased use of it, can significantly raise production. This can be seen in Table 9.3 where productions of wheat, rice and coarse grains are shown for different scenarios for 1981 to 2000. Once again as fertilizer use increases from 4 million tonnes in REFF to 8.6 million tonnes in FR.5 the output of cereals increases by 17 percent from 112 million tonnes to 130 million tonnes. Here also production levels reach a plateau and additional fertilizer subsidies hardly increase output.

The welfare impacts of fertilizer subsidy can be seen in Table 9.4 where the energy intake per capita and the equivalent income of the poorest classes are given.

The aggregate indicators of welfare, average per capita equivalent income and average per capita energy intake, do not show any of the runs to be unambiguously superior over all others. Though a 50 percent fertilizer price subsidy with fixed tax rate, FR.5X, gives higher energy intakes for both 1981 and 2000 than FRA, equivalent incomes in FRA are higher in 2000. In general what one sees is that any short run change in welfare in one scenario compared to another gets reversed in the long run due to differences in the growth of the economy in the two.

Turning now to the impact of fertilizer subsidy on the poor, a 50 percent price subsidy with taxes fixed at their levels in FRA leads to an increase in the equivalent incomes of the rural poorest class in both 1981 and 2000. However, the proportion of population in this class is marginally higher in both the years. The increases in proportion of population are so small that, despite them, the increases of about 3 percent in equivalent incomes could be considered an improvement in social welfare. The impact on the urban poorest is ambiguous. Their equivalent incomes remain almost the same both in 1981 and 2000. But compared to FRA, the proportion of the poorest in 1981 falls or remains the same in all the tax-fixed scenarios though it rises in FR.5. This proportion in the year 2000 is higher or remains the same compared to FRA in all the scenarios except in FR1.5X. Thus, in terms of its distributional impact fertilizer price subsidy does not provide unambiguous results. This is to be expected since it is an output raising measure rather than a redistribution one.

9.5   Concluding Observations

Before concluding, it may be worth emphasizing some of the assumptions behind the analysis.

An important characteristic of the scenarios is that the output price path is kept the same in different scenarios through adjustments in trade flows. Thus, when additional output of foodgrains is produced with a fertilizer subsidy, that output is traded and consumption is altered only to the extent of income effects.

One could have maintained trade at specified levels and let the prices adjust. Such a policy would have produced much larger immediate improvements in

TABLE 9.3 Production of cereals (10^6 tonnes)

	REFF	FRA fertilizer availability Increased	FR.5 fertilizer price 50% of FRA prices	FR.5X fertilizer price 50% and tax rates same	FR.7X fertilizer price 70% and tax rates same	FR1.5X fertilizer price 150% and tax rates same
1981						
Wheat	36.15	44.24	44.96	44.62	44.52	43.38
Rice	48.94	55.20	55.67	55.26	55.28	54.84
Coarse grains	26.74	29.59	30.16	30.16	29.94	28.75
2000						
Wheat	86.88	86.89	88.87	86.58	86.96	85.07
Rice	87.56	87.58	88.87	86.27	87.03	87.01
Coarse grains	34.89	34.90	36.09	35.89	35.57	29.94

TABLE 9.4 Welfare impact of fertilizer prices subsidy

10⁹ Rs. 1970 prices or 10⁶ tonnes	REFF	FRA fertilizer availability increased	FR.5 fertilizer price 50% of FRA prices	FR.5X fertilizer price 50% and tax rates same	FR.7X fertilizer price 70% and tax rates same	FR1.5X fertilizer price 150% and tax rates same
TOTAL POPULATION ENERGY INTAKE (Kcal/person/day)						
1981	2158.0	2144.0	2177.0	2201.0	2177.0	2100.0
2000	2396.0	2396.0	2423.0	2420.0	2410.0	2387.0
EQUIVALENT INCOME (Rs/ Person/day)						
1981	551.0	547.0	547.0	562.0	556.0	536.0
2000	698.0	699.0	694.0	693.0	696.0	704.0
RURAL POOREST CLASS (proportion of rural population)						
1981	0.311	0.310	0.312	0.313	0.313	0.312
2000	0.243	0.243	0.246	0.249	0.246	0.239
EQUIVALENT INCOME						
1981	127.0	126.0	132.0	132.0	129.0	122.0
2000	121.0	121.0	128.0	128.0	125.0	118.0

URBAN POOREST CLASS (proportion of urban population)						
1981	0.019	0.021	0.022	0.020	0.020	0.021
2000	0.004	0.004	0.004	0.005	0.004	0.003
EQUIVALENT INCOME						
1981	165.0	164.0	164.0	164.0	164.0	164.0
2000	172.0	172.0	172.0	172.0	172.0	173.0

domestic consumption when fertilizer price subsidy is given but output prices would have been depressed, lowering future production. Though the long-run impacts would have been similar, the results of such a scenario would have been more difficult to interpret. The chosen policy specifications of maintaining the same prices across runs is easier to interpret as all impacts get directed to investment levels.

The runs demonstrate that:

(1) The short-run elasticity of fertilizer use at the aggregate level with respect to its price is low and is about 20 percent at the level of use in the reference scenarios of around 4 million tonnes of nitrogen in 1981. Fertilizer consumption over the years increases because of an increase in area, irrigation and the spread of HYV use.

(2) The short-run response to fertilizer use in terms of the value of aggregate agricultural output is also very small. Responses of individual crops, however, are more significant.

(3) Though fertilizer price subsidy stimulates immediate agricultural production, the macro-economic consequences lead to lower agricultural output in the long run as well as a lower GDP.

(4) The welfare impacts on the poor in the country are minimal and ambiguous. Thus short run gains are offset by long run effects and while the rural poorest gain, the urban poor lose.

In conclusion, subsidizing fertilizer does not seem to be an attractive policy for India. However, two qualifications to this conclusion should be noted. First, as discussed earlier, we have not accounted for the fact that cheaper fertilizer may promote a faster diffusion of new technology. Second, technical progress in the model shifts the yield-fertilizer relationship without increasing marginal physical product of fertilizer. It is conceivable that agronomic research may develop new varieties that can either increase fertilizer responses or absorb more fertilizer, or both. Such technical progress can alter the conclusion. None the less, we want to emphasize that both the diffusion effect and the different kinds of technical progress may reverse the conclusion but not necessarily so. The case for fertilizer subsidy would still have to be made after accounting for the macro-economic feedback considered here.

10

Development of Irrigation

It is a cliche that Indian agriculture is a gamble on the monsoons. Like most cliches it has a germ of truth. The economic, political and social consequences of the two consecutive and unprecedented droughts of 1965-66 and 1966-67 and of a somewhat less severe drought of 1973-74 are a testament to this. The desire to protect the farmers against the ravages of droughts (and floods) was the driving force behind the development of irrigation in the past. For instance, some of the extant irrigation works in the Cauvery delta are at least a thousand years old. Since the yield per hectare of most crops is considerably increased by irrigation and the associated cultivation practices, farmers naturally will shift their cultivated area towards high value crops (e.g. sugarcane, rice and wheat versus coarse grains) some of which are water- intensive when irrigation becomes available. If they succeed in doing so, water from irrigation works will be used to enhance the average value of production rather than to reduce the variance caused by the vagaries of the weather. That those at the head of irrigation works have first access to the water has often meant that they also appropriate more than their due share of the water at the expense of those at the tail end. Even if such distributional consequences were absent, that reallocation of crop areas will not result in irrigation providing insurance against the weather fluctuations, was considered serious enough in the past, so that measures to prevent such reallocation were often introduced including penalties for cultivating high value crops beyond the extent permitted. Such penalties often were not large enough, nor were thay enforced with vigour, so that reallocation could take place.

In the post-independence era, the focus on irrigation development shifted away from protecting against weather fluctuations to enhancing crop yields and production. This shift in emphasis got accentuated with the introduction of fertilizer-responsive and high yielding dwarf varieties of rice and wheat and hybrid varieties of bajra and maize. Many of these varieties yielded a large output per unit of land even with limited use of fertilizers and under rainfed conditions. Yet their yield performance under irrigated conditions was thought to be much better.

Another distinguishing feature of the post-independence era is the development of minor irrigation facilities for exploiting surface water as well as ground water through deep tube wells. Side by side with the state investment in minor irrigation, there was also a rapid growth in private tube wells and energised wells, particularly during the period and in the areas of the so-called green revolution. While the net area irrigated by all other sources increased only by 50% in the thirty years from 1950-51 to 1980-81, the net area irrigated by wells and tube wells nearly tripled. With increasing intensities of both irrigation and fertilizer use, problems of waterlogging and salinity have emerged in some areas. Also the density of tube wells has increased so much in a few areas that the water table has gone down rapidly.

The problem of a declining water table is an illustration of one of the many externalities in irrigation development. Indeed designing irrigation systems that make optimum conjunctive use of ground and surface water resources through, first, appropriate investment in reservoirs and distribution channels (including those at the field level); second, well formulated rules for allocation of water to different crops at different times; and third, timely and adequate maintenance involving complex technical, economic, political and administrative considerations. The externalities and increasing returns to scale are significant so that private and social costs and benefits can differ substantially. Also irrigation systems have some of the features of public good so that free riding (i.e., sharing in benefits without sharing in the costs) is likely. That many reservoirs in India not only provide irrigation but also help in flood control and are used to generate electricity, introduces conflicts and trade-offs among irrigation, power generation and flood control. Even if one does not wish to go with the characterization by Witfogel of some of the empires of the past as 'hydraulic states', the role of the state in delineating water rights, specifying rates for use of water from public works and in regulating private investment and operation of irrigation facilities and encouraging co-operative/collective management where desirable, can hardly be overstated. However, these issues, though important, cannot be analyzed with our model which is more appropriate for an evaluation of alternative investment and financing strategies for irrigation development.

10.1 Irrigation Development in India since Independence

Out of an ultimate potential of 113.5 million hectares of irrigated area, 67.9 million hectares had been provided with irrigation facilities by 1984-85. The utilization of these facilities led to 60.4 million hectares of land being irrigated the same year. Details of this development and the targets for the Seventh Plan (1985-1990) are given in Table 10.1.

The outlay and irrigation potential development over various Five-year Plans at current prices are given in Table 10.2.

The outlay data include investment as well as some current expenditures. Nevertheless, by deflating the current price values by a suitable price index, one can obtain an idea of the real cost per hectare of irrigation development. This is shown in Table 10.3.

The real cost per hectare of irrigated land from major and medium schemes has increased from about Rs. 2500 per hectare in 1951-56 period to over Rs. 8500 in 1985-90. Since the outlay data in Table 10.2 on minor schemes include only public outlays while the potential created includes what was created also by private investment (for which data are not available), we have not attempted to estimate the real cost per hectare irrigated by such schemes. However, there is no doubt that minor schemes are considerably cheaper.

10.2 Irrigation Development: The Issues

It is useful to begin with some self-evident facts about irrigation. Many of the rivers in India are essentially seasonal streams, flowing with water during the rainy reason and remaining practically dry during the rest of the year. The volume of water flowing in the perennial rivers varies substantially within a year, from roaring torrents to a mere trickle sometimes. Since monsoons can fail and snow packs on mountains can vary in size, there are wide variations in total flows between years as well. Hence a reservoir built on a river can transfer water from the surplus monsoon season to the dry winter season and from years of plentiful monsoon to drought years. Even a reservoir built mainly for irrigation can generate power as long as there is sufficient head by simply letting the water from the reservoirs flow through turbines rather than through sluices before it reaches farmers' fields. Of course, if the reservoir is meant for power generation as well, and if the seasonal pattern of demand for power and water for irrigation is not similar, and if pumped ground water can substitute for water in the reservoir, very interesting issues relating to the operation of the reservoirs can arise including those relating to intra-years, inter-

TABLE 10.1 Irrigation potential and utilization (1950-90) (Million hectares)

Sl. No (1)	Item (2)	Ultimate Potential (3)	1950-51		1984-85		1989-90	
			Potential (4)	Utilization (5)	Potential (6)	Utilization (7)	Potential (8)	Utilization (9)
1.	Surface water							
	(a) Major & medium	73.5	16.1	16.1	40.2	34.3	46.0	39.4
	(b) Minor	58.5	9.7	9.7	30.5	25.3	34.8	29.2
		15.0	6.4	6.4	9.7	9.0*	11.2	10.2
2.	Ground water	40.0	6.5	6.5	27.7	26.1*	34.8	31.9
	Total	113.5	22.6	22.6	67.9	60.4	80.8	71.3

* Since separate utilization figures for minor irrigation have been made available by the end of 1985-90, the related potential and utilization figures are shown separately.

Source : Planning Commission (1985), Vol. II, Ch. 3.

TABLE 10.2 Outlay on Development of Irrigation Potential

(1)	Outlay/Expenditure (Rs. Millions)		Irrigation Potential Cumulative (Mil. Hectares)	
	Major & Medium Irrgn.	Minor Irrgn.**	Major & Medium Irrgn.	Minor Irrgn.
	(2)	(3)	(4)	(5)
Pre-Plan Benefits (up to '50–'51)			9.7	12.9
First Plan ('51–'56)	3800*	760	12.20	14.06
Second Plan ('56–'61)	3800	1420	14.30	14.79
Third Plan ('61–'66)	5810	3280	16.60	17.01
Annual Plan ('66–'69)	4340	3260	18.10	19.00
Fourth Plan ('69–'74)	12370	5130	20.70	23.50
Fifth Plan ('74–'78)	24420	6310	24.82	27.30
Annual Plan ('78–'79)	9770	2370	25.86	28.60
Annual Plan ('79–'80)	10790	2600	26.60	30.00
Sixth Plan ('80–'85)	75160	18020#	30.50	37.40
Seventh Plan ('85–'90)@	115600	28050#	34.80	46.00

* Includes Rs. 800 million incurred during the pre-plan period.

** Government outlays only.

@ Planned outlays and targets.

\# In addition, institutional investment was Rs. 15440 million during the sixth plan, and is expected to be Rs. 35000 million during the 7th plan.

Source: Planning Commission (1985), Vol. II, Ch. 3.

season transfers and inter-year transfers of water. One can complicate matters further by embedding hydro-power in a system consisting of conventional thermal, nuclear and hydro-power and recognizing that river flows, irrigation and power demands are stochastic. An early theoretical contribution to this area was made by Koopmans (1957). In the Indian context Minhas, Parikh and Srinivasan (1974) analyzed the power-irrigation trade-off and conjunctive use of ground and surface water in the operation of the Bhakra reservoir on the Sutlej. We do not go into these issues in this chapter except to note that by making inter-season transfer of water possible, irrigation enables the growing of multiple crops in a year on the same plot of land. Clearly, even if there is no increase in yield per hectare for each crop, by enabling more than one crop to be grown on a plot of land in a year,irrigation increases annual production. In other words, yield per unit of net sown area will go up even though the yield per unit of gross sown area is unchanged. For these reasons, cropping intensity, i.e. the ratio of the gross cropped area to the net sown area, is aꞃ indicator of the benefit of irrigation that we use in comparing scenarios. As described in Chapter 4, in our model, agricultural investment largely determines the irrigated area.

TABLE 10.3   Costs of developing irrigation potential

	Net additional potential created	Outlay on major and medium irrigation	Cost per hectare
	(10^6 hectares)	(10^6 Rs. 1970)	(Rs. 1970)
First plan (1951-1956)	2.5	6440	2580
Second plan (1956-1961)	2.1	6130	2920
Third plan (1961-1966)	2.3	8800	3830
Annual plan (1966-1969)	1.5	4930	3290
Fourth plan (1969-1974)	2.6	11250	4330
Fifth plan (1974-1978)	4.12	14620	3550
Annual plan (1978-1979)	1.04	5060	4870
Annual plan (1979-1980)	0.74	5140	6940
Sixth plan (1980-1985)	3.90	26133	6701
Seventh plan (1985-1990)	4.30	37154	8640

As contrasted with the storage of water in all the operation of man-made reservoirs, exploitation of natural underground reservoirs has additional advantages. We have already mentioned that minor irrigation works are cheaper to construct. While increasing cropping intensity in a fashion similar to that of a surface reservoir, water from a shallow well (energized or not) and deep tube wells can be used much more flexibly than water from the large reservoirs.

Since a well supplies water only to a limited area, one can vary the rate of pumping to suit the changing water needs in that area without affecting other areas. In the canal-based distribution systems of a reservoir such possibilities are obviously limited. Even more important, the control of the operation of a well rests in the hands of the farmer, while that of the reservoir rests with the irrigation bureaucracy.

An important issue then is the relative pace of development of the two types of irrigation and whether private irrigation development should be subsidized. Except indirectly through policy variations in the cost of irrigation per hectare, we do not address the problem of the trade-off between minor and major irrigation in the aggregate irrigation investment.

We already referred to the fact that irrigation not only reduces production uncertainty and so stabilizes production but raises yields as well. A reduction in production uncertainty results because the optimum moisture availability in the root zone of a crop can be achieved with greater assurance if irrigation water is available rather than natural precipitation. This is very likely within a given growing season or even within a year. But over several years, unless storage permits inter-year transfer of water and the reservoir is operated with such transfers in mind, inter-year fluctuations in moisture availability will not be reduced significantly by irrigation. In India, no reservoir is consciously operated with respect to inter-year transfers. The reduced production risk because of irrigation is not captured in our model.

Analyzing the contribution of irrigation to raising yield per hectare requires an understanding of the effect of soil moisture at the root zone and hence, the marginal productivity of water at different stages from sowing to harvest. Not many analytical and empirical studies are available on this topic relating to different crops in different agro-climatic zones. One of the few is by Minhas, Parikh and Srinivasan (1974). They developed a procedure to estimate a yield response function for a crop with dated inputs of water. They used experimental data on periodic soil moisture observations, soil characteristics, rainfall, potential evapo-transpiration and yields to obtain the yield response functions for alfalfa in the USA and wheat in India.

Unfortunately, data for econometrically estimating such functions are hard to find. However, one can use a physical crop production (PCP) model based on agronomic principles (de Wit 1965 and Konijin 1984) for this purpose. A PCP model takes the data on the characteristics of the crop, properties of the soil and climatic conditions to relate inputs such as fertilizer and water to yields. Using such a model, we can generate fertilizer yield responses for a number of years' climates under alternative assumptions about water availability from supplemental irrigation. The results may be represented as shown in Figures 10.1 and 10.2.

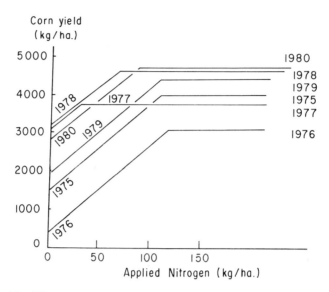

Fig. 10.1 Yield response to fertilizers of corn under climates of different
years – without any supplemental irrigation.

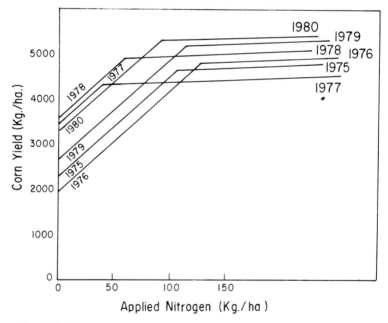

Fig. 10.2 Yield response to fertilizers of corn under climates of different
years – with supplemental irrigation

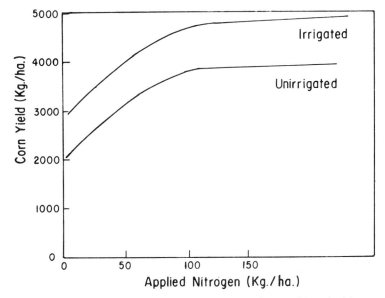

Fig. 10.3 Expected yield-response to fertisers of corn with and without
irrigation – assuming equal probability for all the years

If we now assume that the probability of the climatic conditions for the
various years in our sample are known we can obtain assuming the same
probability for each year, two expected yield response functions from the graphs
of Figures 10.1 and 10.2, one without irrigation and the other with the assumed extent of irrigation. The difference between these curves as shown in
Figure 10.3 tells us the expected additional yield due to irrigation.

The approach, as described above could be very useful for a detailed planning of specific irrigation systems as well as for scheduling the operations of
such systems. However, it is not very practical for the more strategic questions of exploring the extent of development of the irrigation system in the
country as a whole. For such planning purposes, a more aggregated approach
is required for obtaining reasonably accurate estimates of crop yield response
to irrigation.

We have estimated the yield functions of different crops in the country in
which the yield per hectare is related to the proportion of the area irrigated,
the proportion of the area under HYV and to the fertilizer availability. These
functions are estimated using the data of thousands of simple fertilizer trials

(Parikh, Srinivasan et al. 1974 , Parikh 1978) carried out on farmers' fields covering the period 1969 to 1972, and made consistent with the data on time series of these variables at the national level. These yield function estimates are described in detail in Narayana and Parikh (1987). In estimating these aggregate yield functions, we could not distinguish between different levels of irrigation water applications, as usable data on the quantity of water applied are not available. Thus, we had to use the proportion of area irrigated as a variable in the system.

Since these estimates are based on time series data, they provide information on yield responses over the years and annual fluctuations caused by the weather are effectually evened out. Fluctuations are either captured by the weather variable when used, or are in the residuals. As the estimates are at national level they can be used for a strategic analysis of the role of irrigation in national agricultural development.

Apart from yield increases on land sown with particular varieties of crops, changes in irrigation availability will result in a reallocation of crop areas as mentioned earlier, and in the intensity of usage of inputs such as fertilizer. These can be analyzed with our model. The last important issue to consider is the distributional implications of irrigation investment. Of course any increase in production will increase farmers' incomes as iong as market prices do not fall more than proportionately. To the extent equilibrium market prices fall, net buyers of food (landless agricultural workers, small farmers and urban consumers) benefit. Agricultural workers benefit if the demand for labor is shifted outward because of irrigation. However, with no explicit labor market, our model is incapable of directly analyzing this aspect. In India, the proportion of irrigated area in the total area is higher in small farms than in large farms. To the extent this is preserved with further intensification of irrigation (i.e., if the irrigated area in small farms increase more than proportionately to the increase in total irrigated area), small farmers will benefit from irrigation development to a greater degree. Our model is well suited to capture the distributional changes induced by the changes in yields, production and prices.

To summarize, we use the model to analyze the following questions:

(1) What would be the impact of faster development of irrigation on the gross cultivated area, the aggregate cropping intensity, the cropping pattern, crop yields, farm incomes and the welfare of different income groups?
(2) What would be the impact on these of alternative ways in which additional irrigation investment is financed?
(3) Is faster development of irrigation desirable?

10.3 The Scenarios

The following scenarios relating to irrigation development are compared with a reference scenario in which there are no trade bounds, RNQ, so that domestic prices are the same across the runs.

IRO: *Irrigation availability increased:* By earmarking part of total investment for irrigation, *additional* irrigated area is made available each year from 1980 till 2000. This annual *addition* rises linearly from 0.5 million hectares by 0.05 million hectares a year to 1.5 million hectares. This is a substantial step-up over the reference scenario. The rest of the total investment is divided as in the reference scenario between agriculture and non-agriculture.

IRFA: Same as IRO but with increased fertilizer availability. Since additional irrigation induces the adoption of fertilizer intensive high yielding varieties and optimal fertilizer intensities, if fertilizer availability is limited the full output potential of irrigation may not be realized. Hence this scenario.

IRFSX: Same as IRFA but with a 50 percent price subsidy on fertilizer which is financed through a reduction in investment by fixing the tax rates at the levels of FRA of chapter 9.

10.4 The Results

Before we turn to the results of the scenarios, we present illustrative estimates of the rate of return of investment in irrigation. Consider a wheat-growing farmer investing in the irrigation of one hectare of presently unirrigated land. The impact on output from such investment will depend on whether the newly irrigated area will be devoted to the local or high yielding variety. We will consider both alternatives. Yields depend also on fertilizer application. We assume that the farmer will apply a profit-maximizing dose of fertilizer. Given a fertilizer price twice that of wheat, he will then apply 121 Kg/ha, 88 Kg/ha and 120 Kg/ha respectively on unirrigated land sown with local variety, irrigated land sown with local and high yielding variety as per our yield functions.

On the one hectare of land, with irrigation, if he sows the local variety his yield goes up by 0.428 tonnes while fertilizer use goes down by 0.033 tonnes, resulting in a net increase in profit of $(0.428 + 0.033 \times 2)P_w$ where P_w is the price of wheat since fertilizer costs twice as much as wheat per tonne.

With price of wheat at Rs. 2000 per tonne (wholesale prices of local wheat at the end of 1986 ranged between Rs. 1820 and Rs. 2300 per tonne depending on the variety), the additional income amounts to Rs. 988. If we assume that irrigation investment per hectare is Rs. 8500 (the seventh plan figure for major and medium irrigation) and that current costs of irrigation and fertilizer application amount to 10% of Rs. 988, the rate of return of our irrigation investment is about 10.5%.

If the farmers grow a high yielding variety, his additional yield will be 0.928 tonne. His fertilizer use changes only marginally so that his net income goes up to Rs. 1856. His return on investment will then be 19.6%. Similar calculations relating to converting a hectare of unirrigated land growing rice to irrigated land suggest that farmers' net income will go up by Rs. 1863 and Rs. 1769 respectively if he grows local or high yielding variety. The return on his investment is between 19.7% and 18.7%.

It is very likely that investment in minor irrigation which is what a farmer is likely to undertake will cost much less than the Rs. 8500 per hectare assumed above, and the rate of return will, therefore, exceed 20% by a good margin.

Returning to the scenarios, macro-economic indicators are presented in Table 10.4. The impact on area, yield and output of selected crops is presented in Table 10.5. The distributional impact on classwise population proportions, average equivalent incomes, and average energy intakes are presented in Tables 10.6, 10.7 and 10.8 respectively.

Since fertilizer availability did not prove to be a binding constraint after about 1981 as in scenario IRO, increasing the availability as in scenario IRFA makes little difference to any of the indicators as compared to IRO in the year 2000. In what follows we will, therefore, discuss only the scenarios IRO and IRFSX.

Compared to RNQ, there is very little change in any of the macro or micro indicators in IRO for the year 1980. This is as expected since in IRO we simply use a part of essentially the same total investment as in RNQ for irrigation investment. This results in a 1% increase in total irrigated area in 1980 which is allocated among different crops, with sugarcane gaining 3%, jowar 2% and others 1%. By the year 2000, the cumulative effect of investment in irrigation results in a 26% increase in total irrigated area compared to RNQ. The gross cropped area increases by 6%. Irrigated areas of all crops increase with wheat (28%) and bajra (32%) gaining more than the average of 26%. With additional irrigation, fertilizer use goes up by 15% in the year 2000. Crop yields go up in the year 2000 for all crops, and by significant amounts in the case of wheat(9%), jowar(10%), and maize(10%). As expected, real GDP from agriculture goes up substantially (8%) in the year 2000 with non-agricultural GDP going up just by 1%. The average energy intake and the equivalent income increase respectively by 1% and 2% relative to RNQ.

Interestingly, the top three classes in rural areas and the richest class in urban areas gain population from other classes in 2000 as compared to RNQ. However, within each class, average equivalent incomes fall by about 1% for the middle three rural classes. For the poorest it remains unchanged, and for the richest it goes up by 1%. There is no change in the equivalent incomes of the first four urban classes while the richest gain about 1%. The picture with respect to energy intake is the same as that for equivalent incomes.

TABLE 10.4 Macro-economic indicators (ratio to RNQ values)

	Reference run no trade bounds		Irrigation availability increased					
			Fertiliser availability constrained		Fertilizer availability unconstrained		Fertilizer availability unconstrained & subsidized	
	RNQ		IRO		IRFA		IRFSX	
	(Absolutes)		(Ratio to reference run values)					
	1980	2000	1980	2000	1980	2000	1980	2000
GDPA	220.3	340.3	1.00	1.08	1.02	1.08	1.02	1.04
GDPNA	311.2	1081.5	1.00	1.01	1.00	1.01	1.00	0.84
GDP	531.5	1421.8	1.00	1.03	1.01	1.03	1.01	0.88
Total investment	114.2	500.4	0.98	1.01	0.99	1.01	0.87	0.71
Pa/Pna[†]	0.91	0.72	1.00	0.99	1.00	0.99	1.00	0.98
GDP/capita (Rs. 1970 prices)	788.5	1356.3	1.00	1.03	1.00	1.03	1.00	0.88
Equivalent income per capita	542.2	698.4	1.00	1.02	1.00	1.02	0.99	1.00
Energy intake per capita	2145.4	2395.9	1.00	1.01	1.00	1.01	1.00	1.05
Total fertilizer use	3.43	11.0	1.00	1.15	1.47*	1.15	1.47*	1.22
Total cropped area	172.7	201.8	1.00	1.06	1.00	1.06	1.00	1.03
Total irrigated area	45.9	83.8	1.01	1.26	1.01	1.27	1.01	1.14

†   Price index of agriculture/non-agriculture.

*   Though fertilizer availability is increased for the year 1980 it is stll binding and so the price subsidy does not increase its use. From 1981 onwards availability is not binding.

TABLE 10.5 Production indicators (ratio to RNQ values)

	IRO		IRFA		IRFSX	
	1980	2000	1980	2000	1980	2000
Wheat						
Total area	1.01	1.06	1.01	1.06	1.01	1.03
Irrigated area	1.01	1.28	1.01	1.28	1.01	1.15
Yield	1.00	1.16	1.15	1.16	1.15	1.10
Output	1.00	1.09	1.14	1.09	1.14	1.07
Rice						
Total area	1.01	1.15	1.01	1.15	1.01	1.08
Irrigated area	1.01	1.25	1.01	1.25	1.01	1.14
Yield	1.00	1.02	1.08	1.02	1.08	1.03
Output	1.01	1.18	1.09	1.18	1.09	1.11
Bajra						
Total area	1.00	1.03	1.00	1.03	1.00	1.02
Irrigated area	1.01	1.32	1.01	1.32	1.01	1.17
Yield	1.00	1.02	1.02	1.02	1.02	1.02
Output	1.00	1.05	1.02	1.05	1.02	1.04
Jowar						
Total area	0.99	0.85	0.99	0.85	0.99	0.91
Irrigated area	1.02	1.22	1.02	1.22	1.02	1.12
Yield	1.00	1.10	1.06	1.10	1.06	1.09
Output	0.99	0.94	1.05	0.94	1.05	0.99
Maize						
Total area	1.00	1.01	1.00	1.09	1.00	1.05
Irrigated area	1.00	1.09	1.00	1.09	1.00	1.05
Yield	1.00	1.10	1.10	1.03	1.10	1.05
Output	1.00	1.11	1.00	1.12	1.10	1.10
Sugarcane						
Total area	1.01	1.19	1.01	1.19	1.01	1.10
Irrigated area	1.03	1.21	1.03	1.21	1.03	1.11
Yield	1.00	1.00	1.00	1.00	1.00	1.00

TABLE 10.6 Distribution of population (ratio to RNQ values)

		IRO		IRFA		IRFSX	
		1980	2000	1980	2000	1980	2000
Rural class	1	1.00	0.93	0.99	0.93	0.99	0.97
	2	1.00	0.99	1.00	0.99	1.00	1.00
	3	1.00	1.02	1.00	1.02	1.00	1.04
	4	1.00	1.04	1.01	1.04	1.01	1.10
	5	1.00	1.04	1.01	1.04	1.01	0.94
Urban class	1	1.00	0.97	1.06	0.96	1.06	1.79
	2	1.00	0.98	1.01	0.98	1.01	1.52
	3	1.00	0.99	1.00	0.98	1.00	1.31
	4	1.00	0.99	1.00	0.99	1.00	1.11
	5	1.00	1.01	1.02	1.01	1.00	0.86

TABLE 10.7 Equivalent incomes (ratio to RNQ values)

		IRO		IRFA		IRFSX	
		1980	2000	1980	2000	1980	2000
Rural class	1	1.00	1.00	1.00	1.00	1.05	1.17
	2	1.00	0.99	0.99	0.99	1.06	1.19
	3	1.00	0.99	0.99	0.99	1.06	1.19
	4	1.00	0.99	1.00	0.99	1.05	1.16
	5	1.00	1.01	1.00	1.01	1.05	1.04
Urban class	1	1.00	1.00	1.00	1.00	1.00	0.99
	2	1.00	1.00	1.00	1.00	1.00	1.00
	3	1.00	1.00	1.00	1.00	1.00	1.00
	4	1.00	1.00	1.00	1.01	1.00	0.99
	5	1.00	1.01	1.00	1.01	1.00	0.95

TABLE 10.8 Average energy intake (ratio to RNQ values)

		IRO		IRFA		IRFSX	
		1980	2000	1980	2000	1980	2000
Rural class	1	1.00	1.00	1.00	1.00	1.05	1.17
	2	1.00	0.99	1.00	0.99	1.05	1.18
	3	1.00	0.99	1.00	0.99	1.05	1.16
	4	1.00	0.99	1.00	0.99	1.04	1.12
	5	1.00	1.00	1.00	1.00	1.03	1.03
Urban class	1	1.00	1.00	1.00	1.00	1.00	0.99
	2	1.00	1.00	1.00	1.00	1.00	1.00
	3	1.00	1.00	1.00	1.00	1.00	1.00
	4	1.00	1.00	1.00	1.00	1.00	1.00
	5	1.00	1.01	1.00	1.01	1.00	0.98

Thus, these results clearly show that diverting investment for faster development of irrigation increases both growth and welfare, making it is a desirable policy.

Scenario IRFSX differs from IRFA only in that fertilizer use is subsidized by 50% with the cost of the subsidy being financed by a reduction in investment. Although investment earmarked for irrigation development takes place as in IRO, the reduction in total investment slows down the development of irrigation that would have taken place in the normal course. Thus, the gains in irrigated area and gross cropped area over RNQ levels are much less in IRFSX than in IRO. Naturally, fertilizer use is much higher (47% in 1980 and 22% in 2000) as compared to RNQ as well as to IRO. Except for the induced effects of reduced investment on non-agricultural GDP and total GDP, all the macro indicators move in the expected direction.

The pattern of gains in irrigated area across crops is similar to IRO but the gains are quantitatively smaller. With increased fertilizer use, yields go up more in IRFSX (relative to RNQ) than in IRO but this effect is tempered as irrigated area goes up by less. By the year 2000, the combined effect on yield is similar across crops, the only significant change being a smaller increase in yield of wheat (10% versus 16% in IRO relative to RNQ) and of maize (5% versus 10%).

Thus, as far as agricultural GDP and output are concerned, even a 50 percent subsidy on fertilizer does not compensate for the loss in irrigation development resulting from investment reduction needed to finance the subsidy.

The middle two classes in rural areas gain population from the poorest and the richest class. In urban areas, population shifts from the richest class to all the other classes, the bottom two classes gaining 79% and 52% respectively. The changes within class average equivalent incomes and energy intakes are significant in rural areas - all classes gaining equivalent incomes and energy intakes in 1980 and 2000. In urban areas, the changes are less dramatic, with no change in equivalent incomes or energy intakes of any class in 1980 and a significant fall in both for the richest class in 2000. Since urban residents depend entirely on the non-agricultural sector for their incomes, the fall in their average income by 16% in the year 2000 compared to RNQ explains the dramatic shift in population across classes.

The massive fertilizer subsidy, however, does improve welfare of the rural population, though this is at the cost of welfare of the urban population.

10.5 Conclusions

It is clear that investment in irrigation yields handsome returns in the Indian economy. Its distributional effects, while not dramatic, are in the egalitarian direction. Since we have deliberately kept domestic prices the same across scenarios by allowing traded volumes to adjust to any irrigation-induced changes in output, the distributional effect in favor of the poor that may occur because of a fall in domestic foodgrains prices through increased output, is absent.

It appears that a fertilizer subsidy financed through a reduction in investment is not as effective in promoting agricultural development as investment in agriculture. However, it is a policy with a pronounced rural bias.

11

Overview: Insights and Implications

"If you cannot – in the long run – tell everyone what you have been doing, your doing has been worthless"

— Erwin Schroedinger

11.1   Introduction

At the end of the book, it is worth posing some questions. What has been done? What has been learnt? What are the policy insights obtained? Do the results depend on the particular specifications of the model? How do our results compare with those of others? And, finally, where do we go from here?

We shall deal with these questions in turn.

11.2   What Has Been Done?

We have constructed an applied general equilibrium (AGE) model of Indian economy and have used it to investigate a number of policy questions. The AGE model has certain desirable properties for policy analysis in an open (i.e. one which trades with other countries) and mixed (where both public and private sectors co-exist) economy like India's. Particularly, the model described in this book has the following features:

(i)   It identifies a number of specific policy instruments so that a suggested policy can be translated into "who should do what."

(ii)   The model outcome accounts for the behavioral responses of economic agents (such as consumers and producers) to changes in policy.

(iii) The model ensures a consistent income in a number of ways which is important but not normally realized in other analytical approaches. Not only is there consistency among physical flows of commodities, but also consistency in the financial account for each type of economic agent is ensured:

    (a) Quantities produced, demanded and traded balance at the national level.

    (b) For consumers, expenditures, savings and incomes balance.

    (c) Income earned is consistent with income generated by production and trade.

    (d) Prices for producers, consumers and government taxes are consistent.

    (e) Consumer demands and production levels are consistent with the prices.

    (f) Government expenditure balances inflows.

    (g) Balance of trade is realized.

These various consistencies ensure that all the feedbacks are taken into account and that there are no unaccounted supply sources or demand sinks in the system. In other words, there is no free lunch in such a system.

(iv) Apart from the features that the model shares with other AGE models, a distinguishing feature is that as far as possible the parameters are empirically estimated from time series data and not bench marked to one year's data as is the case for many AGE models in the literature. Also the model is in some sense validated and so one can, with some measure of confidence, say that it is a model which produces outcomes which are credible for the Indian economy.

The model has been used to generate scenarios reflecting certain policy changes. The outcome of these policy scenarios has been compared with that of appropriate reference scenarios which describe the state before the policy change to assess the impacts of policy change. To facilitate comparison we have used GDP at constant 1970 prices to reflect on economic growth, energy intake and equivalent income per capita to reflect on consumer welfare, number of persons in the lowest two poorest classes to reflect on poverty, and the Willig-Bailey criteria comparison for ranking social welfare in the situation before and after policy change.

11.3   What Has Been Learnt?

Before describing the insights concerning specific policy issues, we would like to point out some insights concerning the process of policy analysis and regarding the nature of the economy.

Clarity of questions: The very process itself of defining the alternative scenarios to evaluate a policy in the general equilibrium framework of the model is instructive. One is forced to formulate the questions clearly and unambiguously. It also becomes clear that changes in one policy require changes in other policies and hence one has to state what policy package one is assessing. Take, for example, the question of fertilizer subsidy. One is immediately forced to ask the question: How is it to be financed? Will public investment be reduced or new taxes be levied? And, of course, the answer whether fertilizer subsidy is desirable or not can depend on how it is financed. Thus, one recognizes that the question "Is fertilizer subsidy desirable?" is not very meaningful. One should ask the question: "Is fertilizer subsidy financed through reduction in public investment desirable?" The assumption implicitly made in partial equilibrium analysis of such issues is that non-distortionary taxes will be used to finance such subsidies. Not only are such taxes not available in practice, but governments are not always able to raise taxes, distortionary or otherwise.

As another example of how the general equilibrium framework forces one to clarify the question, take the problem of changing terms of trade for agriculture. The moment one tries to define a scenario for change in terms of trade, one is forced to specify how this change is going to be realized. Given a set of world prices, the altered terms of trade can be realized by changes in trade policy or in effective production rates, change in domestic stock policy or a combination of these. And, of course, each of the ways chosen has a different implication for the government budget. Thus, the outcome of a change in terms of trade would depend on the other policies chosen to realize the terms of trade.

Nature of the system - importance of interdependence and need for quantitative assessments: The policy analysis scenarios presented in this book have confirmed the premises with which we began, namely, interdependence and feedback in economic systems are important and quantitative assessments are essential for evaluating policies. Almost every policy scenario produces a desirable impact on some objectives or groups with an adverse impact on others. Also, these effects are sometimes changed as the economy develops differently under the changed policy. A change in policy leads to a change in prices and incomes of different classes. The income effect and the substitution effect often work in opposite directions and the outcome depends on which of the two dominates.

As an example of such interdependence and somewhat paradoxical results flowing from it, take the case of redistributive programs. Giving subsidized food to the poor seems to be politically more acceptable than giving income subsidies. It is somehow felt that the poor would eat more if food is subsidized. And if one can only ensure that the poor do not resell the subsidized food that they buy, that would make them eat even more and a quicker impact on hunger can be realized. The result obtained from the model simulation is that the poor in fact eat less when resale restrictions are imposed than when they are free to resell their subsidized ration. This happens because the income effect of subsidy is not enough for the poor to make them want to buy all the ration they are entitled to. When resale restriction is not imposed, they get the benefit of the subsidy on their full ration entitlement. The result depends on the value of the subsidy and the amount of ration entitlement, as also on the preference parameters of households.

Numerous scenarios show the contrary impact on average income and income of the poor. The average equivalent income increases under free trade but that of the rural poor falls.

Growth-promoting policies: With a constraint on government tax rates the growth rates from the different policy scenarios fall within a relatively small range. This shows the robustness of the system. It also indicates how difficult it is to accelerate growth of the system once the various consistencies are ensured and the feedbacks are accounted for.

In many of the policy scenarios we had imposed the constraint that the government does not raise tax rates. For evaluating specific policy changes this is a reasonable assumption. Only if the policy change considered is such that government's ability (political feasibility) to raise taxes is connected to that particular policy change and contingent on it then one should permit change in tax rates in evaluating that policy. Otherwise one should ask the question: If the government is able to raise additional resources how can they be best used?

The scenarios that show higher growth rates include those in which either the investment rate is increased or exogenous technical progress is introduced. Increases in investment are realized through higher domestic taxes o through increased inflows of capital from abroad. Technical progress in non- agriculture in our scenario is introduced by lowering the capital/output ratio.

Thus, the scenarios show that there is really no magical solution that can give higher growth without major policy changes. Either more investible resources have to be raised, either domestically procured or obtained from abroad and/or organizational reforms have to be introduced that would lead the economy to use capital much more effectively than it does now. The needed reforms may require tough political decisions.

The scenarios show only limited impact on the growth of the economy of some of the price policy measures which are sometimes recommended. In particular, improving price of agriculture relative to that of non agriculture stimulates agricultural growth but has little impact on the aggregate growth. Agricultural growth does not come free; it is realized by shifting resources away from non-agriculture and as long as total resources do not increase, the growth of the economy does not increase much.

The free trade scenario also produces a modest increase in average equivalent income. Here again, changing allocation of limited resources to be more consistent with international comparative advantage helps but not dramatically. One may add, however, that trade liberalization can be expected to eliminate rent-seeking wasteful non-productive activities directed towards seeking advantage by distorting policies in one's favor. These benefits are not accounted for in our analysis. Empirical studies to estimate how significant such benefits are, are not available.

Policies for promoting agricultural growth: The model scenarios show that agricultural growth does respond to policy. A better price for agriculture, greater emphasis on irrigation, cheaper fertilizer - all lead to increased agricultural output. Yet not all these policies can be recommended.

Farmers respond to price incentives, and more acreage is devoted to a crop and more inputs such as fertilizers are applied when its price goes up relative to its competing crops. But such increase in output is at the cost of some decrease in the output of other crops. When prices of all agricultural commodities increase together, relative to the prices of non-agricultural commodities, that attracts more investment into agriculture and the aggregate output of agriculture increases over time. We have seen that such aggregate sector level supply response to price increases is relatively small, though not negligible, and takes time to realize fully. However, such price-induced agricultural output increase does not result in a significant increase in the total gross domestic product, and, in fact, it is marginally lowered if tax rates are not permitted to be raised.

Higher agricultural prices hurt the urban poor as well as the urban population as a whole. Were one to neglect the difference between the rural and urban populations, with higher agricultural prices the poor are better off and the rich worse. It may be pointed out that, in our model, the implicit assumption is that agricultural wages increase immediately with an increase in the price of agriculture. To the extent that, in reality, such wage adjustment takes time, the rural poor could be worse off immediately following an increase in the price of agriculture which also means an increase in food prices.

Agricultural trade liberalization and the consequent changes in relative prices of agricultural commodities compared to non- agriculture, are also not conducive to agricultural growth. In fact, such liberalization reduces the price of agriculture and agricultural output goes down.

Subsidization of fertilizer cannot be recommended as a policy to stimulate agricultural growth. Fertilizer subsidy does result in higher agricultural output immediately, but when the subsidy is financed at the cost of investment, the macro-economic consequences are such that, in the long run, fertilizer subsidy results in lower output. A lower aggregate investment lowers the growth rate of the economy as well as the investment in irrigation. We may point out, however, that any impact that lower fertilizer price might have on diffusion and the adoption of new technology is not accounted for in our analysis. Such effects, however, can be significant only in backward districts. Farmers in the progressive districts who have already reaped the benefits of new technology may already be anxious to adopt newer varieties. Their decision to adopt new varieties may not be critically affected by fertilizer subsidy. Only the dosage gets affected, which is already accounted for.

A greater emphasis on irrigation does seem to be an attractive policy. Irrigation increases not only the growth of agricultural output, but also the aggregate growth. The distributional impact, though not dramatic, is also in the right direction of fostering equality.

These policy explorations show that in stimulating agricultural growth, the development of irrigation and new varieties (scenarios in which the pace of HYV development is stepped up are not reported here but do show a positive effect on agricultural growth), play a more important role than output pricing and input subsidy.

Redistributive policies: Redistributive measures to augment the incomes of the poor are needed to alleviate poverty; otherwise, it will take a long time before all the poor can be brought above the poverty line. Among such measures, we have studied public food distribution to urban and rural areas, income subsidy and the rural works program. These programs all help the poor but their impact on the growth of the economy depends upon the way they are financed. When the government is able to adjust the tax rate to finance the anti-poverty redistributive policies, then the growth rate does not suffer. In fact, then the growth rate marginally improves. A corollary is that anti-poverty programs financed by additional aid would also be desirable. It is not inconceivable that additional taxation and additional aid tied to the expansion of anti-poverty programs, are politically acceptable.

The present food procurement and distribution of food at subsidized prices to urban population in ration shops transfer incomes from the rural population to the urban population. Naturally, the rural poor are worse off. These operations also do not lead to higher agricultural prices in the market so that farmers do not regain the income loss they suffer because of procurement at less than the market price. Thus, the Dantwala (1967) conjecture is not borne out in these simulations.

An extension of subsidized ration to cover the rural population is seen to be desirable as it does indicate a gain in the welfare of the poor. What is seen, however, is that such income subsidy implied by a fixed amount per head of ration given to all, rich and poor, is progressive. However, when restrictions on the resale of such rationed food are imposed, it can be regressive, as under such restrictions the poor purchase less than their full ration entitlement and are unable to avail themselves of the full extent of the subsidy. Under resale restrictions for a given budgetary allocation, it is better to give a smaller amount of grains at a higher subsidy, for then the poor will be able to purchase more of their ration entitlements. In fact, our results show that resale restrictions are not desirable and that it is better to give subsidy directly in the form of income.

Rural works programs, supplementary employment schemes, food- for-work programs or employment guarantee schemes, all have the advantage that one is able to target the benefits to the poor, as only the poor would offer themselves for such work. They also provide the possibility of creating productive assets. On the other hand, the costs of implementing such schemes may be larger than other schemes of administering targeted income subsidy. When the assets created are completely worthless, then a rural works program becomes only an income-subsidy program.

Our analysis shows that a rural works program, that creates productive assets at a scale required to virtually eliminate poverty, involves only a modest reduction in the growth rate, if the government is unable to raise taxes. It is thus an attractive program. It creates demand for perhaps the only endowment the rural poor have, namely, unskilled labor. In the absence of any radical redistribution of rural assets (particularly agricultural land) the main possibility of improving the incomes of the rural poor is by creating additional demand for unskilled labor.

If such programs can be financed by additional taxation or additional aid, they may not only remove poverty but also result in higher growth, provided, of course, that the assets created are as productive as investments made otherwise in the economy.

The effectiveness of planning and execution determines the success of

RWPs. That RWPs were not effectively executed in the past is not an argument against RWPs per se, but only an argument for creating a design and implementation mechanism with less incentives for the diversion of resources to other uses. For instance, the participation of the rural poor in formulating a RWP may help. In any case, it is likely that the efforts and the resources needed to plan and execute RWPs effectively will be modest compared to designing and implementing alternative policies with similar impact on the rural poor.

11.4 To What Extent do these Results depend on the Peculiarities of the Model?

Results often depend critically on the assumptions, frequently implicit, made in the analysis. It behoves us, therefore, to examine whether the results depend on any peculiarities of the structure of the model.

Broadly, the results refer to the process of policy-analysis, the nature of the system, growth promoting policies, policies to promote agricultural growth and redistributive policies. In these, trade-offs between various objectives are important aspects of the results.

Clearer formulations of questions posed and the understanding derived on the nature and the importance of the interdependence of the system would be only accentuated, if we had a model with more detailed representation of the economy.

The stability of the growth rate historically observed as well as in the various model scenarios can be ascribed to the stability of total investments.

The savings behavior in the model assumes that the government is a residual saver which ensures that aggregate investment follows a predetermined path of aggregate savings rate. This is a bit optimistic though not too unrealistic a characterization of India's economy. Efforts to induce additional savings through incentives that make particular forms of savings more attractive often lead to changes in portfolio balances. The government investment adjusts and leads to significant changes in growth rates. The model does not provide for any changes in X-efficiency consequent upon changes in policy. As has already been pointed out, this may, to some extent, account for the small impact of trade policy changes such as free trade on aggregate growth. However, empirical estimates of X-efficiency gains are not available.

Among policies to promote agricultural growth we have considered price policy, fertilizer subsidy and investment in irrigation. The impact of the relative price on agricultural growth and the growth of the economy is affected by the way investment allocation is modeled. The allocation of aggregate investment between agriculture and non-agriculture is not explicitly dynamic in our model. Though it depends on relative prices, it is not affected by considerations of relative expected profitability of the two sectors. The allocation is thus not optimal. However, if farmers invest more in agriculture from their own savings and if they do not consider investment in the non-agricultural sector as an option, and if capital markets are not perfect, optimality cannot be expected to prevail.

None the less, had investment allocation been modeled to be optimal, changes in GDP would have been larger consequent upon changes in prices. However, the changes in GDP have been rather small and our conclusions would not have been very different.

Changes in agricultural GDP itself have, however, been quite significant under a number of policy changes. The extent of these changes but not the direction, would have been different under an optimal allocation of investment. Even then, since the effects of fertilizer subsidy and more investment in irrigation are quite sizeable, our policy conclusions are not likely to change under an optimal allocation of investment.

Evaluation of the various redistributive policy scenarios critically depends on the income distributions in them. There is no explicit modeling of the rural labor market. The assumption we have made is that the share of wages remains constant in real terms in agriculture. This implies a Cobb-Douglas production function and a complete and instantaneous adjustment of wages when prices change. The national income statistics do show a fair deal of stability in factor shares in agriculture. Yet one should keep in mind this limitation of the model that factor markets are not explicitly modeled. Fortunately, evidence from other studies (see Binswanger and Quizon 1984) which explicitly account for factor markets show results similar to ours. We shall return to that later.

Income distribution in non-agriculture resulting from production is stable, and changes only through government transfers. Available empirical evidence does suggest a fairly stable income distribution.

Finally, a major simplification in the model is that there is one aggregated non-agricultural sector all of which is tradeable. Thus, the model does not have any non-tradeables.

For the policy issues explored here, this has an implication for the role of non-agriculture imports. In these scenarios there is mostly a net import of non-agriculture.

Since the model deals with net imports, it is possible to argue that all critical imports of non-agriculture are made and paid for by needed increases in exports of non-agriculture. Thus, macro-economic consistency is maintained. Yet the aggregation masks many needed policy adjustments. Increased exports may not come about by themselves. The various subsectors of non-agriculture may not adjust quickly enough, and the needed imports of specific items may not be available at the implied prices. Thus, this aggregate treatment of non-agriculture, like most aggregation, makes things seem much easier than they actually are. The growth-promoting ability of foreign aid and inflows may not be as high as indicated in our model scenarios, as the needed policy adjustments may not be easy to bring about.

To conclude this section, we feel that, in spite of the various limitations of the model structure, the policy conclusions arrived here are defensible.

11.5 How do They compare with Results from other Models?

Though a number of computable general equilibrium models have become available in recent years, none of them accounts for quite the same set of interdependences and feedbacks. This makes it difficult to see if a different model specification will lead to different results. None the less, it is worthwhile to briefly look at some of these models and their results.

A number of computable general equilibrium (CGE) models constructed around a social accounting matrix (SAM) are available for India.

The model of Janvry and Subbarao (1986) is a static model with seven sectors (rice, wheat, other foods, milk and animal products, other agriculture, industry and services) and seven social classes (landless agricultural workers, small farmers, medium-size farmers, large farmers, urban workers, urban marginals and urban capitalists). The five agricultural sectors have flexible prices, i.e., their outputs are exogenously specified and their prices are determined by the model. The other two sectors have cost plus mark-up pricing and their outputs adjust. Incomes of different social classes are related to sectoral productions through fixed coefficients and pre-determined transfers from the government. Fixed class specific savings rates are used to determine consumer expenditure and class-specific linear expenditure systems characterize sectorwise demands.

The model is truly not a general equilibrium model if one defines it as one which ensures physical and financial flows at the level of each economic agent (in the case, the seven social classes and the government) and in which the behavioral responses of the agents are characterized in some sense to be rational (utility maximization, profit maximization, etc.). The model has a number of imbalances:

(i)   The national accounts are not balanced.

(ii)   The trade does not balance.

(iii) The government expenditure – revenue balance is determined as a residual.

(iv)   Though the consumers pay trade margins, they do not accrue to anyone as income in the model so that income generated in production does not add up to income accruals.

(v)   The balance between savings and investments is not ensured.

(vi)   In addition, even the physical flows do not balance as both changes in stocks and net exports are determined as residuals.

In fact, the model seems to have many solutions because any linear combination of stock changes and net exports of a solution is also a solution of the model.

The model can still be used for analyzing a limited set of policy issues. The one feedback it accounts for satisfactorily concerns the effect of price changes on incomes (assuming that the problem with trade margins does not affect differentially the scenarios being compared) and consumption.

The important policy message that comes out of the book is that, in India, higher food prices hurt the poor because they are net buyers of food. This result, as far as it goes, is consistent with our results. However, when prices change investment and input allocations change and output levels change too. Their model is not able to account satisfactorily for such induced changes in the supply of agricultural commodities.

The authors claim that their results show that increasing output with fixed prices implies significant gains for all social classes and stimulates the growth of the industry and services. Even when one agrees with this conclusion, it cannot be said to follow fully from the results of the model. How does one increase output with fixed prices (presumably low prices to protect consumers)? The implied government policy may have costs with consequences for the growth of the economy. Also, would farmers increase output when prices remain fixed? The supply response behavior is not modeled or estimated, just assumed.

The model of Quizon and Binswanger (1984) is also a one-period static model with four agricultural commodities and one non-agricultural commodity. It distinguishes rural and urban classes by quartiles. A key feature of the model is its explicit modeling of factor markets. This is useful for considering the distributional implication of policy changes. Agricultural supply behavior is modeled by a simultaneous system of factor demand and output supply equations. Agricultural production and prices are simultaneously determined without lags. The neglect of agricultural production lags may make price changes in the model smaller. This may be a problem for a short-term analysis but not if one interprets the results as comparative static scenarios. However, there may be another problem as the Quizon and Binswanger model is an open loop model in which savings do not necessarily add up to exogenously specified investment. Trade levels are also exogenously specified and the government is not an explicit actor in the system.

Thus, while the model cannot analyze a number of trade-offs that our model can, its factor market modeling is at least aesthetically an improvement. As mentioned earlier and as reported in Quizon and Binswanger (1984), their conclusions on the impact of various redistributive policies are similar to ours. They also find that the impact of a redistributive policy on the poor who are net buyers of food, depends critically on other policies, such as trade and tax policies used to finance the redistributive programs, and on the change in the price of food.

In particular, it is interesting to note that they find that the effect on the wage bill in agriculture is relatively small compared to the gains and losses from the price effects of redistributive and ration shop policies.

As Quizon and Binswanger themselves point out, their model does not incorporate the effect of price policies on agricultural investment and is appropriate for an intermediate period of one to four years.

Various versions of the CGE model built at the National Council of Applied Economic Research (NCAER) by Sarkar and Taylor (1981), Sarkar, Panda and Siddique (1986), and Panda and Sarkar (1987) follow the SAM-based approach. These models are also static one-period models with mark-up pricing for many non-agricultural sectors and a usually fixed supply of agriculture. The most elaborate version is the one by Panda and Sarkar (1987). These models are addressed primarily to the issues of industrial policy and their results are not easily comparable.

These models emphasize the rigidities in the structure of the economy more than the behavioral response of economic agents, and so are not appropriate for some of the long-term consequences of policies that we have examined here.

A recursive dynamic version of the NCAER type model is that of Ratso (1986). However, since he does not clearly define the variables and their units, it is difficult to judge his model or results.

Mitra and Tendulkar (1986) have also used a general equilibrium model to assess the impact of internal (agricultural drought) and external (POL price hike) exogenous shocks. In their model, all agriculture lumped into one single sector is represented by a nested CES production function. Only one of the five counter-factual simulations over historical period conducted by them deals with agriculture and assesses the impact of a drought on income distribution. Their results indicating a worsening of welfare because of drought are consistent with the results of our irrigation development scenario.

We do not compare our results with those of the vast literature dealing with these issues in a partial equilibrium framework.

11.6   Some Reflections on Methods of Analysis

Any policy formulation requires an answer to the question, what would happen if policy is changed. One may base the answer on a mental model, an informal back-of-the-envelope calculation, an abstract formal model, an illustrative model, or a descriptive quantitative model such as the one used in this book.

We began with an appreciation that for an analysis of the policy issues that we have posed, an empirical general equilibrium model would be necessary and useful. We feel that this has been borne out.

It is a sobering feeling that in spite of the complexity of our model it is but a pale imitation of the real world and a gross simplification. The directions in which further improvements in the model may be made are obvious from the discussions in section 11.4 above. These improvements may make the model even bigger and more "complex".

This raises some questions.

Empirical general equilibrium models are intricate. Their working is not transparent and requires some efforts to understand it. Even when one has understood and explained a result, how does one make sure that this is the correct explanation? And after confirming that it is indeed so, how does one persuade a reader about it? These difficulties make many people skeptical about complex models and lead them to advocate simple models.

Also, general equilibrium models involve a large number of parameters. Adequate data are not usually available to estimate all of them empirically and it is unavoidable that some parameters are specified arbitrarily. To what extent can one say that the model represents reality? Can one trust the results from such a model?

The modeler also exercises some choice in defining the structure of the model as also in the specifications of the various relationships in the model. It is sometimes argued that with a suitable choice of specifications and parameters, one can get almost any result from a general equilibrium model but the question is: Does one believe in the results?

Whereas the motivations behind these doubts have some validity, the arguments do not go far enough.

Obviously, given a problem, the model should be as simple as possible. No one would argue that just because a model is simple or easy to understand it is a better, more reliable model. Nor would it be correct to say that the more complex a model is, the more reliable it is. One should avoid adding to the model's architecture, unnecessary decorative gargoyles that serve no vital structural purpose. Yet the complexity of the economy that is essential to a particular issue must be reflected in the structure of the model. One may point out that, by appropriately structuring scenarios, it is possible to isolate the effects of specific feedbacks. This was, for example, seen in a number of scenarios in which we kept prices fixed by removing all quotas and trade. Thus, understanding the functioning of a complex system is possible, albeit with some effort.

In any case, it is not easy to define simplicity or to measure the complexity of a model. Does it depend on the amount of effort and time required to construct it? Does it depend on the ease of understanding its functioning? These, however, depend on things such as experience, available computer software, access to data, as also on the training the reader has received. Today's conventional routine and simple models were yesterday's complex models. Thus, if a model attempts to break new grounds, it is likely to be called a complex model.

The question of the credibility of the results is important, for, in the end, a model is useless unless its results are accepted, at least by some people. Once a model is specified to be consistent with economic theory, it incorporates feedbacks and interdependence germane to the problem and the parameters are consistent with available data and knowledge, the results cannot be easily brushed aside. Even when one doubts the numerical values, one has to accept that at least the results emphasize the importance of certain feedbacks and parameters. Recourse to models which do not involve these feedbacks or require these parameters, cannot be easily justified. One has no choice but to improve one's understanding of the mechanism involved and/or to collect data to get reliable information on the questionable parameters.

Efforts towards a better understanding and a more acceptable representation of reality must continue. If it leads to greater complexity, so be it. If it results in elegant simplifications, so much the better.

References

Acharya, K.C.S. (1983): Food Security System of India: Evolution of the Buffer Stocking Policy and its Evaluation, Concept Publishing Co., New Delhi.

Ahluwalia, I.J. (1985): Industrial Growth in India, Oxford University Press, New Delhi.

Ahluwalia, M. (1976): "Inequality, Poverty and Development," *Journal of Development Economics* Vol. 3, pp. 307 - 42.

Ahluwalia, M., N. Carter and H.B. Chenery (1979): "Growth and Poverty in Developing Countries," Chapter 11 in H.B. Chenery *Structural Change and Development Policy*, Oxford University Press, New York.

Alagh, Y.K., G.S. Bhalla and A. Bhaduri (1978): "Agricultural Growth and Manpower Absorption in India", in P.K. Bardhan et.al. *Labour Absorption in Indian Agriculture: Some Exploratory Investigations* ILO, Geneva.

Alain de Janvry and K. Subbarao (1986): Agricultural Price Policy and Income Distribution in India, Oxford University Press, New Delhi.

Arrow, K.J. (1963): Social Choice and Individual Values, Second Edition, John Wiley and Sons, New York.

Bagchee, S. (1984): "Employment Guarantee Scheme in Maharashtra", *Economic and Political Weekly*, September 15, 1984.

Balassa, B. (1981): "The Newly-Industrialising Developing Countries After the Oil Crisis",*Weltwirtschaftliches Archiv,* Band 117, Heft 1.

Balassa, B. (1984a): "Adjustment to External Shocks in Developing Countries", in B.Csikos-Nagy, D.Hague, and G.Hall, ed., *The Economics of Relative Prices*, Macmillan, London.

Balassa, B. (1984b): "Adjustment Policies and Development Strategies in Sub-Saharan Africa", in M.Syrquin, L.Taylor, and L.E.Westphal, eds., *Economic Structure and Performance, Essays in Honor of Hollis B.Chenery*, Academic Press, Orlando.

Balassa, B. (1986): "Policy Responses to Exogenous Shocks in Developing Countries", *American Economic Review*, Papers and Proceedings, Vol. 76(2), pp. 75-78.

Bardhan, P. (1978): "On Labour Absorption in South Asian Rice Agriculture with Particular Reference to India", in P.K. Bardhan, et.al. *Labour Absorption in Indian Agriculture: Some Exploratory Investigations*, ILO, Geneva.

Bardhan, P. *(1984)*: *Land, Labour and Rural Poverty*, Oxford, London.

Bardhan, P.K., A. Vaidyanathan, Y.K. Alagh, G.S. Bhalla and A. Bhaduri *(1978)*: *Labour Absorption in Indian Agriculture: Some Exploratory Investigations*, ILO, Geneva.

Bhagwati, J.N. *(1978)*: *Foreign Trade Regimes and Economic Development: Anatomy and Consequences of Exchange Control Regimes*, Ballinger Press, Cambridge.

Bhagwati, J.N. and S. Chakravarty *(1969)*: "Contributions to Indian Economic Analysis: A Survey", *American Economic Review* (Supplement): Vol.59, September.

Bhagwati, J.N. and P. Desai *(1970)*: *India: Planning for Industrialization: Industrialization and Trade Policies since 1951*, Oxford University Press, New Delhi.

Bhagwati, J.N. and T.N. Srinivasan *(1976)*: *Foreign Trade Regimes and Economic Development*, Macmillan Company of India Ltd., Delhi.

Bhagwati, J.N. and T.N. Srinivasan *(1978)*: "Trade Policy and Development", in R.Dornbusch and J.A.Frenkel ed. *International Economic Policy: Theory and Evidence*, Johns Hopkins University Press, Baltimore.

Bhagwati, J.N. and T.N. Srinivasan *(1984)*: "Indian Development Strategy: Some Comments", *Economic and Political Weekly*, Vol. XIX (47).

Bhattacharya, N., D. Coondoo, P. Maiti and R. Mukherjee *(1985)*: "Relative Price of Food and the Rural Poor - The Case of India", Economic Research Unit, Indian Statistical Institute, Calcutta.

Bliss, C. and N.H. Stern, *(1978)*: "Productivity, Wages and Nutrition," Parts I and II, *Journal of Development Economics* Vol. 5 pp. 331–98.

Box, G.E.P. and G.M. Jenkins *(1970)*: *Time Series Analysis: Forecasting and Control*, Holden-Day, Inc., San Fransisco.

Chandra, N.K. *(1975)*: "Imports: Why and For Whom?", *Economic and Political Weekly*, Annual Number, February.

Chenery, H.B. and Michael Bruno *(1979)*: "Development Alternatives in an Open Economy: The case of Israel", Chapter in H.B. Chenery, *Structural Change and Development Policy* Oxford University Press, New York.

Dandekar, K. and M. Sathe *(1980)*: "Employment Guarantee Scheme and Food for Work Programme", in *Economic and Political Weekly*, April 12.

Dantwala, M.L. *(1967)*: "Incentives and Disincentives in Indian Agriculture", *Indian Journal of Agricultural Economics*, April - June.

Dantwala, M.L. *(1967)*: "Growing Irrelevance of Economics in Planning: Case of Procurement Prices", *Economic and Political Weekly*, October.

Dantwala, M.L. (1978): "Some Neglected Issues in Employment Planning", *Economic and Political Weekly*, Annual Number, February.

Dantwala, M.L. (1979): "Rural Employment: Facts and Issues", *Economic and Political Weekly*, June 23.

Dantwala, M.L. (1983): "Rural Development: Investment Without Organisation", in *Economic and Political Weekly*, April 30.

Dasgupta, P. and D. Ray (1986): "Inequality as a Determinant of Malnutrition and Unemployment: Theory," *Economic Journal* Vol. 96, pp. 1011 - 1034.

de Wit, C.T. (1965): "Photosynthesis of Leaf Canopies," Agricultural Research Report, 663, Wageningen (Holland).

Dharam Narain and Shyamal Roy (1980): "Impact of Irrigation and Labour Availability on Multiple Cropping : A case study of India". Research Report 20, IFPRI, Washington.

Government of India (1964): "Report of the Committee on Distribution of Income and Levels of Living: Part I", (Mahalanobis Committee), Planning Commission.

Government of India (1965): "Report of the Agricultural Prices Commission on Price Policy for Kharif Cereals for 1965-66", Ministry of Agriculture; (and various further issues).

Government of India (1967): "Indian Crop Calendar", Ministry of Food and Agriculture.

Government of India (1967): "Industrial Planning and Licensing Policy" (Hazari Committee), Planning Commission.

Government of India (1969): "Report of the Industrial Licensing Policy Enquiry Committee" (Dutt Committee).

Government of India (1976): "Report of National Commission of Agriculture", Ministry of Agriculture and Irrigation.

Government of India (1978): "Report of the Import and Export Policies", Ministry of Commerce, (Alexander Committee).

Government of India (1979): "Report of the Committee on Controls and Subsidies", Ministry of Finance, May.

Government of India (1980): "Report of the Committee on Export Strategy", Ministry of Commerce, December.

Guhan, S. (1980): "Rural Poverty : Policy and Play Acting," *Economic and Political Weekly*, November 22.

Gulati, Leela, (1977): "Rationing in a Peri Urban Community: Case Study of a Squatter Habitat", *Economic and Political Weekly*, March 19, pp. 501-506.

Hanson, A.H. (1966): The Process of Planning, Oxford University Press, London.

Keyzer, M.A., C. Lemerachal and R. Mifflin (1978): Computation of Economic Equilibria by Nonsmooth Optimization, International Institute for Applied Systems Analysis, Laxenburg, Austria (RM-78-13).

Keyzer, M.A. (1981): The International Linkage of Open Exchange Economies, Centrale Reproductiedienst Vrije Universiteit te Amsterdam.

Konijn, N. (1984): A Crop Production and Environment Model for Long Term Consequences of Agricultural Production, International Institute for Applied Systems Analysis, WP-84-51, Laxenburg, Austria.

Koopmans, T.C (1957): "Water Storage Policy in a Simplified Hydroelectric Systems", Proceedings of the First International Conference on Operations Research held in Oxford, London, Operations Research Society of America, Baltimore, September,

Krishna, K.L. (1987): "Industrial Growth and Productivity in India", included in P.R. Brahmananda and V.R. Panchamukhi (eds.) *The Development Process of the Indian Economy*, Himalaya Publishing House, Bombay.

Krueger, A. (1978): Foreign Trade Regimes and Economic Development: Liberalization Attempts and Consequences, Ballinger Press., Cambridge.

Krueger, A. (1982): Trade and Employment in Developing Countries, 2: Factor Supply and Substitution, University of Chicago Press, Chicago.

Krueger, A. (1983): Trade Regimes and Employment in Developing Countries, 3: Synthesis and Conclusions, University of Chicago Press, Chicago.

Krueger, A., H.B. Lary, T. Monson and N. Akrasanee (eds.) (1981): Trade and Employment in Developing Countries, 1: Individual Studies, University of Chicago Press, Chicago.

Kuznets, S. (1966): Modern Economic Growth: Rate Structure and Spread, Yale University Press, New Haven.

Lakdawala, D.T. (1977): "Growth, Unemployment and Poverty", All India Labour Economics Conference, Tirupati.

Lakdawala, D.T. (1980): "Redistributive Policies and Basic Needs in Indian Planning", Proceedings and Papers of a Seminar held in Trivandrum on the Basic Needs Approach to Indian Planning; ILO, Bangkok and Geneva, 1980.

Lal, R.N. (1977): Capital Formation and Its Financing in India, Allied Publication, New Delhi.

Leibenstein, H. (1957): Economic Backwardness and Economic Growth, John Wiley and Sons, New York.

Majumdar, K.C. et al. (1977): "Employment Structure and Planning Policy", Chapter 3 in *Studies on the Structure of Indian Economy and Planning for Development*, Planning Commission, Government of India.

Malinvaud, E. (1970): *Statistical Methods of Econometrics*, Elsevier - North Holland, Amsterdam.

Mann, J.S. (1967): "The Impact of PL 480 Imports on Prices and Domestic Supply of Cereals in India", *Journal of Farm Economics*, February.

Mehra, S. (1976): "Some Aspects of Labour-use in Indian Agriculture", *Indian Journal of Agricultural Economics.*

MHJ (1980): "Maharashtra II: Employment Guarantee Scheme: An Evaluation", *Economic and Political Weekly*, December 6, pp. 2043-45

Minhas, B.S., K.S. Parikh, and T.N. Srinivasan (1974): "Towards a Production Function of Wheat with Dated Inputs of Water", *Water Resources Research*, Vol.10, No.3, June.

Mitra, P. and S.D. Tendulkar (1986): "Coping with Internal and External Exogenous Shocks: 1973-74 to 1983-84", First Draft, March.

Narayana, N.S.S. and K.S. Parikh (1981): *Estimation of Farm Supply Response and Acreage Allocation: A Case Study of Indian Agriculture*, International Institute for Applied Systems Analysis (RR-81-1), February.

Narayana, N.S.S. and K.S. Parikh (1987): "Estimation of Yield Functions for Major Cereals in India" in *Journal of Quantitative Economics*, Vol.3, No.2, July.

Narayana, N.S.S., K.S. Parikh and T.N. Srinivasan (1984): "An Indian Agricultural Policy Model: Preliminary Results of an Analysis of Some Redistributive Policies"; Economic Analysis Unit, Indian Statistical Institute, Bangalore (EAU-DP28-1-84), January.

Narayana, N.S.S., K.S. Parikh and T.N. Srinivasan(1984): "Income Generation and Income Distribution in the Model for Indian Agricultural Policy" (mimeo), June.

National Council of Applied Economic Research (NCAER) (1969): "Export Strategy for India", New Delhi, June.

National Council of Applied Economic Research (1980): *Household Income and Its Disposition*, New Delhi.

National Council of Applied Economic Research (1981): "A Computable General Equilibrium Model of Indian Economy: Structure and Sensitivities", by Sarkar et al., New Delhi, September.

Parikh, K.S. and T.N. Srinivasan (1974): *Optimum Requirement of Fertilizer for the Fifth Plan Period*, Indian Statistical Institute and Fertilizer Association of India, New Delhi.

Parikh, K.S. (1978): "HYV and Fertiliser: Synergy or Substitution", *Economic and Political Weekly, Review of Agriculture*, March.

Parikh, K.S. and Wouter Tims (1986): "From Hunger Amidst Abundance to Abundance Without Hunger", Executive Report 13, International Institute for Applied Systems Analysis, Laxenburg, Austria, December.

Parthasarathy, G (1978): "Interstate Variations in Rural Unemployment and Growth of Agriculture", Occasional Paper 6, Agro Economic Research Centre, Andhra University, Waltair.

Planning Commission (1983): "Sixth Five Year Plan: 1980-85, Mid-Term Appraisal", Government of India.

Planning Commission (1985): "Seventh Five Year Plan: 1985-90," Government of India, Vols.1 and 2.

Quizon, Jaime B. and H.P. Binswanger (1984): "Distributional Consequences of Alternative Food Policies in India", Report No. ARU20, World Bank, Washington D.C., August.

Quizon, Jaime B. and H.P. Binswanger (1984): "Income Distribution in India: The Impact of Policies and Growth in the Agricultural Sector", Report No.ARU21, World Bank, Washington D.C. November.

Quizon, Jaime B. and H.P. Binswanger (1986): "Modeling the Impact of Agricultural Growth and Government Policy on Income Distribution in India", *The World Bank Economic Review*, Vol.1, No.1, September.

Radhakrishna, R. and K.N. Murty(1980): "Models of Complete Expenditure Systems for India", International Institute for Applied Systems Analysis, Laxenburg, Austria, WP-80-98, May.

Raj, K.N. (1966): "The Current Economic Crisis", *The Times of India*, February.

Rajkrishna and Ajay Chibber (1982): "Policy Modeling of a Dual Grain Market: The Case of Wheat in India", Stanford Food Research Institute (Mimeo.).

Rajkrishna (1967): "Government Operations in Foodgrains", *Economic and Political Weekly,* September.

Rajaraman, I.(1984): "Wages and Labour Supply: Rural Labour in India", Bangalore, Indian Institute of Management (Mimeo.).

Rattso, Jørn (1986): *Macrodynamic Adjustment Mechanisms in India: A Model Analysis Based on 6th Five Year Plan*, University of Trondheim, Norway.

Ray, S.K. (1977): "Variations in Crop Output", Institute of Economic Growth, Delhi.

Reserve Bank of India (1985): "Report of the Committee to Review the Working of the Monetary System", (Chakravarty Committee).

Reutlinger Shlomo (1978): "The Level and Stability of India's Foodgrain Consumption" : Occasional Papers, World Bank Staff Working Paper No. 279, May, Washington.

Reynolds, N. and P. Sundar (1977): "Maharashtra's Employment Guarantee Scheme: A Programme to Emulate?", *Economic and Political Weekly,* July 16.

Rosenzweig, Mark (1988): "Labour Markets in Low-Income Countries: Distortions. Mobility and Migration," in H.Chenery and T.N.Srinivasan, (eds.): *Handbook on Development Economics*, North Holland, Amsterdam.

Rudra, A. (1981): *Indian Agricultural Economics: Myths and Realities*, Allied Publishers, New Delhi.

Sah, R.K. (1987): "Queues, Rations and Markets: Comparison of Outcomes for the Poor and the Rich", *American Economic Review*, Vol. 77(1), pp. 69-77.

Sah, R.K. and T.N. Srinivasan (1988): "Distributional Consequences of Rural Food Levy and Subsidized Urban Rations", *European Economic Review*, Vol. 32(1), pp. 141-159.

Sah, R.K. and J. Stiglitz (1987): *Peasants Versus City Dwellers: Taxation, Pricing and the Burden of Economic Development*, Oxford University Press, New York.

Sau, Ranjit (1978): "Growth, Employment and Removal of Poverty", Economic and Political Weekly, Special No. August.

Schumpeter, J. (1961): *The Theory of Economic Development*, Oxford University Press, New York.

Sen, A.K. (1979): *Collective Choice and Social Welfare*, North-Holland, Amsterdam.

Sen, A.K. (1983a): "Poor, Relatively Speaking", *Oxford Economic Papers*, 35.

Sen, A.K. (1983b): "Goods and People", Plenary Address to the Seventh World Congress of the International Economic Association, Madrid.

Sen, A.K. (1983c): "Rights and Capabilities", in Ted Honderich (ed), Morality and Objectivity: Tribute to J.L. Mackie, Routledge and Kegan Paul Ltd., London.

Sinha, J.N. (1978): "Rural Employment Planning: Dimensions and Constraints", *Economic and Political Weekly*, Annual Number, February.

Sinha, J.N. (1981): "Full Employment and Anti-Poverty Plan: The Missing Link", *Economic and Political Weekly*, December.

Srinivasan, T.N. (1965): "The National Council's Strategy for the Fourth Plan", *Economic Weekly*, January. Also "A Rejoinder", in *Economic Weekly*, April.

Srinivasan, T.N. and P.K. Bardhan (1974): *Poverty and Income Distribution in India*, Statistical Publishing Society, Calcutta.

Srinivasan, T.N. and N.S.S. Narayana (1977): "Economic Performance since the Third Plan and Its Implications for Policy", *Economic and Political Weekly*, February.

Srivastava, Uma K., Earl O. Heady, Keith D. Rogers and Leo V. Mayer (1975): *Food Aid and International Economic Growth*, Iowa State University Press, Ames, Iowa.

Stiglitz, J.E. (1976): "The Efficiency Wage Hypothesis, Surplus Labour and the Distribution of Income in LDCs", *Oxford Economic Papers*, 28: 185-207.

Sundaram, K. (1967): "P.L.480 Imports: Efficiency in Purchase and Distribution", *Economic and Political Weekly*, March.

Sundaram, K. (1970): "The Relationship Between P.L.480 Transactions, Money Supply with the Public and Prices: An Analysis", *Indian Economic Review*, 5 (NS),1.

Sundaram, K. and S.D. Tendulkar (1983): "Poverty Reduction and Redistribution in Sixth Plan: Population Factor and Rural Urban Equity", *Economic and Political Weekly*, September.

Taylor, L. (1980): "Food Subsidy Programme: A Survey", Ford Foundation, New York.

Taylor, L.L.S. Horton and D. Raff (1983): "Food Subsidy Programs - Practice and Policy Lessons," Department of Economics, Massachusetts Institute of Technology.

Tendulkar, S.D. (1987): "Economic Inequality and Poverty in India: An Interpretative Overview", in P.R. Brahmananda and Panchamukhi, V.R. (eds.): *Development Process in the Indian Economy*, Himalaya Publishing House, Bombay.

Vaidyanathan, A. (1978): "Labour Use in Indian Agriculture: An Analysis Based on Farm Management Survey Data", in P.K.Bardhan et al. *Labour Absorption in Indian Agriculture: Some Exploratory Investigations*, ILO, Geneva.

Verghese, S.K. (1978): "Export Assistance Policy and Export Performance of India in the Seventies", *Economic and Political Weekly*, Annual Number, February.

Visaria, P. (1981): "Poverty and Unemployment in India: An Analysis of Recent Evidence", *World Development*, Vol.9, No.3.

Visaria, P. and L. Visaria (1973): "Employment Planning for the Weaker Sections in Rural India", *Economic and Political Weekly*, Annual Number, February.

Vyas, V.S. and Mathai (1978): "Farm and Non-Farm Employment in Rural Areas: A Perspective for Planning", *Economic and Political Weekly*, February.

Wall, John (1978): "Foodgrain Management: Pricing, Procurement, Distribution, Import and Storage Policy in India", Occasional Papers, World Bank Staff Working Papers No. 279, World Bank, Washington D.C.

Willig, R.D. and E.E. Bailey (1981): "Income Distribution Concerns in Regulatory Policy Making" in Fromm G. (ed.) *Studies in Public Regulation*, University of Chicago Press, Chicago.

SUBJECT INDEX

AUTHOR INDEX